WILLIAM STUKELEY

Stuart Piggott

WILLIAM STUKELEY

An Eighteenth-Century Antiquary

REVISED AND ENLARGED EDITION

WITH 44 ILLUSTRATIONS

THAMES AND HUDSON

First published in 1950
Revised and enlarged edition published in the USA in 1985 by
Thames and Hudson Inc.,
500 Fifth Avenue, New York, New York 10110
©1950 and 1985 Stuart Piggott

Library of Congress Catalog Card Number 84-51643

Printed and bound in Hungary

Contents

Preface to the Revised Edition

The original version of this book was published in 1950, and at that time represented something of a pioneering effort in British antiquarian studies as a part of the history of ideas in the seventeenth and eighteenth centuries. Since that time, however, interest in this field has greatly developed, while the picture of British prehistory within which William Stukeley's work needs to be assessed has, with over thirty years of active research, altered beyond recognition. So far as the main biographical scheme is concerned, new unpublished manuscript material has become available, some of it throwing light on two important aspects of Stukeley's life, on the one hand the original book he drafted on Avebury and Stonehenge in 1723, and on the other, the part he played in the notorious 'Richard of Cirencester' forgery in the 1750s. It was therefore felt that a new and revised edition of a biography, long out of print and unobtainable, of one of the main figures of British antiquarianism was worth presenting to a new generation of readers.

In the first edition appendices, proper to the publication of the academic thesis in which the book originated, listed extant MS sources *in extenso* and provided a topographical index to these. Since its publication, numerous new MSS have been reported, widely scattered in public and private collections, but with few notable exceptions they throw little light on anything more than the increasing vagaries of Stukeley's antiquarian and religious speculations in his later years. It has therefore been decided not to attempt the considerable task of incorporating these in revised catalogues, while making full use of such as illuminate the main narrative. There has been an inevitable migration of some MSS since 1950, notably the incorporation of the great Alexander Keiller collection into the Bodleian Library, and all references to locations and shelfmarks have been appropriately revised.

In the preface to the first edition its genesis at the instance and with the encouragement of the late Alexander Keiller and its emergence as an Oxford B.Litt. thesis were set out, and my acknowledgment to the help of others recorded. To these, in the preparation of this new edition I would add with gratitude my indebtedness to many colleagues, especially Professor R.J.C. Atkinson and Dr Iain Brown. My thanks are due, as before, to the Bodleian Library, Oxford, and to the Cardiff Public Library and the Royal Library of Denmark.

West Challow, 1984   STUART PIGGOTT

1 *Stukeley at Avebury, dozing after a day's fieldwork: pen sketch by Gerard Vandergucht in 1722 (see page 63 below). The artist wrote on the drawing the Latin tag about even Homer nodding* (quandoque bonus dormitat Homerus: *Horace,* Ars Poetica *359).*

Introduction

'IF ANY MAN WAS BORN for the service of Antiquity, it was Dr. Stukeley', wrote Richard Gough in the late eighteenth century,[1] and a hundred and fifty years later, when the study of British antiquities had developed from an amateur's hobby to a branch of learning employing the rigorous disciplines of modern science, one of its most outstanding exponents wrote: 'Let us once for all pay a tribute of esteem and gratitude to Stukeley's memory.'[2] Between these two pronouncements, however, we have a century in which fictitious and imagined descriptions of Druids and their temples became increasingly popular, whilst a wider and wider publicity was given to fantastic ideas which can all be traced back to the theories of the same William Stukeley in the second half of the eighteenth century. Nor can we forget that in the late nineteenth century critics were able to demonstrate in detail how a certain alleged Itinerary of Roman Britain to which Stukeley had stood sponsor was in fact an impudent and complete forgery. How then can we resolve the inconsistencies which appear inherent in the work of this eighteenth-century antiquary, to which praise and blame seem equally applicable?

It is partly to explain this curious mixture in Stukeley's work that this study was undertaken, for at a very early stage of investigation it became apparent that the intellectual development of the man during his lifetime of antiquarian studies would in itself give a clue to the varying quality of his work and explain its lamentable decline in his later life. From the archaeologist's viewpoint, Stukeley was a worker whose place in contemporary and subsequent antiquarian studies needed evaluation. His splendid contributions by fieldwork and survey to our knowledge of the great monuments of Stonehenge and Avebury had not been studied in detail, and his debt to previous workers in the same field was obscure. As a central figure in the

9

antiquarian studies of the early eighteenth century he would afford an opportunity for an appreciation of this circle, and its relationship to the high tradition of historical studies of the Restoration and to the decline of such scholarship after about 1730.

But no biography of Stukeley could remain a merely archaeological document. The wide interests of the man, and his curious professional career, first as a doctor of medicine and subsequently as a clergyman of the Church of England, meant that the social and intellectual life of the early eighteenth century would be touched at many points. Through Stukeley's eyes it is possible to see the changes of taste and fashion which lie behind the growth of antiquarian interests in Britain, changes partly scientific, partly aesthetic. Science is predominant in his life at the University of Cambridge at the beginning of the century, and with the great figures of Georgian medicine – Sloane and Mead particularly – it continues during Stukeley's younger days as a London doctor. He now begins his friendships with painters and engravers, and is admitted to the circle of intellectual nobility which included Lord Winchelsea and Lord Pembroke.

His entry into Holy Orders throws a curious light on the conditions upon which candidates for ordination would be welcomed into the Latitudinarian Church in 1725–30, and is the more interesting since this welcome comes from that great figure of the early Georgian Church, Archbishop Wake. Stukeley's sermons, of which some were published and others remain in manuscript, are only touched upon here; they would probably repay a separate study by one tracing in detail the vagaries of belief and doctrine tolerated within the Church of England at this period.

Stukeley's interest in architecture led him not only to make a large series of topographical and architectural drawings throughout his life, but also to more practical essays in actual construction, and of these, the designs in the Gothic manner dating from the 1740s have a considerable importance in the history of eighteenth-century architectural modes.

And as a person, Stukeley emerges as one of the most curious and complex of the English eccentrics, pathetic, charming, admirable, and laughable by turns. One becomes very endeared to the Archdruid, so enthusiastic in everything he does, whether it is riding in search of antiquities, building a hermitage in his garden, watching an eclipse of the sun (postponing his morning service so that his congregation can see it too), or writing, writing away at the extraordinary fancies of his later years, where the Druids are lurking everywhere, though they may sometimes be Moses, sometimes Apollo or Horus. He is so essentially English, and although representative of his century, yet possessing a certain timeless quality which brings him very close to us. The modern counterparts of William Stukeley still look for earthworks on the downs and write papers for the local Field Club.

In Stukeley we see, thanks to a remarkable volume of evidence, the eighteenth-century antiquary larger than life-size. He is unrepresentative and yet representative: individual, eccentric, an 'original', but with all his characteristics no more than a slight exaggeration of those of his fellow antiquaries. He is almost a corporate sum of his contemporaries, with all their achievements and their intellectual crotchets concentrated and magnified in one man. The good and bad qualities of his work, as we judge them today, have an equal importance if we are to attempt any balanced picture of antiquarian studies in the eighteenth century. In his life every aspect of these studies is illustrated – sound scientific observation and theory developed to the point of fantasy, an intuitive grasp of some problems and an almost unbelievable credulity in dealing with others.

It is with a conviction of Stukeley's value as an individual that I have shaped this book around his own life and given it an essentially biographical framework. In any account of the growth of antiquarian studies of his time Stukeley would play an important part, though in some respects he is not typical, and always individual. It is his idiosyncratic approach to every problem that makes him so fascinating and gives a peculiarly characteristic flavour to his work. He is often slightly out of period. He appears as a scientist in the good seventeenth-century tradition, belated and unappreciated in the 1720s: a romantic before his time, he anticipates Blake, and designs Gothic revival buildings, twenty years later. To exclude Stukeley's personality from an account of his antiquarian work would be to make the narrative not only the poorer in humanity, but misleading in emphasis. It is easy to admit the value of his early archaeological fieldwork while ridiculing or ignoring his later theories, but to do this can only produce an unbalanced picture. We select, as praiseworthy and 'scientific', certain aspects of Stukeley's antiquarianism, but forget that all such studies were in origin episodes in the history of taste, and remained as such until comparatively recent years. To appreciate the eighteenth-century antiquarians and their work, we must remember that there are associations between surveying stone circles and landscape gardening, Druids and Deists, sketching in watercolours and excavating tumuli. We are dealing with an antiquarianism that was partly involved in the search for the newly discovered picturesque in nature; prehistory was non-Roman, excitingly barbarian, and so scarcely to be distinguished from Gothic in its appeal.

The importance of antiquarianism in the eighteenth century is more than the dawning of modern archaeology. For 200 years the objective fieldwork at Stonehenge and Avebury was forgotten, nor was it thought important in Stukeley's own day. But his speculations on Druids, which seem to us so childishly fantastic, played a very considerable part in shaping the literary moods of the Romantic Revival, and Collins, Mason, Gray, and Blake all owe him an unacknowledged debt.

More than this, it is to Stukeley and his contemporaries that we owe so much of our unconscious attitude towards the history and landscape of our country today. The historian works from documents and not from the soil, but the antiquarians and their descendants, the archaeologists, since the time when the Tour in search of the Picturesque and the Prehistoric was one, have brought a sense of history into our conception of the countryside. To our ideas of what is beautiful in landscape Stukeley as well as Uvedale Price contributes his share, but above all to our appreciation of the intimate links between the countryside of England and its antiquities. This has not come from the scientific archaeology of the last few decades, but is inherent in the eighteenth-century attitude that accepted antiquarianism as a part of the Romantic Movement. This aspect can hardly be dismissed as unimportant – it has coloured English thought for two centuries – and it inevitably forms the background of this book.

I

The Antiquarian Background
1660–1730

IN THE YEAR 1738 Francis Wise, Fellow of Trinity College, Oxford, and later to be the first Radcliffe Librarian, found occasion to review the advances made in antiquarian studies 'in the several periods of our more early History and Antiquities' since the publication of Camden's *Britannia* in 1586.[3] Wise was not himself a profound scholar[4] and his review is sketchy, but it probably does represent fairly enough the average of intelligent opinion on the matter at his time, which is more important in the present context. 'If any part was obscure, the British must have been remarkably so,' he writes, 'the times preceding Julius Caesar's invasion being a dark, and impenetrable, wild, without letters, and almost without documents, save what later antiquaries have discovered to belong to it.' But now, says Wise, our knowledge of prehistoric Britain has been remarkably increased – 'upon the whole, I cannot think that any branch of our Antiquities has received greater improvements than this'. Stonehenge, Avebury, and Rollright have come to be recognized as prehistoric temples, and of these and other monuments 'we may expect a still much better account, from a very learned and celebrated pen'. At this dramatic point our eye is directed to a footnote, 'Dr Stukeley'. The central figure of early eighteenth-century archaeology has been appropriately introduced.

At the time of Wise's writing his *Letter to Dr Mead*, William Stukeley was fifty-one years of age, Vicar of All Saints, Stamford, and the author of a book and a few pamphlets dealing with antiquarian matters. His two major contributions to these studies (hinted at by Wise) were not to be published until 1740 and 1743, but he was already established as the outstanding British antiquary of his time, Fellow of the Royal Society and of the Society of Antiquaries. Whatever Hearne might have said of his being 'not much admired among judicious Men, being an hypothetical, fancifull Man',[5] he was certainly regarded by

Ars longa. Vita brevis. Judicium fallax. Memoria labilis.

30 Junij 1720.   Isaac Newton.

Dona præsentis cape lætus horæ

Jan.to 172½   Edm: Halley

Pondere Numero et Mensurâ.

Cr: Wren. Mar: 10: 1721.

— *Sequiturq̄ Patrem non Passibus Æquis*

Chr: Wren. C. Fil.

ὁ Θεὸς ἀεὶ γεωμετρεῖ.

Sept. 20 1731.   Gul: Whiston mathescos Professor Lucasianus apud Cantabrigiensis

2 *Page of Stukeley's* Liber Amicorum, *with the signatures of Sir Isaac Newton (1642–1727); Sir Christopher Wren (1632–1723) and his son (1675–1747); Edmund Halley, the astronomer (1656–1742); and William Whiston, divine and mathematician (1667–1752).*

most of his contemporaries as the one man who understood the ancient monuments of pre-Roman Britain. His antiquarian investigations had started when he was in his twenties and a doctor of medicine practising in Lincolnshire: from 1718 to 1725 he was actively engaged in the fieldwork which can now be recognized as the main scientific achievement of his archaeological career. By the 1730s we find him married and in Holy Orders, and producing works of half-religious, half-antiquarian speculation; such productions occupied the remainder of his life (from the middle of the century in London), and though even his admirers could not conceal the fact that his theories were becoming increasingly fantastic as time went on, he still retained an unchallenged position as practically the only antiquary in England whose main theme of interest was the pre-Roman period. An old man, he found himself in the vastly changed intellectual atmosphere of the later eighteenth century, visiting 'Mr Hor. Walpole in his most elegant Gothic Seat at Strawberry Hill' and writing as his last published work a dissertation on Macpherson's *Ossian* poems which had recently appeared. After his death in 1765 we have to wait until the nineteenth century before we find men taking up the tradition of archaeological fieldwork where he left it, and until the twentieth before the worth of his work was realized and the sound observations of his earlier years disentangled from the very curious speculations of his later life.

Stukeley is a link between two worlds. Brought up in the scientific and scholarly traditions of the late seventeenth century, the world of Newton and Wren and of the great historians such as Dugdale, Hickes, and Wanley, he lived to see the Royal Society in decline, lampooned for its ridiculous *Transactions*, and history in the hands of the dilettanti. He began his intellectual life in an age of Palladian architecture and Augustan verse, but by his later years the poems of Gray and Macpherson's *Ossian* were on the tables of drawing-rooms furnished in contemporary 'Gothick'.

To appreciate Stukeley's work and the position he held in the antiquarian world of the first half of the eighteenth century, some historical retrospect is necessary before we discuss his life in detail and his entry into the learned circle of his time. The formal founding of the Society of Antiquaries in 1717, with Stukeley as its first secretary, was in the view of many of its members rather a refounding of an institution which had its origins in Elizabethan times, when 'there was such a Society, made up of right learned Antiquaries'.[6] This Society had not survived, and so, although there was no direct continuity between the two institutions, there was not, on the other hand, any break throughout the seventeenth century in the succession of antiquaries whose studies were not confined to historical records or classical texts but were directed towards '*Archiology*, which consists of Monuments . . . still subsisting'.[7] Even though no formal association of scholars brought them together except in so far as the wide range of scientific interests of the new Royal Society included archaeology (like so much else), yet, particularly in the last third of the seventeenth century, antiquarian scholars were as much linked by the amenities of learned correspondence and informal meetings in colleges, taverns, or coffee-houses as was the great band of contemporary historians.

With the exception of William Camden, there are practically no works of historical or antiquarian learning of the late sixteenth and early seventeenth centuries in England which do not show, in their approach to the subject, a very practical and utilitarian viewpoint. Here are the ancients, here we are – how can we profit from the works of our forefathers? The *Curious Discourses* published by Hearne in 1720, which were in fact papers offered to the original Elizabethan Society of Antiquaries, are almost all written with an eye to determining and confirming by historical or archaeological precedent the institutions of the contemporary England of the writers. The antiquity of shires, of land dimensions, the office and privilege of heralds, the etymology, antiquity, and privilege of castles – the titles show immediately the antiquarians seeking to contribute to the formalization of custom and tradition into instruments of government and a defined code of laws. As David Douglas[8] stressed, the great output of immense and accurate historical learning at the end of the seventeenth century was in fact the result of the search for precedent in ecclesiastical and political controversy, and this was itself but following an Elizabethan form.

It is especially interesting to turn to a peculiarly archaeological subject, the study of Roman Britain and its topography. In Elizabethan times two of the most important texts of the Roman historians concerning Britain were translated with commentaries – the *Agricola* of Tacitus and the *Gallic War* of Julius Caesar. The Tacitus translation,[9] published in 1591, was an early work of that great scholar, Sir Henry Savile, and contains no reference whatever to the problems of topography involved in the course of Agricola's campaign in Britain. The preface makes its contemporary application clear in such phrases as 'If thou mislike their warres, be thankfull for thine owne peace; if thou doest abhore their tyranies, loue and reuerence thine owne wise, just and excellent Prince.' And this lack of interest in the archaeological aspects of the earliest writers on Britain is even more apparent in the manner in which Clement Edmonds[10] dealt with Caesar' Commentaries in 1604, the very subtitle of his book being sufficient advertisement of its intention – 'setting forth the Practise of the Art militarie in the time of the Romaine Empire for the better direction of our moderne Warrs'. After this declaration, it is perhaps hardly surprising that the account of the Druids in Book IV calls forth no comment, nor is the British campaign discussed in detail, but is dismissed with the words 'And thus ended the warre in Britanie, which afoordeth little matter of discourse, being indeed but a scambling warre.' Edmonds, in fact, was not for nothing a contemporary of the creator of Capt. Fluellen, and would have thoroughly concurred in the latter's condemnation of Macmorris for having 'no more directions in the true disciplines of the wars, look you, of the Roman disciplines, than is a puppy-dog'.[11]

But by the first decade of the eighteenth century it would have been almost impossible to publish commentaries on the classical texts relating to Britain and Gaul without an elaborate disquisition on the topography and the identifications of the Roman towns with their modern counterparts. This linking of text to countryside dates from the great pioneer efforts of Camden, but the real developments in the study of British archaeology belong to the period 1670–1740 and form in fact a phenomenon lesser than but parallel to the rise and decline of English historical studies over the same period.[12] To some degree the historians and prehistorians covered common ground, and Dugdale could make notes and plans of stone circles and similar prehistoric monuments while conducting a Herald's Visitation of Cumberland in 1664–5[13] or Aylett Sammes print a text of Ine's Laws at the end of his entertaining and speculative *Britannia Antiqua Illustrata* (1676), which purports to deal with prehistoric Britain and its monuments rather than with Saxon history. But on the whole the two groups of workers, those who dealt with manuscript sources for history and those who were trying to construct prehistory from field monuments, were distinct, except in so far as students of Roman Britain naturally utilized the writings of Caesar and Tacitus, or the Itineraries, in interpreting the extant inscriptions or the remains of buildings. It must be emphasized, too, that the general standard of historical studies rose during the Restoration period to a height far above that of contemporary archaeological work, and giants of the stature of Hickes or Wanley are hardly to be found among the antiquaries. Yet the objective field surveys of Aubrey and Stukeley at Stonehenge and

Avebury are today more valuable and reliable than nearly the whole of the huge output of nineteenth-century literature on the same monuments, and Haverfield was able to say in 1907 that John Horsley's *Britannia Romana* of 1732 'was till quite lately the best and most scholarly account of any Roman province that had been written anywhere in Europe'[14] – high praise enough coming from such an authority,

Of the thirty or forty books published between 1670 and 1740 concerned with British or Romano-British antiquities, about half appeared around 1710–30 and are, I think, to be related to the stimulus given to such studies by the appearance in 1695 of Edmund Gibson's great enlarged and annotated English edition of Camden's *Britannia*. This remarkable work, undertaken by a young man in his early twenties, provided a comprehensive topographical and antiquarian background embodying the then available knowledge, printed or in manuscript, of the antiquities of the British Isles. Though himself primarily an historian, Gibson (who had shown his interest in Roman Britain by his notes to Brome's edition of Somner's *Roman Ports and Forts in Kent* a couple of years before the appearance of his *Britannia*) had devoted particular attention to such archaeological matter as he could collect to amplify Camden, including extracts from the famous *Monumenta Britannica* manuscript of John Aubrey.[15]

By producing this edition of Camden, so augmented as to constitute something approaching an original work, Gibson placed in the hands of the country gentry, doctors, and clergymen, a basic summary against which they could set the results of their own local inquiries in history and archaeology. An annotated copy of the 1695 or subsequent editions of Camden formed the almost inevitable nucleus around which comment and additions would grow as local investigations were carried out by these amateurs who were beginning to build up the tradition which crystallized into the great nineteenth-century county histories and the foundation of regional archaeological societies.

When we come to consider the early study of prehistoric monuments in Britain, we must for a moment turn from history to prehistory and to the actual type of the monuments themselves. It is obvious that attention would first be attracted towards ancient structures which were in some degree recognizable as architectural performances in themselves, however rough and primitive. The deliberate setting of stones into a circle (as at Rollright in Oxfordshire), or even more, with the provision of lintels, as at Stonehenge, attracted attention even in the Middle Ages[16] and entitled these monuments to a place among the wonders of Britain. Stone circles, therefore, or conspicuous single or grouped standing stones, and the remains of Neolithic collective burial chambers built of megalithic slabs (the 'dolmens' and 'cromlechs' of nineteenth-century antiquarianism) were likely to attract attention at an early stage in archaeological field studies before the recognition of less obviously artificial remains such as barrows and earthworks.

The circumstances of geology coupled with the settlement patterns of the builders of megalithic tombs and stone circles in western Europe from the fourth to second millennia BC result in these structures being concentrated, as a whole, in the 'Highland Zone' of western and northern Britain. Rollright is indeed fairly near Oxford, but antiquaries in London or Cambridge, or those in midland or east English parishes such as Browne Willis in Buckinghamshire, or Morant at Colchester, would encounter no obvious prehistoric antiquities in their journeys about the neighbourhood. It is therefore hardly surprising to find that the study of prehistoric antiquities in the late seventeenth century was largely centred on megalithic monuments and was carried out in the main by men whose accident of birth or residence connected them with the areas of western Britain in which conspicuous stone circles or chambered tombs form a striking part of the local scene.

The volumes of notes and drawings of prehistoric antiquities made by the Garter King of Arms, John Anstis (1669–1744) are the work of a Cornishman:[17] John Aubrey (1626–97) discovered Avebury on a day's hunting with his neighbouring Wiltshire squires;[18] Edward Lhuyd (1660–1709), though working at Oxford, was a Welshman – 'I don't profess to be an Englishman', he once said, 'but an old Briton.'[19] He made large collections of drawings of megaliths in western Britain in connection with his topographical researches described below: John Toland (1670–1722), that shabby firebrand with a mind of curious ability which turned to Druidism and Celtic antiquities as searchingly as it had to religious controversy, was an Irishman.[20] Andrew Paschal, William Musgrave, John Strachey, and Walter Moyle, living in Somerset and Cornwall, described local megaliths and inscribed stones at the turn of the century,[21] Henry Rowlands, friend of Lhuyd, those of his parish and adjacent regions of Anglesey in 1723,[22] and when Roger Gale edited his father's commentary on the Antonine Itinerary in 1709[23] he included in it drawings and descriptions of the standing stones known as the Devil's Arrows at Boroughbridge, not far from the Gales' Yorkshire home. In Scotland, Professor Garden of

Aberdeen corresponded with Aubrey on the east Scottish 'Recumbent Stone' circles, and the outstanding monuments in Orkney and the Hebrides had been described by Wallace (1693)[24] and Martin (1703).[25] Sir Robert Sibbald described some Roman and prehistoric sites and finds, especially in his *Miscellanea quaedam Eruditae Antiquitatis* of 1710.

In addition to these studies on the megalithic monuments of the north and west, Roman antiquities were relatively obvious objects of antiquarian comment. Alexander Gordon in 1726 published his folio on Roman Scotland, and his patron, Sir John Clerk of Penicuik, was himself a zealous recorder of Roman antiquities and inscriptions.[26] In England, there were the accounts of Somner and Batteley of the Richborough and other Kent sites in 1693 and 1711,[27] as well as Horsley's great book of 1732 and Ralph Thoresby's work in Yorkshire.[28]

It is not the place here to analyse this remarkable body of local archaeological studies, almost all dating from the thirty years following the publication of Gibson's edition of Camden. It not only clearly justifies Francis Wise's claim in 1738 that British prehistoric studies had, over the past generation, made a significant advance, but it also indicates the material already available to William Stukeley when he began his own studies of prehistoric and Roman field monuments around 1715–20. Characteristically, he is an exception in having, as a Lincolnshire man, no territorial associations with the megalithic monuments he studied to such good effect: he approached them from the outside, and his original plan of research seems to have been to compile some sort of objective synthesis of the whole known range of such structures in Britain. How far he succeeded in this ambitious plan we shall see later – the final result bears but little resemblance to such a project.

John Aubrey before him, in his *Monumenta Britannica*, had, in his own incomparable blend of diligence and wayward inconsequence, attempted something similar, which had come as near completion in a manuscript draft as any work of Aubrey's ever could, but which got no nearer printing than a prospectus and specimen page issued in 1693.[29] Much of Stukeley's work did appear in print, 'each instalment deviating more and more from the original intention; some, fortunately, remains in early manuscript draft where the main purpose of objective record and comment is not swamped by accretions of theory or dimmed by the dust arising from forgotten religious controversy. The study of William Stukeley's intellectual life and the estimate of his contribution to British archaeology largely depends on the separation of these two strains in his work.

The bulk of the archaeological literature on which I have very briefly commented above seems to be the outcome of a genuine scientific curiosity about the local antiquities of the countryside as a part of that investigation of all phenomena of the visible world which is so well mirrored in the early transactions of the Royal Society. It took a practical form at the end of the seventeenth century when more than one set of questionnaires were sent out to country squires and clergy by scholars intent on compiling topographical accounts of the various regions of Britain in which they might be interested. These may find their origin in the 'General heads for a Natural History of a Countrey' issued by the Royal Society at Robert Boyle's instance in 1666.[30]

The earliest set of queries I have been able to trace is that issued in 1673 by John Ogilby, 'His Majesties Cosmographer', who was engaged upon a survey and road-book of Great Britain including '*An Historical and Geographical Description* thereof, more Accurate than whatever has been heretofore done, in a fair large Volume, stil'd BRITANNIA.' To this end a printed broadsheet of 'QUERIES In Order to the Description of BRITANNIA' was sent to 'the Nobility and Gentry and all other Ingenious Persons'. There were some twenty short queries, which included a few antiquarian subjects such as 'Castles, Churches, Chappels, Monasteries, Hospitals, Schools, Colleges', or '*Roman* Ways and Stations, Coyns and Monuments &c.'[31]

The parochial inquiry then seems to have been taken up in Oxford, where Thomas Machell, of Cracanthorpe in Westmorland and a Fellow of Queen's, issued in January 1676–7 a broadsheet of queries headed *That the Northern Counties which abound in Antiquities and Ancient Gentry, may no longer be bury'd in Silence*, and presumably intended for circulation to the ancient gentry themselves. It is a rather breathless production, with the queries crowding upon one another in close and sometimes startling juxtaposition – 'What Horse-Races?' Machell asks: 'Where? for what prize? by whom first appointed, and how long ago? What memorable places where ́Battles have been fought? Round heaps of stones, or Earth cast up in Hills, trench'd round about, or otherwise? What fortifications, Camps?'[32] About this time another Oxford man, Dr Richard Parsons, Chancellor of Gloucester, issued an undated sheet of *Queries in Order to a Survey of the County of Gloucester*, and from 1670 until his death in 1711 used this as a basis for his county notes.[33]

Two years after Machell the questionnaires of Robert Plot of the Ashmolean were compiled, also in Oxford, entitled *Enquiries to be propounded to the most Ingenious of each County in my Travels through England and Wales in order to their History of Nature and Arts* and printed in February 1678–9. References to antiquities are more specific here, if rather more romantically phrased than Machell's terse questions: Enquiry viii runs 'Are there any ancient *Sepulchres* hereabout of Men of *Gigantick stature*, *Roman Generals* or *others* of ancient times? has there ever been any *apparitions hereabout?*', and Enquiry x continues:

Are there the remains of any ancient *Castles* or Fortifications hereabout, any ancient *Ways* or *Banks* of Land now remaining, and *Barrows*, or ancient *Monuments* of stone? . . . Find you hereabout any ancient *Mony*, *Urns*, Lamps, *Lachrymatories*, *Pavements*, *Bracelets*, *Rings*, *Seals*, or other *British*, *Roman*, *Saxon* or *Danish*, antiquities?

Partly as a result of such inquiries Plot produced the well-known *Natural Histories* of Oxfordshire and Staffordshire, in which echoes and chalybeate springs, fossils and artificial water-works, stone circles and prodigious births all get a place and a grave disquisition appropriate to each. Contemporary gossip said that he was over-credulous, easily and not infrequently hoaxed by those to whom he addressed his queries, but his Oxfordshire volume has the merit of containing a drawing and description of the Rollright stone circle for the first time. Plot's work is in fact sensible and often percipient: Aubrey modelled the plan of his *Memoires of Naturall Remarques in Wilts* (final version 1685) on Plot's scheme. Ten years earlier he had offered to hand over to Plot his Wiltshire notes.[34]

The best known of these comprehensive topographical inquiries was that compiled by Edward Lhuyd, Plot's successor as Keeper of the Ashmolean Museum, and issued in 1697. Lhuyd, a Welshman and a Celtic scholar, planned an ambitious work on the antiquities and topography of Wales, of which an important part was to be an *Archaeologia Britannica* divided into four parts. The first only was completed, and published in 1707, two years before his death, dealing with the Celtic languages and their vocabularies and grammars. The second part was to contain a comparison of the customs and traditions of the Britons with those of other nations, while the third was to be:

An Account of all such Monuments now remaining in *Wales*, as are presumed to be *British*; and either older, or not much later than the *Roman* conquest:

viz their Camps and Burial Places; the Monuments called *Cromlecheu* and *Meineugwyr*; their Coyns, Arms, Amulets *&c.*

The fourth and last series dealt with the Welsh Princes of the Roman and Sub-Roman Dark Ages.[35]

To obtain material for this work, Lhuyd issued his *Parochial Queries*,[36] which contain in all thirty-one inquiries dealing with antiquities, the two most interesting for our purpose running as follows:

VI – A Catalogue of the *Barrows*, or those artificial mounts distinguish'd by the several Names of *Krigeu*, *Gorsedhau*, *Tommenydh*, *Beili* &c, as also of the *Camps*, and all old *Entrenchments* whatever.

VII – Roman *Ways*, *Pavements*, *Stoves*, or any Under-ground Works: Crosses, Beacons, Stones pitch'd on end in a regular Order; such as *Meinihirion* in *Caernarvonshire*, *Karn Lhechart* in *Glamorgan*, and *Buarth Arthur* in the County of *Caermardhin*; As also those rude Stone-Monuments distinguish'd by the several Names of *Bedh*, *Gwely*, *Karnedh*, *Kromlech.* . . .

In these inquiries we see the systematizing mind at work, and the collection of information concerning antiquities as a part of the general world of natural and artificial phenomena. What is important is that field antiquities – barrows or megalithic tombs or entrenchments – were recognized as fit objects for scientific study. The first field archaeologists were the equivalent in their own studies to men such as John Ray in natural history, and the search and record of megalithic monuments runs parallel to the collection and classification of plants and insects, especially butterflies, from the late seventeenth century onwards.[37] Stukeley as a young man collected additions to Ray's *Catalogus Plantarum Circa Cantabrigiam*, and Locke's friend, John Strachey, to whom Stukeley owed his first plan and account of the Stanton Drew circles in Somerset, read to the Royal Society a paper which Lyell claimed as the first explicit treatment of the theory of geological stratification.

Archaeological studies were part of the discovery of England which the gradually improving means of transport and roads[38] coupled with the mental temper of the time were bringing about – the tour was beginning, whether by Defoe in 1724 writing as a competent journalist of the trades and manufactures of the country, or Roger Gale chatting about his visit to Oxford in 1705, with its new buildings '*a-la-Romain*, of neat architecture', and to Stonehenge.[39] Alexander Gordon was in love with the study of antiquities for its own sake – 'Seeing Reason and Knowledge are the Characteristicks which distinguish Mankind from the more ignoble Part of the Animal Creation', he writes in his preface in 1726, 'those Studies, which are the most improving, deserve our greatest application: In the number of which, *Antiquity* claims a great share, particularly *Archiology*, which consists of Monuments, or rather Inscriptions, still subsisting.' The defence of antiquarian studies continues in this delightfully enthusiastic vein, but he regrets that others may not always share his view:

I know, that there are People to be found, and it is to be regretted, some of them of Birth and Fortune, who expose their own Ignorance, in discountenancing this Kind of Knowledge, giving out, that Antiquity, and such like branches of Learning, are but the Chymeras of *Virtuosi*, dry and unpleasant Searches; So, because they themselves are blind, and uncapable to relish such Pleasures, they have the Imprudence to betray their own Weakness to the World. Hence we observe, That Things which are in their Nature rough, unpolish'd, vicious and cruel, these fit their Genius the best; violent Hunting, Bear-Gardens, Gaming-tables, Quarrelling, and Midnight Revellings, are their Darling Delights.

After this rake's progress for those who are not interested in archaeology, Gordon goes on to say that he feels sure that the Society of Antiquaries, which has recently elected him a Fellow, will come to the rescue, and 'that by them Antiquity and Learning may flourish in this Island, to the total Extirpation of *Gothicism*, Ignorance and a bad Taste'.[40]

This reference to 'Gothicism' is interesting, and deserves comment. Gordon was dealing with Roman antiquities, and, as we shall see later, Stukeley had founded in 1723 a society for the study of Roman Britain, of which Gordon was a member, and which had an avowedly anti-Gothic standpoint. The prevailing classicism of the early eighteenth century endowed the remains of the Roman occupation of Britain with a peculiar importance: they were the only surviving remnants of our former allegiance to the great traditions of Greece and Rome before the links were severed by the Gothic barbarians of the Middle Ages. Stukeley and Gordon in the 1720s were still consciously heirs of Rome and the Renaissance, and just as John Toland had found in contemporary architecture that "'tis still so difficult a thing to get rid of Gothic oddnesses',[41] they felt that the Middle Ages were the destroyers rather than the creators of art and architecture, and the cause of Roman Britain must be upheld. But Stukeley had always had an interest in medieval architecture for its own sake, and this militant classicism did not last. We shall see how he and others threw in their lot with the barbarians, and prehistoric stone circles and medieval churches soon became as fit objects of study as any Roman altar. There is an interesting contemporary parallel in classical archaeology for this movement to go behind the Roman Imperial façade, in the revived interest in ancient Italy brought about by the publication by Thomas Coke in 1723–6 of Thomas Dempster's work of a century before on Etruscan antiquities, the *De Etruria regali*. Here again was a new and considerable impetus to the study of the forerunners of the Romans in another field.

There seems little or no evidence that archaeology might be used in the search for legal or ecclesiastical precedent that had actuated so much of the fine historical research of the Restoration – its material did not admit of it – but religious controversy at last involved even prehistory in the early eighteenth century. Toland's studies in comparative religion led him to the Druids, and Stukeley's antagonism to what he conceived to be the Deistic doctrines led him to find in this half-forgotten Iron Age priesthood justification for his ideas on natural religion.

The evidence of archaeology and of the classical texts enables us today to see the Druids in their rightful setting, a primitive priesthood which had accidentally appeared in the literary record as a result of the contact of the Mediterranean civilizations of Greece and Rome with the northern barbarians in the first few centuries B C. Druidism was the religion of the Celts, especially in Gaul and Britain, which in Britain at least traces its origins back into Neolithic contexts of the third millennium B C. But the eighteenth-century antiquaries, by no means uninfluenced by the contemporary growth of romanticism, found in the scanty and often ambiguous references to Druidism in the classical writers evidence of a mysterious priesthood to which every virtue could be attached, every ruined and romantic megalithic monument attributed. Before long Druids and Deists were competing for attention, and in their claims to enduring public recognition the former won. The Deistic controversy is now a remote lost cause, enshrined in the faded pages of unread sermons and pamphlets, and alive only to the ecclesiastical historian. But the Druids die hard, as every British archaeologist knows to his cost, and even recently could appear without warning in the pages of some journal in the very guise in which they were decked by Dr Stukeley 200 years ago.

II

Childhood and the University

LINCOLNSHIRE IN THE late seventeenth century, and for many generations after that, was perhaps one of the most remote regions of England other than those cut off from outside contacts by mountain or moorland. The still very imperfectly drained fens made it, like the adjacent parts of Cambridgeshire, a land of marsh and heavy winter fogs:

> Nay, tis as vain to wish for Sunny Days
> Altho' the God of Light condense his Rays
> And try his Pow'r, so must in Water lie:
> All still is marsh, the Fen will ne'er be dry.

So the pedestrian poet of 1720: these marshlands were ideal breeding-places for mosquitoes, and malaria was endemic in the fens until the nineteenth century:

> Here Gnats surround you with their humming Drone
> Worse than e'er plagued th' *Egyptian* Tyrant's throne
> In vain the weary limbs expect Repose,
> Their Din invades your Ears, their Stings your Nose.

> Agues and Coughs with us as constant reign
> As Itch in *Scotland*, or the Flux in *Spain*.

And the peasantry, too, at least to the prejudiced eyes of this author, were even more boorish than those in other parts of England:

> The *Goths* were not so barbarous a Race
> As the grim Rusticks of this motly Place,
> Of Reason void, and Thought, whom Int'rest rules
> Yet will be Knaves tho' Nature meant them Fools,
> A strange half-humane and ungainly Brood
> Their Speech uncouth, as are their Manners rude.[42]

Holbeach is today a small country town in this fenland area of Lincolnshire, northwards of which rise the chalk uplands of the Lincolnshire Wolds; in the middle of the seventeenth century it had some standing as a market town. A John Stukeley was born at Holbeach in 1623 and seems to have been a country gentleman with a small estate at Uffington. He was a likeable character, 'of great Agility and vivacity, very quick in speech and ready witt, particularly facetious' and 'mighty fond of making extempore Jokes and verses upon Company', but this easy manner, if it brought him into friendly contact with the neighbouring nobility, also led him to follow them in their expensive pastimes, and on his death in 1675 the family estates had been sorely diminished and were encumbered by debts. He is like a character sketched by Aubrey in his *Brief Lives*, and one thinks of him with sympathy, forgetting the enforced sale of farms and mills and remembering rather the 'verses which he made upon a great Eclipse of the sun, which were not contemptible'.[43]

His elder son, Adlard, had been apprenticed to the law in the days when the family fortunes were presumably showing signs of declining, while the younger, also christened John, was to be brought up to 'country business and Grazing' – in other words as a small farmer. But the boy destined for this employment contrived to defer his actual entry into farming by continuing to attend Stamford Grammar School clandestinely and with the contrivance of his mother, and later persuaded old John to allow him to join his brother in the study and practice of the law.

Adlard and John Stukeley set up their business in the family house at Holbeach: John married, and in 1687 William Stukeley, later to become by far the most distinguished member of the family, was born, the eldest son of a family of four boys and one girl. His father had become a person of standing in the town, concerning himself with building up the family firm, planting trees, laying out gardens, interesting himself with the town drainage, and rebuilding the various pieces of house property he acquired in Holbeach. He was obviously a solid, honest person, well respected in his native town. As might be expected, he was a sound Church-and-State man – 'Loyal to his Prince, a Zealous enemy to Popery and Tyranny, attached to the Church of England, and against persecuting the Dissenters' – and his son was to represent just this essentially English religious viewpoint in later life.

At the age of five William was sent to the Free School at Holbeach under Edward Kelsall. His writing-master, Mr Coleman, had 'a mighty knack of drawing with the pen' and William was taught by him the rudiments of drawing which were to be brought to a pitch of real ability within the next ten years and were to serve him in excellent stead as an anatomist and later as an archaeologist. He seems to have been a solitary child and to have lived very much apart from the rest of the Stukeley children, learning what he could of the arts and crafts from anyone who would teach him. He was eager to make or do almost anything with his hands – he goes 'simpling' with the apothecary, learns the rudiments of surveying (and some astrology) from the parish clerk, talks to the tiler employed on his father's houses, picks up something of painting from someone else, and carves heads out of stone. A puppet-show came to the town, and young William had soon made one for himself; he learnt to dance, and to play the flute (a volume of manuscript flute music written out by him as a young man still survives),[44] and he tells how he listened enraptured to an old man who remembered the traditional ballads of Robin Hood and that of the Elizabethan hero, his namesake, Bold Stukly. His boyhood interest in mechanical contrivances inevitably recalls another and more famous Lincolnshire, man, Newton.

At the age of thirteen he was top of his school, and in this year (1700) he was taken into his father's legal business. The work at first appealed to William, but the law and its interpretation were not very congenial subjects to his already inquisitive and discursive mind. He often turned from the leases and contracts to peep at the schoolbooks he had brought with him into the office and secreted in his desk; the affairs of John Doe and Richard Roe were forgotten as he found to his delight an epithet in Plutarch which could be applied to Whaplode Wood. In London during the law terms with his father he escaped from the routine of his legal duties to climb about the scaffolding of the new St Paul's, then building, or he made his way to bookshops and to the dealers in scientific instruments: at the Lincoln Assizes he confessed that he spent more time in the cathedral and other ancient buildings of the city than attending to the courts.

Restless and unsatisfied with the monotonous drudgery of a country lawyer's office, William begged his father to send him to the university, where he might learn the discipline of those scientific studies that in his boyish way he was trying to grasp. To train as a doctor would, he felt, bring together his interests best – the botany learnt from the Holbeach apothecary would be valuable with a Materia Medica that still mainly relied on medicinal plants or 'simples', crafstmanship would help the anatomist, and skill with the pencil could record his observations. His father no doubt felt that from an uninterested clerk William might easily grow to a moody and disgruntled one; perhaps, too, he remembered how he himself had rebelled against the 'country business and Grazing' which his own father had intended should form his occupation in life, taking instead to the law as a fitter outlet for an active mind, though now his son found it offered little scope for his restless scientific curiosity. To exchange a clerk for an undergraduate meant a financial loss, but the business appeared to be a sound one, and the eventual upshot was that William was sent to Cambridge in 1703, his younger brother, John, taking his place in the family firm.

William Stukeley was admitted a pensioner of what is now Corpus Christi College, then known as Bene't College, matriculating in 1704 at the age of seventeen. His delight knew no bounds: his enthusiastic letters to his old school-friend, Ambrose Pimlow, are full of a jubilant mixture of boyish excitement and such charmingly pompous statements as 'O Philosophy (says Tully) thou empresse of life, one day spent in thy studys is to be preferred before an idle eternity.'[45] He found congenial companions with whom he could talk for what seemed a far from idle eternity; they would meet in his rooms and 'the entertainment was jugs of mild and stale, pipes and tobacco' – tea was just becoming a fashionable drink at Cambridge in his last year.[46] Life was very full and very delightful: there were two or three lectures to attend a day, and reading with his tutor, Mr Fawcett, in Classics, Ethics, Logic, Metaphysics, and Divinity, and with Mr Danny in Mathematical Studies and Philosophy. He went out hunting plants and fossils in the country around, and drew landscapes everywhere, even the bathing-places of Freshmen's and Soph's Pool and Paradise, where swimming and bathing were now becoming common and no longer frowned on as in the days of that eccentric Fellow of St John's, Everard Digby, who caused a scandal to his college and to Cambridge University by publishing in 1587 a book advocating swimming for young men.[47]

Dissection and chemical experiments were at this time beginning to win encouragement at Cambridge as a result of Richard Bentley's patronage of scientific studies in the university, and a new laboratory was formed out of an old lumber-house in Trinity under the supervision of the Italian Vigani,[48] appointed Professor of Chemistry in 1703 and described by Abraham de la Pryme as 'a very learned chemist and a great traveller but a drunken fellow'. He was a friend of Isaac Newton for a time, but the friendship was abruptly terminated by the shocked mathematician when Vigani one day ventured to tell him 'a loose story about a Nun'.⁴⁹ Stukeley attended Vigani's lectures, and his notes taken on the Materia Medica course remained in his library until his death. His tutor gave him a room in Corpus where he could carry out experiments and dissection – it had, he records,

a very strange appearance with my Furniture in it, the wall was generally hung round with Guts, stomachs, bladders, preparations of parts and drawings. I had sand furnaces, Calots, Glasses, and all sorts of Chymical Implements. . . . Here I and my Associats often dind upon the same table as our dogs lay upon. I often prepared the pulvis fulminans and sometime surprised the whole college with a sudden explosion. I cur'd a lad once of an ague with it by a fright.

But in 1705 his father died, and his uncle Adlard (who was 'but weakly') broke down completely and died himself three weeks later. William had to go to Holbeach to help his younger brother and his mother with the family affairs as best he might: his father had become inattentive to his business in his later years and his financial affairs were not so sound as had been thought. He returned to Cambridge again, probably with some monetary sacrifice on the part of his mother. There had never been much of a margin for William's expenses in his undergraduate days, and the few letters from his father which survive show the boy hoping to be sent a watch but disappointed in the expectation,⁵⁰ and conscious of his clothes which were becoming too short for him, though thoughtfully provided by the country tailor at Holbeach with enough in the seams to make them capable of being let out 'and the sooner you doe it the better, before they are thred bare, to prevent being so easily perceived', writes his careful father in the year of his death.⁵¹

Less than two years later, Mrs Stukeley died, and shortly after, John, William's younger brother. Once again he had to make the melancholy journey to Holbeach and to cope, now almost single-handed, with the settling up of the family business and estates. The affairs were in disorder, there were debts of £400 and more to be settled: he managed to let the family house in Holbeach, and had to sell up the furniture and even dispose at Stourbridge Fair of the silver bequeathed to him by his father. Just as his father had found himself starting afresh after the extravagance and mismanagement of John Stukeley of Uffington, so William came of age as an undergraduate with dependent younger brothers and a sister. He seems to have resumed his studies once again without discouragement, however, and created a local sensation by dissecting 'Old Hoyes', a local suicide who received a roadside burial and was therefore available for the eager medical students who could so rarely obtain a human body for examination. In 1708 he began taking his degree and 'kept his Act' according to the grotesque ceremonies of degree-conferring which survived until 1827, with Mr Danny making the customary 'jocular speech' in Latin, full of reference to the thick country air and the frog-ridden marshes of Lincolnshire.[52] He returned triumphant to Holbeach and contrived to give his tenants an entertainment to celebrate the occasion, with a hogshead of ale, and 'tea by Bucketts full' for the ladies.

While at Cambridge he had already begun to take a particular interest in antiquities, and as early as 1708 made careful pen-drawings of medieval buildings such as Boston Stump. A little pocket-volume of these survives, drawn with some skill in a neat, rather dry architectural manner belonging to the seventeenth-century tradition.[53] He was making a romantic approach to ruins which would be in place a century later – 'I frequently took a walk', he says, 'to sigh over the Ruins of Barnwell Abby, and made a Draught of it, and us'd to cut pieces of the Ew trees there into Tobacco Stoppers, lamenting the Destruction of so noble monuments of the Piety and Magnificence of our Ancestors' – sentiments which would have won the approval of Catherine Morland herself.

In the mode, too, of the later eighteenth and the early nineteenth century is the following charming and well-known vignette, written after his stay with friends in Northamptonshire and excursions with Martha Lucas, sister of his host. She

had somewhat of an airy temper, and accompanyd me in several of my Rambles in that Country to view Antiquitys, Roman Camps, and the like. We traveld together like Errant Vertuosos, and when we came to an old ruind Castle, etc., we climbed together thro' every story and staircase, mutually helping one another, and pulling each other over the gaping arches and rugged heaps of rubbish, and when I had occasion to draw a view of them out, as we sat upon a stone or the grass, she held my ink horn or my paper, and was very serviceable and assistant in taking my designs, and all without any reserve or immodesty; nor could any aged Philosophers have conversd together with more innocent familiarity or less guilt even than in thought or intention. Nor could travailing curiosity or Antiquarian Researches be rendered so agreeable as with a fair and witty Companion and Fellow Labourer, and when we returnd home my young disciple could entertain the Family with so very curious Relation of the curiositys we had seen, that it would be difficult to say whether so nice taste in the Remains of Ancient Time most recommended a young Lady, or that Refined Study became more lovely and delightful for her sake.

But this idyllic holiday came to an end, and in August 1709 he took himself to London, to continue his medical studies at St Thomas's Hospital under the great Dr Mead. He took with him from Cambridge a scientific training probably as good as any that could be obtained at that time: he had learnt to observe accurately and to record his observations in writings and by drawings. A country boy, he was at home in the open air, on foot or horseback, looking eagerly about him at ruins or wild flowers, Roman roads or landscape gardening, with alert eyes in the face that could be sullen or suddenly animated which we see in the portraits of ten and fifteen years later. For fifteen years, from 1710 to 1725, he was to make one or more expeditions on horseback across the English countryside every summer, noting, sketching, measuring, and conjecturing upon antiquities. His notes, which nearly all survive, form a topographical record of great importance, but there is more than that in his Stonehenge and Avebury work. Here we have a major contribution to British archaeology.

PORTRAITS OF STUKELEY

1 Sketch portrait in pen and wash by Sir Godfrey Kneller of William Stukeley at the age of thirty-four. This informal profile, without a wig, gives a more convincing impression of the man than the rather bland formal portrait Kneller painted in the same year.

2 Self portrait in pen and wash of Stukeley aged forty in 1727 – a rather surly figure, two years before leaving London and taking Holy Orders.

3 Full length formal portrait by an unknown artist of William Stukeley in the 1720s.

4 (*left*) Sir John Clerk of Penicuik (1676–1755), oil portrait by William Aikman. Sir John was the leading Scottish antiquary of the day and his diary records two visits to Stukeley.

5 (*below left*) Portrait of Roger Gale (1672–1744). A Yorkshire country gentleman and MP for Northallerton, he was a longstanding friend of Stukeley, who married his sister in 1739.

6–9 (*opposite*) Pen and wash drawings by Stukeley around 1722–3 of four of his friends in classical guise as Roman Knights: (*top left*) Thomas Herbert, eighth Earl of Pembroke (1656–1733) (Carvilius); (*top right*) Algernon Seymour, Lord Hertford (1684–1750) (Segonax); (*below left*) Ralph Thoresby (1658–1725) the Leeds wool merchant and antiquary; (*below right*) Andrews Jelfe (?–1759), architect and builder whose drawings of the Roman temple of Arthur's O'on Stukeley published in 1720.

magnus Carvilius.

SEGONAX

Ld. Hartford

ob. 1749-50.   Stukeley f.

R. Thorelby

23. May 1723

ob. Oct. 1725.

Stukelsy f.

A.J. 6 Jan 1722.   andrew jolf.

10 Replica of Arthur's O'on, the Roman temple near Falkirk destroyed in 1743, incorporated by Sir John Clerk's son, Sir James, as part of his design for the stable block of Penicuik House, Midlothian. For Stukeley's engraving of the original, see fig. 5.

TOPOGRAPHICAL SKETCHES

11 (*below*) Pen and wash drawing by Stukeley of Malvern, 1721, representative of his ability and charm as a topographical draughtsman.

Prospect of Malvern Church.

the ground in Abury declines very much e. & w. moderately n. & s.

13. May 1724 this day I saw several of the few stones left on overton hill carryed downwards towards w. Kennet & two thirds of the temple plowd up this winter & the rest thrown into the cavitys so that next year it will be impossible ever more to take any measure of it.

this afternoon I pacd over Kennet avenue, the intermediate distance betw. overton hill & Silbury thence to the termination Bekampton avenue thence along bekampton avenue to Abury again I find each avenue is 8000 f. long, from Silbury to either of the extremitys 6000. the whole making 30000 foot or 6 miles. I drank at Swallow head to the pious memory of king cuneda it runs pretty strong now out of the solid chalk & the water is altogether as clear as Horace's fons Blandusia & admirably soft. I found some parony clia hereabouts upon the north sides of banks a palm long & flowers extravagantly large the folio rutaceo I mean a palm long & about this bulk much brook lime watercresses at Swallow head thalictrum call the meadow plants hereabouts the temple at the end of Bekampton avenue was at the extremost corn field just under a square enclosure at the S. side of bristol road betw. it & Bathroad in a streight line with Silbury & overton hill. the ditch round Abury is not so broad as the vallum by a great deal but very deep & sloop cut out of the solid chalk very curiously tho' they have not been so carefull in heaping up the vallum but left it irregular this is the profile of it

tho' the stones of the avenue are but 100 on a side & generally 70 f. interval yet 1000 f. is gaind by the curvity of those avenues for sometime the two stones are near 100 f. asunder perhaps they regarded the harmonic number of 8 or the proportion of Silbury. the entrances to both druids house that under overton way hill & that S. of Stonehenge is under with a sort of causway.

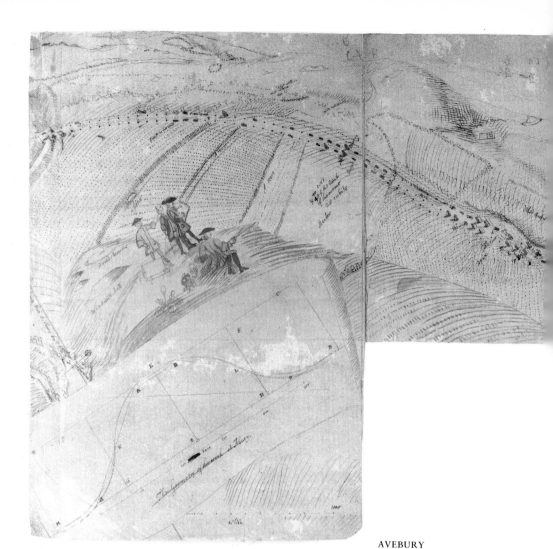

AVEBURY

14 (*left*) Destroying a fallen stone at Avebury by fire and water, 20 May 1724. Stukeley has titled his splendid drawing an 'Atto de fe' in reference to the 'auto da fe', the sentence given by the Spanish Inquisition resulting in the burning of a heretic.

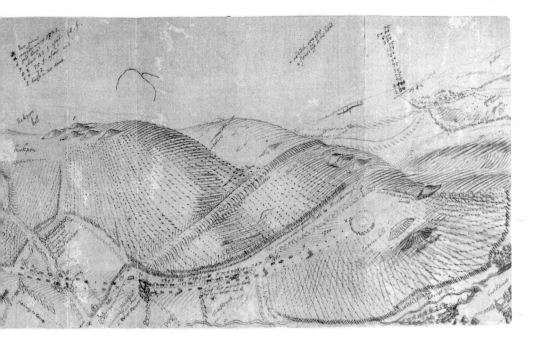

13 (*above*) The right-hand wing of a great triptych of Avebury and its avenues, undated but drawn by Stukeley almost certainly in 1723, with the main circles on the extreme left, Stukeley and his friends on what is now Waden Hill, and on the right the Sanctuary circles and the barrows on Overton Hill.

15 (*below*) Drawing by Stukeley of Avebury from the south, 19 July 1723, with instructions to the engraver, though no engraving of this drawing was published.

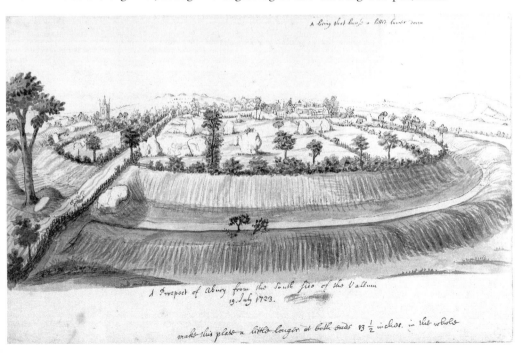

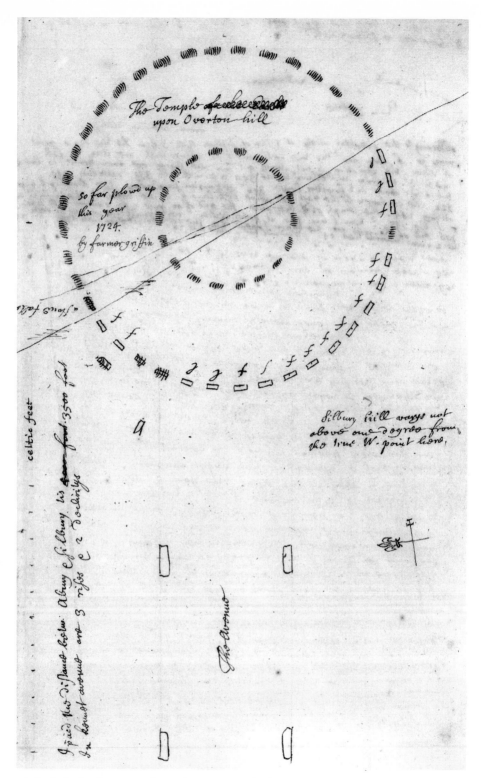

The Temple ~~of~~ upon Overton hill

So far plow'd up this year 1724. by farmer griffin

Silbury hill varys not above one degree from the true W. point here,

celtic feet

16 Stukeley's plan recording what remained of The Sanctuary stone circles immediately after Farmer Griffin's depredations of 1724. The remaining stones were soon destroyed.

III

The Doctor
and the Field Archaeologist

To sit at the feet of Dr Richard Mead, F.R.S., must have been a remarkable experience for William Stukeley, now a young man of twenty-two, fresh from Lincolnshire and the comparative provinciality of the University of Cambridge. Dr Mead moves across the eighteenth-century scene as a splendid, stately, glittering embodiment of the fashionable physician, the patron of the arts, and the friend of everyone, from the Court to his students at St Thomas's. There is a cosmopolitan polish to the great man – had he not been educated at Utrecht, and taken his degree at Padua? – and his antiquarian interests were those founded on his Italian travels, while his collections of books, sculptures, and gems were in the Renaissance manner; he was no great scholar, and one feels that this urbane physician is of another age than that which delighted in the barbarous gothicisms of our Saxon forefathers and encouraged the work of such as Humphrey Wanley. Yet if Richard Mead was no Robert Harley he had the golden touch. He could be a staunch and discerning friend to any intelligent young man, and could help to bring him into the company of the most interesting and influential society of London. The abundance of dedications to him (among which comes Francis Wise's *Letter* about the Berkshire White Horse quoted at the beginning of Chapter I) bear testimony to the place he held in the minds of contemporary writers and scholars.[54]

Stukeley pays a tribute to Mead's 'Innate goodness and sweetness of temper', while the older man (himself only in the middle thirties) must have found an answering charm in his pupil. They made the rounds of the coffee-houses together and this did not escape the comment of the other medical students. It was due to constant dinners with Dr Mead, says Stukeley, 'where we drank nothing but french wine', that he was 'every winter laid up with the gout: and that sometimes for three or four months together. In the spring, I was oblig'd to ride for my health, and that brought me in the humour and love of travelling; whereby I indulg'd myself in the study of the antiquities of my country.'[55] Fortune so smiled on friends of Dr Mead that even the gout produced by his convivial dinners could be no common disorder, but one conducive to antiquarian fieldwork, and one still feels across 200 years a certain benign glow diffused from this periwigged Maecenas with his gold-headed cane and his coach-and-six. Mead 'lived more in the broad sunshine of life than almost any man', Dr Johnson was to say after his death, and he had the capacity of enabling his friends to share its warmth.

But in March 1710 Stukeley decided to leave London and to practise medicine in the country. He was to come back to London in 1717 only to leave it again ten years later for another period of country retirement until 1748. The years from 1710 to 1717 are probably the most obscure in the whole of his extraordinarily well-documented life. Apart from two tours in search of antiquities, the first of many, we know he took a practice in Boston, in his native Lincolnshire, and that he was made a Freeman of that town in 1713. He dedicated a print of Boston church to the Marquis of Lindsey in 1715 and wrote an account of the Roman remains of Richborough in September 1716. Clearly he was becoming more and more interested in the serious study of British antiquities, and, as we shall see, already concerning himself with Stonehenge.

He had made friends with Maurice Johnson of Spalding, who in 1710 had just been called to the Bar and was only a year Stukeley's senior. Johnson had returned to his family seat of Ayscoughfee Hall at Spalding and was largely instrumental in founding, 1709–10, one of the most famous of the local antiquarian and literary societies, The Gentlemen's Society of Spalding, an institution still happily surviving after a continuous life of over 270 years. It numbered among its early members Newton, Bentley, Pope, Gay, Samuel Wesley, and Rysbrack (to select from a notable list), and had not started as an institution primarily antiquarian in its objects, but as a group of local gentry who met at the coffee-house to read, and listen to reading, from the *Tatler* and *Spectator*. But with Maurice Johnson as its secretary for the first thirty-five years of its life, and with such members as Stukeley, the Gales, Beaupré Bell, Sir John Clerk, and Alexander Gordon, it is not surprising that it devoted considerable attention to such studies and kept in the closest contact with the Society of Antiquaries of London, which could only claim to be a junior foundation, dating from 1717.[56]

The minute-books of the Spalding Gentleman's Society are continuous from 1712, and constitute a remarkable record of a provincial antiquarian and literary society's activities over more than two centuries. At the early meetings at Mr Younger's Coffee House in Spalding explicit rules for the conduct of the meetings were laid down, and merit quotation in full. 'The Oeconomical Rule', as it is headed in the 1712 Minute Book, runs as follows:

The Society must meet or assemble at Four.

When the Season requires there must be a Table, Two Candles, a Pair of Snuffers, and good Fire dureing the Society.

There must be a Pot of Coffee, of an Ounce to Eight Dishes, or in proportion.

There must be a Pot of Bohee Tea of ½ oz. to Twelve Dishes.

There must be Twelve clean Pipes and an Ounce of the best Tobacco.

There must be a Chamber Pot.

There must be a Latin Dictionary, a Greek Lexicon All the Printed Papers ordered by the Society not read Publickly and this Book of Injunctions.

The Coffee and Tea must be ready exactly at Five and taken away before Six which Done a Paper must be read by some member.

Then a Tankard of Ale holding One Quart and No More must be set upon the Table.

The President must always sit on the Right-Side of the Chimney and take care of the Fire.[57]

There is in existence a most interesting letter from Maurice Johnson to Stukeley in 1714, advising him on books to read on British history and antiquities, apparently in response to an inquiry for such a reading-list.[58] Caesar, *De Bello Gallico*, Book VI, will inform him 'as to the Druids and Religion (if your Profession will permit You to look into that)' – a comment not without its amusing side when one considers his passionate absorption in later life with just this subject, and containing a mild gibe at the atheism popularly attributed to the medical profession in his day as in Sir Thomas Browne's time, when the phrase *ubi tres medici, duo athei* was current. From Caesar, he can go on to Tacitus, with Savile's commentaries (the Elizabethan translation to which reference has been made above), Milton's *History of England*, Richard Verstegan's *Restitution of Decay'd Intelligence* (1605), the preface to Camden (presumably in reference to Gibson's edition), the *Introduction to the Old English History* by Robert Brady (1694) – Brady whom Professor Douglas has likened to a Horace Round of the Restoration, accurate and acrimonious in controversy – and Peter Heylin's *Help to English History* (1652).

Johnson then goes on to urge that historical studies must always be considered in their geographical context, a remarkable early appreciation of a factor which Gibbon was later to turn to such magnificent effect and which today has become a fundamental of historical research. He is even moved to verse on this subject:

> . . . Geography must show
> In exact Plans what Watry Currents flow
> Dividing Provinces, the various Name
> Each Province hath assum'd, the Land the same,
> Must fix the Boundaries each Century knew
> Where Cities have been, And where Forest grew.

I have quoted from this letter at length, both on account of its intrinsic interest as an expression of the view of a young man, who was not an historian, on historical studies in the early eighteenth century, and also because it helps to build up a picture of what Stukeley's background of reading was at the time when he came to study the ancient monuments of Britain at first hand. At a later stage I propose examining in detail the evidence we have for Stukeley's reading and knowledge in general of early antiquities at the time he was working at Avebury and Stonehenge, but for the present it is convenient to trace the course of his numerous journeys in which he made first-hand observations of field monuments in various parts of Britain.

The raw material on which our knowledge of these tours is based is varied. The period covered is 1710 to 1725, during which time Stukeley made ten or a dozen excursions of varying length and extending from Kent to Devonshire, Wrexham to Lincolnshire, and north to the Roman Wall. For some of these tours (e.g. those of 1710 and 1725) he kept a consecutive journal in a notebook from day to day – the original books for these two expeditions survive and may have existed for others, though they are not now traceable. From 1722 to 1724 Avebury and Stonehenge took up much of his time each year, though other places were visited as well and for these years, and for the two journeys made in 1712, and 1719–21, we have to rely partly on the published versions of the tours which (excluding Avebury and Stonehenge matter) were printed in his *Itinerarium Curiosum* of 1724,[59] and partly on incidental references in letters or other similar sources. One outstanding source, however, is afforded by his drawings, which he made at every place he visited and which he generally dated, and which constitute therefore almost a diary in themselves. Many of these drawings survive in the original, and others were engraved and published either in the 1724 edition of the *Itinerarium* or in the second and posthumous edition of 1776, which contains a mass of engraved plates bound together without any accompanying text. Not only did he date his original drawings, but he also dated the alterations he made to the proof engravings. At Avebury, at least, he took these proofs with him the year after they had originally been drawn and checked them against the landscape. As we shall see, this meticulous noting down of the date enables us to chart with some assurance the changing shoals and quicksands of his theories during the years he worked on megalithic monuments.

The tour of 1710 was that of an 'Itinerant Society' consisting of Stukeley and seven friends and was presumably on horseback.[60] They started from Boston, and went through Deeping, Uffington (Lincs.), and Stamford. Thence they struck westwards towards Northampton-shire through Fotheringay and Oundle, and came to Boughton, the seat of the Duke of Montagu. This was a place destined to play a very important part in Stukeley's later life and he was to acquire an intimate knowledge of the great gardens and parks laid out like another Versailles, where (as he noted in 1710) 'Nature is rack'd and improv'd ten thousand ways and made to submit to the powerful Laws of Mechanism' and where the fountains were controlled by 'an Engine of neat workmanship, to force up Water in great Draughts, which cost above a thousand pounds'. Stukeley's interests had not at this time become predominantly antiquarian, and his tour notes are those of one intrigued by everything remarkable or unusual – the gardens at Boughton, the fact that at Geddington 'we met with some excellent Ale', or the new buildings at Northampton going up after the recent fire. His love of architecture, which had begun in his boyhood at Holbeach, never left him, and never degenerated into mere antiquarianism. He was interested in building for building's sake and had a fine eye for structure and solidity which comes out in his drawings. He could admire (as at Northampton) the 'very fine Assize House, of Corinthian work' or 'Allhallows built after a new modell . . . a curious and very beautiful church'.[61] Equally could he appreciate the essential constructional features of Gothic beneath the surface ornament, unlike so many antiquaries of the eighteenth century who never succeeded in piercing the screen, but accepted instead the accessories of the style as its whole content.

After Northampton, the party made its way to Naseby, Towcester, and Buckingham, and so to Oxford. Here they met that successful opportunist and polemical preacher, Dr Sacheverell, then the hero of the hour after his impeachment for seditious libel expressed in his high church sermons, and took snuff from his box of Boscobel oak, while Stukeley was so impressed by the new buildings going up from the designs of Hawskmoor, Townesend, and Aldrich that he has to insert after his panegyric an apology to his own university for such disloyal sentiments. This was the great period of rebuilding in Oxford, and Stukeley had no time for antiquarianism in the reconstruction of colleges – the new quadrangle of All Souls, of Hawksmoor's designing, he regarded as 'an anachronism of the *Gothic* degenerat taste' and thought with regard to the work at University College that 'uniformity in this and other structures in the university, is no sufficient reason for using the old style of building'.[62]

Near Oxford he was able to examine some Roman and prehistoric sites, at Alchester the Roman town, and earthworks at Blenheim, where he noted that Plot had confused the Grim's Ditch with a Roman road – 'it was doubtless some division of the antient *Britons*', he sensibly comments, anticipating in a lucky guess the result of the excavations of the 1930s when the earthwork was shown to date from the immediately pre-Roman Iron Age.[63] But the most significant antiquity he saw was the Rollright Stones – an Early Bronze Age stone circle standing on the ridge of the Cotswolds above Chipping Norton.[64] This had been known to Plot, and to Stukeley was 'the greatest Antiquity we have yet seen', the stones being 'corroded like wormeaten wood by the harsh Jaws of Time', and altogether they made 'a very noble, rustic, sight, and strike an odd terror upon the spectators, and admiration at the design of 'em'. 'I cannot but suppose 'em', he goes on, 'to have been an heathen temple of our Ancestors, perhaps in the Druids' time.' Despite his profession he had read his Caesar and meditated on ancient religion already: in this remark was the germ of his lifetime's work.

In 1712 Stukeley made an extensive tour to the west of Britain.[65] He had, he says, long wanted to go to Wales, 'and longed to hear at least a language spoke soon after the deluge': the Celtic languages were still a great mystery to the learned, and, as we shall see later, philology was in a state of delightfully irresponsible conjecture which could happily equate Welsh and Hebrew and assign both to the primeval ages of mankind. It was indeed possible to produce such oddites as David Malcome's *Essay on the Antiquities of Great Britain and Ireland* (1738), which sought to establish 'a relationship between the languages of China and St. Kilda, promising eventually to demonstrate a like connexion between those of St. Kilda and the

Isthmus of Darien'[66]. Stukeley was no student of languages, though an undaunted interpeter of place-names and other words by means of any language which could provide four or five letters in common with the word under debate. Edward Lhuyd's *Archaeologia Britannica* of 1707, the first attempt to correlate the known grammars and vocabularies of the Celtic languages, seems to have been beyond his superficial range in these matters. He preferred instead the speculative and unreliable *Glossarium Antiquitatum Britannicarum* published by William Baxter in 1719, to which he subscribed, and which he subsequently annotated with even more dubious etymologies than those of the author. Lhuyd's book, however, does not seem to have been in his library[67].

The tour of 1712, later published as the *Iter Cimbricum*, was not only made in search of spoken Welsh. He proceeds through Grantham to Derby, Buxton, the Peak, Chatsworth, and Manchester, noting some antiquities, but only as a part of the general 'curiosities' of the journey – the silk mills at Sheffield, the baths at Buxton, the house and gardens at Chatsworth. At Manchester, 'the most rich, populous and busy village in *England*', industries and the new church 'after the London models' receive comment in a manner as unantiquarian as that of Defoe, though naturally the Roman remains at Chester are noticed. Welsh was at last heard spoken at Wrexham. He detected enough accidental coincidences in superficial sounds to convince him that several Lincolnshire dialect words had their origin in pre-Roman Celtic speech, and was appropriately pleased with this discovery. He returned through Lichfield and Tamworth back to Boston again. The general impression one forms of this tour as one reads it in the *Itinerarium Curiosum* is that it differs little from that which could be written by any intelligent gentleman of the period with a slight, and understandable, antiquarian bias and an interest in ancient sites as a part of the countryside at large. It is not yet the characteristic product of a field archaeologist.

From the time of this tour until the year 1717 we know, as I have said, very little of Stukeley's life as a country general practitioner in Boston. The first *Iter* of the published series is an *Iter Domesticum*,[68] and in its published form has no precise indication of date, but must have been formed from notes made in Lincolnshire at this time. He made some sensible comments on the earthwork known as the Car Dyke in Lincolnshire, which he thought was likely to be a Roman canal used, among other purposes, for transporting corn from Cambridgeshire northwards. Recent archaeological evidence of the extensive Roman agricultural system in the Fenland supports this view, and the Roman date of the work is proven in Cambridgeshire and extremely likely in Lincolnshire.[69]

With regard to his professional activities, he is known to have encouraged the drinking of the chalybeate waters of Stanfield, near Polkingham; the practice of resorting to spas was now rising in popularity after its beginnings in the previous century.

There are a few surviving letters to Maurice Johnson that throw light on Stukeley's intellectual interests during these years. Writing in May 1714, he tells Johnson how he has compiled a great series of chronological tables[70] of all the British kings from the time of the legendary Brutus. This has obviously been based on the famous medieval fabrication of Geoffrey of Monmouth, which is accepted whole-heartedly by Stukeley, who strives to vindicate Brutus as an historical figure. References to the Druids show that they, too, were claiming his attention, but in 1716 he is more explicit about his immediate interests. 'Happening to fall' he writes:

into a Set of thoughts about Stonehenge in Wiltshire, by a prospect of Loggan's which I met withall, I undertook to make an exact Model of that most noble and stupendous piece of Antiquity, which I have accomplish'd, and from thence drawn the groundplot of its present ruins, and the view of it in its pristine State, and propose from thence to find out the original Architectonic Scheme by which it was erected, together with its design, use, Founders etc and thereby do justice to so wonderful a Curiosity which Mr. Camden passes over so slightly (as usual in things ancienter than the Romans) with such a wretched anile account, as tis hard to say whether that or his draught of it be most false and trifling.[71]

David Loggan (1635–93) engraved two views of Stonehenge which are certainly more satisfactory than the odd fantasy engraved in the early editions of Camden and based apparently on a Dutch original.[72] Stukeley's criticism of Camden's description and illustration is quite justified, and one can see that he is intending to repair the omissions in the *Britannia* of 'things ancienter than the Romans' by some sort of work of his own. He was fortunately encouraged in his resolution to write a new account of Stonehenge by Lord Pembroke, whose acquaintance he made within the next few years in London, for by 1719 he is again writing to Johnson:

One thing I believe I must be forc'd to bring to some kind of a head which is Stonehenge. My Lord Pembroke, in whose neighbourhood that Noble Antiquity stands, and I, have had a deal of talk about it and he generally either comes to me or sends for me two or three times a week to discourse concerning it. He has been three times this Summer and taken accurate measures of it which my short stay would not permit me and given me thereby an opportunity of finishing my Drawings.[73]

He had decided to return to London in 1717, and by 18 May of that year we find him established at a house in Great Ormond Street, near that which his old friend and patron Dr Mead had taken shortly after his retirement in 1715 from the post of Physician to St Thomas's Hospital.

We do not know the reasons for this decision to return to London, though we may infer that, as at Stamford thirty years later, he had grown weary of the provinciality of his neighbours and become restive for the company of congenial friends and a life in the more invigorating atmosphere of the circle of the London intelligentsia. Whatever the reason, the move was to have a profound influence on his future life and work, and the obscure young country doctor is well on the way to becoming Dr Stukeley of London, Fellow of the Royal Society and of the Society of Antiquaries, the friend of the intellectual nobility and the acknowledged authority on the Ancient Britons and their temples. Despite his frequent asseverations that he loved the solitary retreats of the country, William Stukeley was really a gregarious creature. He liked conversation, and he liked a little flattery; a pleasure in debate was to make him self-opinionated and dogmatic in later life, but now, in his thirties, he must have been an entertaining talker and full of an intellectual curiosity that would have made him move in the most varied circles of learned conversation. That charm and pleasant oddness, the cheerfulness and disarming ingenuousness which Warburton was to set on record after his death[74] as his most endearing characteristic in middle and later life, must have made him popular from the first. Now he had returned to London we see Stukeley not as an isolated individual, but for a time a member, and often the leading figure, of a group of friends and fellow antiquarians.

Of these friends we have already encountered Lord Pembroke, and the benign figure of Richard Mead, now a neighbour in Bloomsbury and setting up his picture-gallery and collection of works of art where students could come every morning to copy and examine the pictures, and Watteau came for professional advice.[75] But one of the most important friendships formed by Stukeley during this period was that with the two sons of Thomas Gale, the eminent scholar who died as Dean of York in 1702. Roger Gale, the eldest son, was fifteen years older than Stukeley and had inherited the family estates of Scruton in

Yorkshire, had represented Northallerton as a Member of Parliament intermittently between 1705 and 1710, and was in 1717 a Commissioner of Excise, dividing his time between London and Scruton.[76] 'This cultured country gentleman', wrote Professor Douglas, 'moves freely if with a certain stiffness among the scholars of the time',[77] but though he may be faintly patronizing to Hearne or off-hand to Wanley, there is little in his recorded contacts with Stukeley to suggest anything but a warm friendliness with nothing of the grand manner. Roger Gale was not a profound scholar like his father, and his habits of mind were more of the eighteenth-century dilettante than of the heroic scholars of the Restoration. He is likely to have found a more sympathetic reaction in Stukeley with his discursive interests and, in the field of historical or classical studies, shallow scholarship, than in those who, like Thomas Hearne or Humphrey Wanley, were carrying on the great tradition of immense industry and patient research founded by that band of historians of which Thomas Gale had himself been a member.

Roger Gale was in 1722 to publish the important twelfth-century documents contained in the *Registrum Honoris de Richmond*: in the field of more ancient studies he had already in 1709 published, with his own additions, his father's commentary on the Antonine Itinerary of Roman Britain. His younger brother, Samuel, only five years older than Stukeley, has even less claim to fame in antiquarian studies, to which he was, however, much attached. From the glimpses one gathers of Samuel Gale, however, he seems a rather pleasant man: he was in the Customs House in London and his connoisseurship was recognized in his appointment as examiner of books and curiosities imported into England from abroad. He was the constant companion in the later days of young Dr Ducarel, with whom he went on antiquarian tours with a coachman and a footman, travelling fifteen or twenty miles a day and staying at small inns where, after dinner, Gale would smoke his pipe while Ducarel wrote out his notes on the day's tour. His godfather and relative had been Samuel Pepys, a link with the great days when Gibson was editing the *Britannia* and dined with Pepys to discuss its progress.

Stukeley's friendship with Lord Pembroke and the brothers Gale must have been an immediate passport into the antiquarian circles of London. He was elected a Fellow of the Royal Society early in 1718 on Mead's nomination; Sir Isaac Newton was president and the Society was at the height of its reputation.[78] But in the previous year a group of historians and antiquarians, which included Humphrey Wanley and the Gales, were discussing the formation of a society solely devoted to antiquarian subjects. 'It was first begun by a few gentlemen', Roger Gale wrote ten years later, 'well-wishers to Antiquities, that used to meet once a week, and drink a pint of wine at a tavern for conversation'.[79] This informal club had in fact been formed as early as 1707 by Wanley, John Bagford, and John Talman, who had met every Friday at six in the evening at the Bear Tavern in the Strand: other members were collected, such as Peter le Neve, William Elstob, and Thomas Madox, and the venue moved first to the Young Devil, and then to the Fountain, in the Strand. In 1709–10 Maurice Johnson and Stukeley copied from the Cottonian Library the original Elizabethan project for an Antiquarian Society contained in MS Faustina C5 and drew up proposals based on this.[80] The Society was by the winter of 1717–18 settled on this more formal basis, with those minute-books begun which now form a continuous series to the present day.[81]

The foundation of the Society of Antiquaries of London, as it became called, with Stukeley as its first secretary, was in fact due to the last representatives of the fine tradition of historical scholarship in the late seventeenth century, and although in the matter of precise dates its beginnings fall within the first two decades of the eighteenth century, the spirit which brought it into being is that of the days of George Hickes and the Saxonists; the medieval historians such as Tanner, Gale, and Madox; the palaeographical studies of Wanley and the minute textual care of Thomas Hearne. Something of this spirit still remained alive in the 1720s when William Stukeley was beginning his serious antiquarian studies, and his inevitable inclusion in the newly founded Society of Antiquaries brought him into close contact with those who carried on the tradition from the previous century. But by 1730 it was almost extinct – in November 1726 the engraver Elisha Kirkall was to write to Stukeley, 'I suppose you have heard, Humphrey Wanley is dead, he undertook a second Wife who Laid him flat on his Back in a fortnight's time,'[82] Madox died in the following January, and William Elstob (brother of Elizabeth, the 'Saxon Nymph', who was publishing critical texts of Saxon documents in the first decade of the century) had died in 1715. Stukeley was able to touch the hem of the mantle of good scholarship, but no more, and by the time he came to write his two major archaeological works in the 1740s the intellectual atmosphere was sadly changed, and he with it.[83]

Despite his position as secretary, Stukeley seems to have taken little part in the business of the Society of Antiquaries, nor did he communicate to them the results of his important fieldwork in

1719–25 except by exhibiting a model and drawings of Stonehenge and the Avenue on 14 February 1721–2. In Soc. Ant. MS 265 he gives two lists of 'English Drawings', one of which can be identified with Bodl. MS Top. gen. d 13, a book of drawings made when with Roger Gale in the summer of 1721; and the other, 'English Drawings Summer 1722', some of which are contained in Bodl. MS Top. gen. b 53, a scrapbook of drawings of various dates. Whether these drawings were merely laid before the Society or were at one time in their possession is not clear. He was partly instrumental in setting up the committees on coins in 1721–2, referred to below, but otherwise it is difficult to trace the part played by him in the Society's affairs. He resigned from the secretaryship on moving to Grantham in 1726 and seems to have discontinued his subscription, with the result that he was 'amoved' in 1740 and not re-elected until 1754. We shall see that there is reason to think that Stukeley found the Society more interested in medieval than in prehistoric or Roman studies, and so played a minimum part in its affairs.

Dr Thomas Gale has been described as 'in many ways almost a Renaissance figure',[84] with his immense breadth of knowledge and interests, ranging from the classical scholarship that made him Professor of Greek at Cambridge in 1666 to his profound medieval English studies which led to his editing the great series of chronicles in 1684–91. In English history his special interests lay in the pre-Conquest period: he edited Gildas and Nennius, and, as we have seen, his edition of the Antonine Itinerary was published posthumously by his son Roger. It is hardly to be wondered at that he was known to John Aubrey, who refers to Dr Gale as 'my faithfull friend' in a letter to Anthony Wood in 1692,[85] or that he was interested in the work that Aubrey had been so long compiling, the *Monumenta Britannica*.[86] This remarkable discursive work on British antiquities, of which an important section was that entitled *Templa Druidum*, contains the results of Aubrey's fieldwork at Avebury and Stonehenge. (A letter from Aubrey to Anthony Wood written in March 1679/80 implies that the original title of the whole book was to be *Templa Druidum*, later altered to the name under which the work is now known.)[87] It appears that Thomas Gale had added some notes to Aubrey's work, and as we shall see he had certainly made a transcript of much or the whole of it. In 1692 a scheme was on foot to publish the *Monumenta* with some unspecified additions of Gale's, for Aubrey wrote to Wood on 19 May of that year saying that:

Dr. Gale accepts your proposall, and is y^r servant. Mr. Wilkinson has a mind to print my Monumenta Britannica and Dr. Gales's, he is an honest man, and fitt to undertake it. Dr. Gale has promised me to assist me in it but would not have me carry them to Oxon but I will bring my Templa Druidum to be perused by you and Mr. Collins of Magd Coll.[88]

In the following year a printed sheet of Proposals for printing the *Monumenta* appeared, and Wood dated his copy as 10 April 1693,[89] but in August of the same year Ralph Bathurst wrote to Aubrey (who from the address was at that time staying with Dr Gale) referring to the work with Gale's annotations as still not printed.[90] As is well known, the *Monumenta* long remained unpublished in its entirety, though it was used by Gibson in his 1695 edition of Camden, where large extracts are printed from the *Templa Druidum* section, among others.

The annotated transcript made by Thomas Gale of Aubrey's *Monumenta Britannica* cannot now be traced,[91] but there is no doubt that Roger Gale, who had inherited his father's library, showed it to Stukeley in 1717 or 1718, for in December of the latter year Stukeley retranscribed a great part of this manuscript into a folio commonplace-book[92] with a note at the end 'Thus far Mr. Gales' Notes out of Mr. Aubrey's Collections'.[93] It seems, pending an exhaustive collation, substantially the text of the *Monumenta* as it survives in Aubrey's holograph, but there are a few notes against which Stukeley has written 'T. Gale' or 'T. Gale 1697'.[94] It includes a miscellaneous selection of antiquities scattered all over Britain, but most important are the notes on Avebury and a copy of the small-scale plan of the stone circles and Kennet Avenue at that place, though there is no copy of Aubrey's large plane-table survey of the circles in detail which is contained in the original manuscript of the *Monumenta*.

Nowhere in his published work does Stukeley give an indication as to the events which led up to his fieldwork at Avebury, on which his fame as a field archaeologist today mainly rests. More than twenty years later, when he was writing up a retrospective journal of his earlier life, he put in an entry – 'In 1718, Mr. Roger and Sam. Gale and I took a journey, through my eager desire, to view Abury, an antiquity altogether unknown',[95] and again in his published book of *Abury* (1743) he says 'when I first went thither about 1718'[96] without further explanation. Now these dates, unsupported by any other evidence, do not seem to me to fit in with the facts – they imply a visit to Avebury before the transcript from the Gale MS, and as he certainly made a visit there with the two Gales in May 1719, I believe the 1718 date to be a mistake of a year in the memory of an event twenty years old.

There is little doubt, I feel, that Stukeley's attention was directed to Avebury by Gale's transcript of the *Monumenta Britannica*, and that the connection between the two great pioneer tasks of fieldwork on this monument was a close one. The description of Avebury in the 1695 Camden, taken from Aubrey's notes, is jejune enough and would hardly fire one with an intense desire to visit the site, but the drawings and details in the original account are another matter. In a later chapter I propose examining in detail the extent of general antiquarian knowledge, and of Stukeley's in particular, with regard to stone circles and allied monuments in the early eighteenth century, but for the present it is sufficient to indicate that references to Avebury, other than those made by Aubrey, were scanty and uninteresting. Stukeley had seen Rollright, and as we have noted was already contemplating preparing a new account of Stonehenge. The extraordinary monument revealed by Aubrey's description – stone circles that 'exceed Stonehenge as a cathedral doth a parish church' – must have filled him with the 'eager desire' he records to examine the site personally. It was now winter, but here was an incentive for another tour when the warm weather came again in 1719.

The present village of Avebury lies in the high, windswept chalk downs of North Wiltshire, west of Marlborough. It was established as a village by the time of Domesday Book; the church retains pre-Conquest work, and though probably none of the cottages surviving today are earlier than the seventeenth century, there is archaeological evidence from pottery and other finds made during the recent excavations of intensive habitation from the time of the Norman Conquest onwards. The position of the original village was clearly determined by the more ancient structures over which it now largely sprawls, for the vast, roughly circular bank and ditch enclosing nearly thirty acres of ground and delimiting the original prehistoric site provided an obvious ready-made enclosing rampart within which the Saxon settlement could be placed, and the presence of the ancient earthworks was echoed in the place-name with its suffix of *burh*, a defended camp. Today, the name of Avebury is associated primarily with these remarkable prehistoric structures of chalk-cut ditch and piled rampart, and the huge stones set up in circles and rows within and about the earthwork.

After its initial record by Aubrey, and Stukeley's work of surveying and description with which we shall deal in the next chapter, sporadic digging took place in the nineteenth century, but systematic excavation did not take place until the twentieth century, initiated by the work of St George Gray in its first decade. In 1934–8 large-scale excavation, accompanied by a judicious policy of conservation and restoration, was undertaken by Alexander Keiller, and the problems of Avebury were for the first time attacked on a wide front. As a result of this work, and of subsequent smaller operations, it is possible to construct a fairly coherent account of the site, and its probable sequence of construction.[97]

Avebury is in itself a complex of structures covering several square miles, and mainly consisting of circles or double rows of standing stones, of local 'sarsen', natural but artificially erected in their present positions. The main group of circles is contained by the enormous ditch with external bank which formed the shelter within which the Saxon village was placed, and round the inner lip of this ditch stood a circle originally of about a hundred huge upright stones of which thirty are visible today standing or fallen. Within this are two smaller circles, set side by side, with approximate diameters of 320 and 340 feet, the southern retaining five and the northern four stones out of an original number of about twenty-five to each circle. In the middle of the northern circle stood three stones, of which two remain, in the southern a single upright, now destroyed. All these stones lie among the cottages, gardens, and fields of the village, and in the eighteenth century the subdivision of the present fields into small, hedged, and tree-lined 'closes' must have rendered the ground-plan very difficult to disentangle.

There are four gaps in the great bank and ditch, approximately at the points of the compass. Excavation has shown that three at least of these are original features, with causeways of solid chalk left in digging the ditch on the north, west, and south: presumably that to the east is also part of the original layout. In the seventeenth and earlier eighteenth centuries the Bath Road ran across the downs west of Marlborough on a line still represented by a grass drove-way, and passed through the Avebury circles by the eastern and western entrances through the bank and ditch, but, as we shall see, few of the travellers along this highway noticed the prehistoric monument through which they passed on horseback or in a coach.

From the southern entrance there ran a double line of standing stones towards the village of West Kennet in the valley of the Kennet river, and then, turning south-eastwards, the double line continued up to the crest of Overton Hill, where two small concentric stone circles

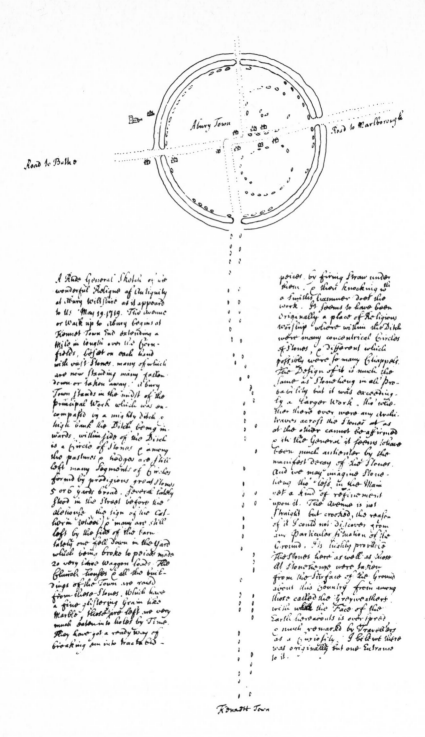

3 *Stukeley's first sketch plan of the Avebury circles and the West Kennet avenue, made on 19 May 1719.*

stood until 1725, to be recorded by Stukeley. The lines of standing stones he named the West Kennet Avenue, by which name it has since continued to be known, and the stone circles on Overton Hill were, he states, known locally as 'The Sanctuary' – a rather improbable name for rural folklore, and suggesting some seventeenth-century antiquarianism at work.

From what we now know to be an original entrance in the west of the great circle, Stukeley believed that he had discovered another avenue leading towards the village of Beckhampton. Near this village still stand two out of an undoubted original setting of three stones, but the remaining stones claimed by Stukeley as representing the remnants of the Beckhampton Avenue have been destroyed or buried since his day. The existence of such an avenue has therefore been much disputed: it would have to cross very marshy ground immediately outside the main circle, in the neighbourhood of the hamlet of Avebury Trusloe, and it has been suggested that the standing stones at Beckhampton represent the remains of a circle which may have had a separate avenue of approach from the Avebury Trusloe area. Recent work has however suggested that the evidence is in favour of Stukeley's claim.

The evidence of excavation is consistent in showing that Avebury, like other embanked circles or 'henge monuments', is of Late Neolithic date, around the middle of the third millennium B C. It had a complex building history, spread over two or three centuries into the period when Beaker pottery was in use, and burials of this date were found at The Sanctuary and against stones of the West Kennet Avenue.

This archaeological excursus is necessary to explain the monument to which Stukeley gave so much attention in the 1720s. His devoted record of the then extant remains, far more considerable than they were to be two centuries later when scientific work on the site first began, leaves archaeologists permanently in his debt.

Pausing long enough at Basingstoke to draw the Chapel of the Holy Ghost,[98] Stukeley and the two Gales made for Avebury in May 1719, and on the 19th he was able to make the first of his innumerable drawings of the great stone circles and avenues.[99] In the early eighteenth century, as we have seen, the main road ran through the circles of standing stones within their enormous encircling bank and ditch,[100] and it is a tribute to the indifference of the average British traveller that nobody seems to have been struck by the remarkable nature of the site they traversed further than to notice, perhaps, with Philemon Holland, that they had come to 'an uplandish village, built in an old camp, as it seemeth, but of no large compass' and to regard the standing stones as 'rather natural, than artificial'.[101] We are today as puzzled as Stukeley was that no comment was made on the regular setting of the stones, nor on the huge chalk-cut ditch and its massive rampart – 'of this at least one might think', he observes, that 'its oddness would arrest one's attention, if the stones escap'd it'.[102] But no; Stukeley and the Gales standing there in May 1719 seem to have been the first to appreciate the true nature of Avebury since that memorable day in 1648 when John Aubrey unsuspectingly discovered it on a day's hunting.

It is not to be wondered at that Avebury, in the early eighteenth century incomparably more complete a monument than it is today, even after the excavations and restorations of 1934–9, should have stirred the imagination of William Stukeley and caught him in the web of that strange fascination it still possesses. There are a few details of this first visit of 1719, less of that of 1720, but from 1721 to 1724 we can build up a diary of his work here and at Stonehenge after he had made a decision to prepare for both monuments a detailed record of their every feature. It was an ambitious task, and one for which there was little precedent save that of Aubrey, little guide save common sense. We do not know how consciously the plan was formulated in Stukeley's mind in 1719–20, but it is certain that the destruction which he saw going on around him at Avebury was a powerful incentive to the preparation of a record in writing and in drawings before all should be lost. He was powerless to prevent the breaking up of the stones which was taking place yearly, but he knew that a record on paper was better than the total loss to the learned world of an obviously outstanding ancient monument.

In 1723 Stukeley wrote, in the unpublished draft of an account of Avebury,

The particularity of this description is designed to preserve the memory of this most illustrious Work of the highest Antiquity, & writing it upon the spot made me catch at every appearance that I thought tended that way & had a regard in the eye of the Founders. If it be not too dry for the entertainment of the present age it may assist in their contemplation of what reality remains & I hope will tempt them strictly to survey it, which may rescue some part from impending ruin when the Country finds an advantage in preserving its poor reliques, but future times may hence be able to ascertain its purport, when this sort of learning will be more cultivated.[103]

He had, he felt, discovered Avebury himself – it was easy to forget Aubrey, dead a generation ago and with his notes still unpublished, when this fabulous work of remote antiquity revealed itself bit by bit, as stones were seen to form new circles or unrecognized alignments as he walked about the village and the fields around. These stone circles of Britain – Avebury the giant of them all, Stonehenge, Rollright, Stanton Drew, of which Mr Strachey had told him at the Royal Society, the others in Wales and Cornwall with queer names which had been sketched by Aubrey, and in those notes of Edward Lhuyd's he had been shown by Anstis, Garter King-of-Arms – what were they? *Templa Druidum*, so Aubrey thought: the Druids, about which Maurice Johnson advised him to read in Caesar many years ago. Here was a field of research untouched by anyone, work that could pleasurably be combined with those tours on horseback in the spring and summer for which the gout induced by Dr Mead's claret offered a more convincingly scientific excuse than his natural, almost boyish enthusiasm and intense love of the English countryside and its antiquities.

These are the thoughts which seem to run behind the notes systematically compiled in 1718–20 on stone circles and other allied structures in Britain and incorporated by Stukeley in his folio commonplace-book and the draft *History of the Temples of the Ancient Celts* written at Avebury in 1723, from which a quotation has just been given. The extent of the knowledge he collected, and his interpretations, will be discussed later in an appraisal of the whole Avebury and Stonehenge fieldwork, and it will be convenient to consider now this particular work only in its general setting of the pattern of his life from 1720 to 1725. Tours were to be made to other sites than those of megalithic monuments, new friends formed, and some hostile criticism encountered: he was still a practising doctor, and could find intellectual outlets in scientific as well as antiquarian researches. The years before he left London again in 1726 were to be crowded and enjoyable.

After the visit to Stonehenge and Avebury in the early summer of 1719 Roger Gale went to Oxford, there to call on Thomas Hearne, that curious crabbed figure who was now an established eccentric in the Oxford scene. 'He tells me', Hearne wrote in his diary, 'Dr. Stukeley is about a new Discourse upon Stone Henge, and y^t he will give a new Draught. He says Inigo Jones's Account is all wrong, as well as the Draught, and y^t it is founded altogether upon an Hypothesis.'[104] Hearne was suspicious of most people, and he was not prepared to think that Stukeley's views might be any sounder than those of Inigo Jones, however enthusiastic Gale might be. He was also rather suspicious of Gale, and though he walked with him to University College, would not go in, lest he should meet his enemy, the Master, Dr Arthur Charlett – a needless precaution as it happened, since Charlett was away. Gale was later to write to Charlett about Stonehenge, assuring him that 'in a little time you will have a most accurate description of it,∗ with nice plans and perspectives, and a learned dissertation upon those sorts of Circular Antiquitys from my friend Dr. Stukeley'.[105] Whatever Stukeley may have been saying himself, his friend seems to have been acting as an effective publicity agent, and helping, however unconsciously, to build up in the minds of the intelligentsia the picture of Stukeley as the one great authority upon Druids and ancient British monuments.

Such an impression was really fair enough: there were no obvious competitors in this field of studies, and since the classical sources were both exiguous and ambiguous, and the study of the actual stone circles such a novelty, no one was in a position to dispute anything Stukeley might say. The disadvantage of being a pioneer is that one has no colleagues engaged on the same researches who can effectively criticize one's work as it progresses.

In the summer of 1719 Stukeley had been able to make a very interesting observation in field archaeology at Great Chesterford in Essex. The Roman town at this place was in great part under the plough, though much of the town wall remained, with the Crown Inn on its line.

> Thither [wrote Stukeley to Roger Gale] I summoned some of the country people, and, over a pot and a pipe, fished out what I could from their discourse, as we sat surveying the corn growing upon the spot . . . the most charming sight that can be imagined is the perfect vestigia of a temple, as easily discernible in the corn as upon paper. . . . The people say, let the year come as it will, this place is ever visible, and that it has been so ever since the memory of man, and fancy the fairies dancing there causes the appearance.[106]

Stukeley was in fact describing a 'crop-mark' of a type well known today from archaeological air survey, where the presence of ancient wall-foundations beneath the soil causes parching and a poorer growth of the crop along their lines, which show up as lighter streaks. He was able to make a sketch-plan of the building at Chesterford, and makes half a dozen references to similar phenomena at other sites in the *Itinerarium Curiosum*: these must rank among the earliest uses of the observation and record of such indications. With the advent of archaeological air photography they have become a standard tool of investigation.[107]

Among the eight or ten books which constitute the literature of Druidism and the ancient Celtic religions from the Renaissance to the end of the seventeenth century, one delightful small quarto seems to have taken Stukeley's fancy. It was written by a doctor of medicine at Dijon and was published in 1623, but described a find made in 1598 of a glass cinerary urn within a stone cylinder with a Greek inscription recording the name of a priest, Chyndonax.[108] Dr Guenebault devoted many pages to the discussion of this remarkable discovery, making allusions to the burial customs of the Scyths, the Indians, and the Ethiopians and tentatively concluding that the priest Chyndonax was a Druid. Archaeologically the whole find is suspect, and the name of Chyndonax the Druid does not appear in the august pages of Holder's *Altkeltischer Sprachschatz*: Kendrick, however, thought that a case might be made for regarding it as a genuine antiquity.[109]

It has long been known that Stukeley was called 'Chyndonax' by his friends, and the name in fact appears on the engraved portrait by Vandergucht which forms the frontispiece to *Stonehenge* (1740). But behind this nickname, so appropriate for the Archdruid, lies a remarkably interesting episode in early eighteenth-century archaeology. In July 1722 Stukeley and a group of friends formed an antiquarian club for the study of Roman Britain, under the extraordinary name of the 'Society of Roman Knights', the members taking titles chosen, so far as possible, from those of Celtic princes or notables associated with the Roman Conquest of Britain.[110] Such a use of assumed names was not unknown in contemporary clubs of intellectuals – the Zodiac Club, founded at St John's College, Cambridge, in 1725, named its members from the planets or the zodiacal signs.[111] But in the Society of Roman Knights the jest was carried to an ingenious conclusion by choosing names more or less associated with the homes or country seats of the members. Lord Winchelsea takes the name of Cingetorix, a Belgic prince of eastern England; Roger Gale that of Venutius, the Brigantian ruler whose territory included Yorkshire; and Alexander Gordon was Galgacus, as befitted a Scot, though his patron, Sir John Clerk, had to be Agricola, as Celtic names were by then running short.

To the original sixteen members,[112] others were added in the next two years, and as it was specifically laid down in the constitution of the Society that it would include members of both sexes, the Duchess of

ILLVSTRISSIMVS e Excellentissimus Dominus Dns.
THOMAS Comes Pembrokiæ &c &c &c CARVILIVS Magnus, Aug.
Supremus ORDINIS Equitum Romanorum, Dominus &c
                                    LONDINIO AVGVSTA.

Illustrissimus e Excellentissimus Dominus Honorius comes de
Winchilsea &c &c &c CINGETORIX D.s de Romani Portu DVROLENO

Illustrissimus e Excellentissimus D. Algernonius Comes de Hartford &c.
BEGONAX D.s de VENVTIVS   CVNETIONE
D.s Rogerus Gale CASIVELAVNVS D.s de ISVRIO VEROLAMIO
D.s Wittus Stukeley Cancellor CHVNDONAX D.s de DVROCINONTE
D.s Jacobus Hill CARADOCVS D.s de ARICONIO
D.s Samuel Gale CVNOBELINVS D.s de Colonia CAMVLODVNO
D.s Wittus Hulet BRENNVS D.s do PONTIBVS
D.s Gerard vander queth INDVTIOMARVS D.s do BRAGE
D.s Johes Pine ADMINIVS D.s de SORBIODVNO
D.s Thomas Bawtre SCRIBONIVS D.s do CAMBORITO
D.s Johes Warburton Fenith ASCLEPIODOTVS D.s do CANONIO
D.s Alexander Gordon GALGACVS D.s de BREMENIO
D.s Nicholaus Hayn VARRO D.s do CAESAROMAGO
D.s Johes Clark AGRICOLA D.s do CASTRISALATIS
)(Mauritius Johnson PRASVTAGVS 8.s &c CAVSENNIS

        In Romanos Equites, Antiquitatis Britannicæ vindices.
Multa reposta diu veteris vestigia ROMAE
    servat in annoso terra Britanna sinu.
Antiquam Romani Equites, exquirite matrem,
    Eruite o tenebris hæc monumenta suis.
Hæc honobræ lucem nostris annalibus addant,
    Et Britonum historiam diruta Roma struat.
Vt Romam videas, patria, Brito, cedere noli,
    Roma domi, peregre quam tibi quæris, adest.
                        M. Mettairs. 12 Dec. 1722.

4 List of founder members of the Society of Roman Knights, 1722.

Hertford was elected in 1723 under the title of Bonduca, and at some time Stukeley's future wife (see below) was also admitted as Cartismandua. This inclusion of women in a learned society of the 1720s is so unprecedented that we may be sure that it was a direct outcome of Stukeley's characteristically unconventional approach.[113] The women members of the Roman Knights take their honourable place as the first of their sex to belong to an English archaeological society: the Society of Antiquaries waited for almost exactly 200 years before admitting its first woman Fellow.

But the Society of Roman Knights was not intended as a joke, however playful the nicknames. In 1723 Stukeley made a remarkable statement of policy to the 'pretorium', assembled in the Fountain Tavern in the Strand.

With what grief [he said] have these eyes seen the havoc, the desolation, the fate of Roman works, owing to the delusion and abominable superstition of cloyster'd nuns and fryers, what the fury of wars could not demolish, their inglorious hands have destroyed. . . . Whilst others therefore are busying themselves to restore their Gothic Remnants, the glory is reserved for you to adorn and preserve the truly noble monuments of the Romans in Britain. . . . The business of this Society is to search for and illustrate the Roman monuments in the Brittanic Isles. The name of Knights (equites) dictates to us that travelling is part of our province and we are so far to answer our title of Roman, as never to return home without conquests. We are to encounter time, Goths and barbarians . . . we are to fight, pro ara et focis, to save citys and citysens, camps, temples, walls, ampitheatres, monuments, roads, inscriptions, coyns, buildings, and whatever has a Roman stamp on them. . . . The motto is Temporis utriusque vindex, which intimates to us that we are able to be the Secretarys, the interpreters and preservers of the memorials of our ancestors.

Perhaps the most curious thing about this admirable manifesto for a nascent Society of Roman Studies is the attack on those who are concerning themselves with 'Gothic Remnants'. We have seen that Alexander Gordon, Galgacus of the Roman Knights, publicly expressed a hope in 1726 that the Society of Antiquaries would 'extirpate *Gothicism*', and it is likely that Stukeley is in fact referring to this Society in his speech, and that his formation of the Roman Knights two or three years after the foundation of the Antiquaries was prompted by the lack of interest in Roman and pre-Roman studies he found in the senior body. In this context we can appreciate the underlying significance of Sir John Clerk's complaints about the Society of Antiquaries made to Roger Gale in 1736.

I am sorry to find [he writes] that Gothicism prevails so much in your Society. If your Antiquarians won't entertain a just opinion of it, they won't believe it to be only the degeneracy of Greek and Roman Arts and Sciences. In this view I my self have admired the laborious Dullness and Stupidity which appear in all the Gothick contrivances of any kind. These Barbarians had the originals in full perfection and yet could discover no beauties for their imitation, but Goths will always have a Gothick taste.[114]

The Roman Knights did not survive long as an organized body, though the nicknames did, and produced such odd passages in letters as that in the following from Cunobelin (Samuel Gale):

Having been inform'd since the arrival of Prasutagus from the Girvii, of the never enough to be lamented Miscaridge of the incomparable Cartismandua, a Misfortune wch not only myself but all Albion must be seriously touch'd with, since without doubt we have lost a second Chyndonax, or at least another Boadicea.[115]

Some of these personages we know already, but with such figures as Segonax and Cingetorix there enter into the Stukeley circle new friends with whom he was to be intimate during the next few years from 1720 onwards. Segonax is Lord Hertford, later to become Duke of Somerset and Earl of Northumberland, a man a few years Stukeley's senior: his country seat was at Marlborough, within a few miles of Avebury and not more than thirty from Stonehenge.[116] The other is 'Winchelsea, as an Englishman; And as a Briton, Cyngetorix', as the signature runs to a letter from the fifth Earl of Winchelsea to 'Chyndonax'.[117] The earl was a man of over sixty at this time, but his warm friendship with his 'dear Brother and Venerable Druid' thirty years his junior is apparent in all his letters.[118] He and Lord Hertford will be in London soon and 'intend to beat up your quarters' at ten o'clock next Monday morning;[119] Lord Hertford has asked them both to dine – he will call for Stukeley in his coach and they will go together, taking 'a book of your drawings, and the book in which we write our names and mottoes'[120]: the *Liber Amicorum* now in the Bodleian Library.[121]

Lord Winchelsea lived in Kent: his wife, the famous Anne, had died in 1720, and now he and his chaplain, Mr Creyk, are alone at Eastwell, where they drink the healths of Stukeley and Roger Gale every night, and during the day explore for antiquities. He writes as a pupil to a master, reporting his activities and hoping they are on the right lines. They set out 'in my chaise, where that will go; and where not, upon our horses', they make notes and take bearings of the Roman road when they come upon it, 'and I have been at Julaber's Grave, which I formerly measured only by my paces but I have now taken it with my measuring-chain, and have all its dimensions very right; and I took its bearings with my compass, and from the top of it I have drawn out a prospect of the country'.[122] Could an apt pupil, even though twice one's own age, have done better? The notes, the measurements, the bearings, the prospect – these are so closely similar to Stukeley's own mode of work that they can only have been the result of explicit directions given by him to Lord Winchelsea. And they are more than that. They are first beginnings of the great tradition of archaeological fieldwork and survey foreshadowed by Aubrey and continued in Britain to our own times.

In February 1726 Allan Ramsay published a 'Scots ODE to the *British* Antiquarians',[123] dedicated to Lord Hertford who was at that time President of the Society of Antiquaries, and celebrating the learned circle of which he was so distinguished a member:

> To HARTFORD, and his learned Friends
> Whose Fame for Science far extends,
> A *Scottish* Muse, her duty sends,
>   From *Pictish* Towers:
> Health, Length of Days, and happy Ends,
>   Be ever yours.

Thus the opening stanza, and the ode proceeds to more antiquarian detail:

> When you the broke Inscription read
> Or among antique Ruins tred,
> And view Remains of Princes dead
>   In Funeral Piles,
> Your Penetration seems decreed
>   To bless these Isles.
>
> Where Romans form'd their Camps of old,
> Their Gods and Urns of curious Mold,
> Their Meddals struck of Brass or Gold,
>   'Tis you can show
> And Truth of what's in Story told,
>   To you we owe.

Then follows praise of the other noble antiquarians:

> BARDS yet unborn shall tune their Lays
> And Monuments Hermonious raise
> To *WINCHELSEA* and *DEVON's* Praise –

nor is Sir John Clerk of Penicuik forgotten among the antiquaries 'Be North the Wall' who are:

> No Strangers to each antique Stage
>   And Druids Cells,
> And sacred Ruins of each Age,
>   On Plains and Fells.

It is interesting to see that Druids are appearing as an essential part of an antiquarian performance as early as 1726, before Stukeley had published his Stonehenge and Avebury books, but Ramsay seems to have known something of his work, for there is a verse:

> PEMBROKE's a Name to *Britain* dear
> For Learning and brave Deeds of War;
> The Genius still continues clear
>   In him whose Art
> In your rare Fellowship can bear
>   So great a Part –

and against the words 'In him' Stukeley has placed an asterisk in his own copy of the Ode with the simple footnote in naïve pride – 'Stukeley'.[124]

Stukeley's boyhood interest in architecture had led him to friendships with designers and builders of houses – the two were hardly yet distinct and though there was 'a small number of men who specialized in architectural design and supervision . . . gentlemen by birth who supplemented their inadequate private income by acting as architects and artistic advisers, most people . . . still thought it unnecessary to consult anyone but a master workman when undertaking building operations'[125]. Such an architect-mason was Andrews Jelfe, 'my Ingenious Friend', says Stukeley, 'who was sent by the Board of Ordnance to repair and make some Forts in *Scotland*' at this time.[126] Jelfe's work took him to the Antonine Wall, then more usually known as Graham's Dyke, and at Stukeley's request he made measured drawings of a remarkable building which stood not far from Falkirk on the bank of the Carron River. This structure, known locally as 'Arthur's O'on', or 'Oven', was circular, stone-built of good ashlar, and with a domed roof with central opening, and some sort of much-weathered relief carving over the doorway. It had been known to antiquaries for centuries, and the first literary record is indeed as ancient as a thirteenth-century gloss on MSS of the Historia Brittonum of Nennius which refer to *domumque rotundam politis lapidibus*

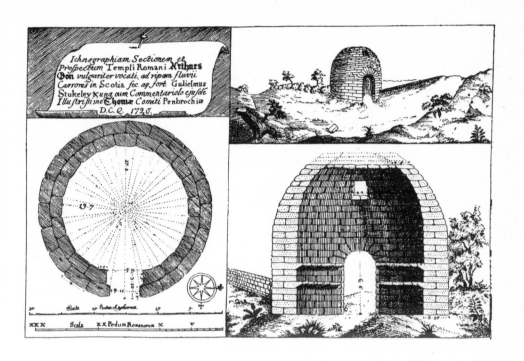

5 *Stukeley's engravings of Arthur's O'on, the Roman temple near Falkirk destroyed in 1743, published in 1720 and based on drawings by Andrews Jelfe. Compare with plate 10.*

super ripam fluminis Carun, which can hardly be other than Arthur's O'on. The medieval Scottish historians such as John of Fordun mentioned it, and it was an object of antiquarian interest to the traveller by the end of the seventeenth century. Jelfe's drawings, which were published by Stukeley with a commentary in 1721, are, with those of Alexander Gordon, among the only records of the structure which exist, for it was demolished in 1743 to repair a mill-dam by Sir Michael Bruce of Stenhouse, 'an ignorant sordid and ungenerous man who, abandoned to covetousness', pulled down this unique monument amid the outcries of the Scottish antiquaries of the day.[127]

Stukeley, in common with other antiquaries of the time, believed Arthur's O'on to be a Roman temple or shrine. This is in fact the modern view, and it has been suggested that we might see in it 'a war memorial, or *tropaeum,* erected to commemorate a victory . . . crowned by the completion of the Antonine Wall'.[128] At all events Stukeley's first archaeological publication was to be our primary source for this extraordinary structure, followed by Alexander Gordon in 1726, and the remarkable full-sized replica erected as a dovecot and as a part of the stable block at Penicuik House, Midlothian, by Sir James Clerk in 1763.[129] Stukeley was thus prompted to make his first published appearance as an antiquarian; he etched plates from Jelfe's drawings himself and added a map of the Antonine Wall.

In May 1720 he was at Stonehenge and Avebury with Roger Gale, and in October came a fine surprise to gratify his medical interests. An elephant brought to England from Bencoolen had died after being a very popular public exhibit in London, and Stukeley notes that the beast's disorders had been 'heightened by the great quantity of ale the spectators continually gave it'.[130] Sir Hans Sloane secured the carcass and had it brought to his garden in Chelsea where, in bad weather, it was dissected by Sir Hans, Stukeley, and other medical men. Stukeley's skill in drawing was brought to bear on the elephantine anatomy, and he wrote an *Essay towards the Anatomy of the Elephant,* illustrated by his diagrams, which was to be printed in 1723 as an appendix to his other published medical treatise *Of the Spleen, its description and history, uses and diseases, particularly the Vapors, with their remedy.* It was more than fitting that this essentially eighteenth-century production should have prefaced to it Anne, Countess of Winchelsea's *Ode on the Spleen,* inserted by the express leave of the earl. The book consisted of three Gulstonian Lectures read to the College of Physicians in March 1722 and is illustrated with fine, accurately drawn plates. Someone was to tell Hearne in 1725 that this book was 'much commended . . . as having very nice and exact Cuts', but Hearne, who by this time had decided to rank Stukeley among his arch-enemies, rounded on his informant, declared the doctor to be as useless in his own profession as in antiquarian studies, and finally extracted the tactful admission that Stukeley 'had some skill, tho' he was far from being a topping or an eminent Physician'.[131]

In the summer of 1721 Stukeley set out with Roger Gale on another tour which began with brief visits to Avebury and Stonehenge on 16–18 August.[132] On his way down the Kennet valley between Newbury and Marlborough he felt the need of a geological map – 'I have often wished', he wrote, 'that a map of soils was accurately made, promising to myself that such a curiosity would furnish us with some new notions of geography, and of the theory of the earth, which has only hitherto been made from hypotheses.'[133] He always tended to think in terms of maps and plans and drawings rather than of the written description, and on this is based the greatness of his work as a field archaeologist. Even the fantastic religious theorizing of his later life was as often as not visually presented in elaborate plans of the Ark of the Covenant or Solomon's Temple, drawn with the same precision as he had used in surveying the Avebury circles.

The tour continued to the west, to Gloucester, where he confesses that he is 'much in love with Gothic architecture (as called)',[134] and on by early September to Hereford; Ludlow by the middle of the month. Then they turn north to Wolverhampton and Derby, and so to Grantham by the second week in October. The notes of this tour were put together as the *Iter Sabrinum* of the published collection and it is still the journal of the ordinary educated tourist of the eighteenth century rather than that of an archaeologist, with plenty of room for descriptions of how 'Mr. Gale and I disputed a good while about borage quite grown out of cognizance', of the Euonymus growing in the Ludlow hedges, or the Welsh harper who played at Leominster 'and at proper intervals threw in many notes of his voice, with a swelling thrill, after a surprising manner, much in the tone of a flute'.[135]

The next summer, that of 1722, saw him once again taking to horseback in search of antiquities, and in July he and two friends were making for Avebury.[136] The friends were artists: one was Gerard Vandergucht, of Dutch ancestry though born in London where he had a business as an etcher and engraver; he was now a young man of twenty-six, and was later to engrave many plates for Stukeley's

6 *One of the two engraved tail-pieces in the published* Abury *of 1743, from a sketch by Stukeley in 1722 of Reuben Horsall, the parish clerk of Avebury who tried in vain to prevent its destruction.*

7 *The second tail-piece shows by contrast the smug Tom Robinson, active in destroying the stones by fire and sledge-hammer, with an attendant Fury and ill-omened bat. 'Jerostratus' refers to the legendary Herostratus who burnt the great temple of Ephesus as an act of self-advertisement.*

publications.[137] The other was John Pine, like Stukeley in his early thirties and within the next few years to establish his reputation as an engraver of great precision and excellence, to become a personal friend of Hogarth, and, stout and jovial, to be painted as the fat friar in 'The Calais Gate'.[138] Both were to become Roman Knights that summer.

It seems to have been a light-hearted expedition, perhaps rather less restrained and conventional than those made with the Member for Northallerton. They all could draw, and this made a form of entertainment that could be shared – Vandergucht sketched a Mr Holland of Amesbury on the back of the hotel bill there,[139] and when at Avebury they were settled in the Catherine Wheel inn, and one evening as Stukeley, sleepy after a hard day's fieldwork, drowsed off in his chair so that the candle-light threw the modelling of his face into interesting chiaroscuro, Vandergucht made a brilliant pen-portrait sketch on a page of the doctor's field-notes and measurements.[140] And though undated, I think it was on this visit that Stukeley made the amusing little drawings of the Parish Clerk, Reuben Horsall, and of Tom Robinson the 'Stonekiller', which were to be engraved as tailpieces in his published account of Avebury, and the sketch of Reuben Horsall's little mongrel dog, which turns up impudently among the Avebury field-notes.[141]

Stukeley's drawings of the 1720s, of which so many survive, show a delightful natural style of draughtsmanship which has become freer and less dry than the careful pen-drawings in the notebooks of 1708–10. He now often uses a sepia or grey wash in addition to a sensitive pen-outline – 'My friend, Dr. Stukeley, draws with a pen, without shading, unless with a little Indian ink or soot wash', wrote Maurice Johnson some years later[142] – and his 'Prospects' often have a great feeling for the country, and I think are not unworthy to take an honourable, if minor, place in the early history of English landscape drawings. His engravers seldom did justice to his original drawings when translating the mobility of pen-and-wash into the rather arid contemporary technique of line engraving, and Vandergucht alone seems to have preserved something of the odd charm and mystery of the drawings made within the Avebury circles. Stukeley's figure-drawing was always poor, and sometimes grotesque, but at least lively, and in his wash-drawing of the destruction of a great stone at Avebury, by building a fire under it, he has made a splendid spirited composition with an imaginatively decorative handling of the swirling masses of black smoke dominating the scene, with its ant-like men furiously stoking the blaze under the enormous recumbent stone.[143]

The Catherine Wheel at Avebury (which stood on the opposite side of the road at the central village cross-roads to the present inn, the Red Lion) now displayed on its walls drawings presented to the landlord by Stukeley – a view of the south entrance of Avebury drawn in 1722, and one of the stones in the centre of the north inner circle, made in the previous year, and a portrait of Reuben Horsall. These were seen there seven years later by a Mr Loveday, and he passed on the information to Hearne, who, allowing his passion for accurate record to get the better of his dislike of Stukeley, carefully transcribed in full the titles of the drawings into his diary.[144]

From Avebury Stukeley went on to Stonehenge, perhaps by himself, as from now on there is no record of Pine and Vandergucht accompanying him. They may well have taken a coach back to London after seeing Avebury, to which they must have come as a result of Stukeley's enthusiastic conversation in London. Even the single visit would have helped Vandergucht to preserve, in his engravings of Stukeley's drawings, something more of the spirit of the place than might otherwise have been possible.[145] Stukeley then returned to London via Silchester, and seems to have set off almost immediately on another tour, which took him to Cambridge, Boston, Lincoln, Dunstable, and Leominster, where he arrived on 14 September, but by the beginning of October he was in Rochester, and made a Kentish tour which lasted until the middle of the month.

The greater part of this year's expeditions, omitting the Avebury and Stonehenge work, he combined into one *Iter Romanum* which was dedicated to the Earl of Winchelsea.[146] It was made almost entirely along the lines of Roman roads, the larger part between London and Lincoln, and the Kentish part of the tour continuing to Dover. This, then, was an avowedly archaeological tour, and the published account leaves no doubt in the mind of the reader that he is being taken along the Roman road by a guide who has little time for antiquities after the Occupation, or for curiosities by the wayside. Stukeley's eye for the geography of archaeology appreciated the antiquities he saw in their relation to the countryside – at Royston he noted how: 'These high chalk hills, having a fine prospect northwards, are covered with a beautiful turf like the Wiltshire downs, and have such like barrows here and there, and indeed are but a continuation of them quite a-cross the kingdom',[147] and one meets with passages of accurate and enthusiastic description as when he observes the Roman road in section near Lincoln:

I saw the true profile of the road broke off by the wearing away of the ground: it is about thirty feet broad, made of stone piled up into a easy convexity; there is likewise generally a little trench dug in the natural earth along both sides of the road, which is of great use in conducting the water that falls from the heavens into the vallies upon the long side of the road both ways, and prevents its lodging and stagnating against the side of their work: the turf that came out of those trenches they threw upon the road to cover it with grass: thus had they all the curious and convenient ways for beauty, use and perpetuity.[148]

One regrets to notice, however, that although he has in his possession a 'long and particular catalogue' of coins from Castor, he thinks it a 'nauseous formality to print them', and only gives a selection of silver types.[149] At Barrow-on-Humber he construes certain probably medieval earthworks into 'a temple of the old Britons' – the first of the 'alate temples' upon which he was to speculate so long and so unwisely in later years.[150] He does not describe it in detail, deferring it to another occasion and so indicating that the idea of a book dealing with the ancient British sacred sites was already in his mind.

At Dunstable he gives once again a good instance of his sound topographical and common-sense approach to prehistoric monuments. The prehistoric hillfort of Maiden Bower had been claimed as Roman, but

I am persuaded it is a British work, like that at Ashwell, at like distance from the Chiltern, and of like form, but more circular. . . . Between here and the town is a long barrow called the Mill-hill, no doubt from a mill which was afterwards set upon it: it stands east and west: the ends of it ploughed somewhat: I have no scruple in supposing it Celtic. A high prominence of the Chiltern overlooks all, called the Five Knolls, from that number of barrows, or Celtic *tumuli*, round, pretty large, and ditched upon the very *apex* of the hill. . . . This great tract of chalk comes from the eastern sea, and traverses the kingdom in a like direction with the Icening-street.[151]

With 'Celtic' as a quite reasonable non-committal word for 'Pre-Roman' this account is really surprisingly adequate and most sensible, and any archaeologist who has an acquaintance with the older literature of British antiquities will admit that far less satisfactory passages are the common form of much nineteenth- and even early twentieth-century productions.

The tours of 1723,[152] which were published as the *Iter Dumnoniense* and the *Iter Septimum Antonini Aug.*, were purely archaeological except for an inserted account of the eclipse of the sun which he recorded on Haradon Hill in Wiltshire and dedicated to Halley. The first tour deals almost entirely with pre-Roman sites: he had gone to Marlborough via Newbury at the end of June and probably stayed with Lord Hertford, but went on to spend about three weeks at Avebury again, staying at the Catherine Wheel.[153] He made a short excursion from here to Stanton Drew, in Somerset, to see the remarkable stone circles there under the guidance of his friend, John Strachey, a neighbouring landowner of antiquarian and scientific interests who had probably come in contact with Stukeley at the Royal Society,[154] and Stukeley was back in Wiltshire by the beginning of August. The stone circles at Stanton Drew[155] have never received modern scientific excavation: they present most interesting analogies to Avebury in having avenues of approach as well as a setting of three stones similar to that in the centre of the northern inner circle at Avebury. Like Avebury, they are presumably Early Bronze Age in date, and probably monuments of the Beaker culture, but without excavation we can advance little from Stukeley's original description two centuries ago. The results of all this fieldwork, and some at Stonehenge, are omitted from the *Itinerarium Curiosum* and reserved for a separate work. The *Iter Dumnoniense* is dedicated to Lord Pembroke, with whom he stayed at Wilton after his return from Stanton Drew and who seems to have suggested some of the places to visit in Dorset. While at Wilton in this and the following year he commenced a catalogue of the antique marbles and sculpture there, but this was to come to little, for he noted some years later:

> I intended to have wrote an account of my Lord Pembrokes Antiquitys about this time, with good designs of them, and had taken many drawings of them. This book was the groundplot. My Lord sent for it and transposed the leaves, put out and in, what he pleased, and so confounded my scheme that I left it off.[156]

Some account of the collection was, however, included in the *Itinerarium*.

The greater part of these two tours, however, deals with earthworks, mainly hillforts, and barrows, and contains some interesting comments on these antiquities. The archaeological research of the last few decades has resulted in a broad dating for the majority of hilltop fortifications, so often miscalled in the past 'Roman Camps', as the work of Late Bronze and Early Iron Age peoples between the eighth and first centuries BC, while in the main the round barrows of the Wessex chalk are attributable to the Bronze Age, ranging over the wide chronological limits of *c*.2000–1000 BC. Stukeley thought that many of the Iron Age hillforts of Wessex must be Roman – even Maiden Castle has 'a double ditch savouring of inferior times of the empire'[157] – though he thinks some of them may be attributed to the Belgae (an Iron Age tribe of the first century BC). Stukeley's views on the course of prehistory in Wessex, as he held them in the 1720s, can be pieced together from several scattered references in his writings, and are of some interest. 'The incredible number of barrows that over-spread this country from the sea-side to North Wiltshire', he writes, 'persuades me a great people inhabited here before the *Belgae*, that came from Spain, which we may call the *Albionites*.'[158] The Belgic invasion, documented by Caesar, was the one fixed point he could turn to before the Roman Conquest. Later he was to identify the Albionites with the Phoenicians,[159] but, however fantastic all this may sound today, it is important to appreciate that he had some grasp of a prehistoric perspective back beyond the Romans, back even beyond the Belgae. Stone circles and barrows he considered pre-Belgic, therefore presumably Albionite, though the word is not used except in the one quotation made above, and 'Celtic' or 'Druidic' seems to take its place. He rightly noted from field observations that at Vespasian's Camp near Amesbury, and at Poundbury near Dorchester, Bronze Age ('Celtic') round barrows are earlier than the Early Iron Age hillforts, though he seems to regard both these examples as Roman.[160] He further noted that Roman roads cut through Bronze Age disc ('Druid') barrows near Beckhampton in north Wiltshire[161] and at Oakley Down on Cranborne Chase.[162] To successive stages in the Belgic occupation of Wessex he attributed the series of large banks and ditches, or dykes, with a general east to west line and represented by Combs Ditch near Blandford, Bokerly Dyke along the north edge of Cranborne Chase on the Dorset-Wiltshire border, the dykes running south of Stonehenge, and finally Wansdyke along the crest of the North Wiltshire Downs above the Vale of Pewsey – not really an unreasonable interpretation considering the knowledge at his disposal. One of his reasons for making Stonehenge pre-Belgic is that, as its sarsens are derived from north Wiltshire, this area would be beyond the final territorial limits of Belgic power as defined by Wansdyke, and therefore free access from the site of Stonehenge impossible except at an earlier date.[163]

Of these four dykes, all falling into the class known to archaeology as linear earthworks, Bokerly Dyke has been shown to be a Romano-British work of three periods within the fourth century AD. Wansdyke was built in the fifth or sixth century AD as a northern frontier-work defending the still romanized province lying to the south against the Saxons of the Upper Thames. Combs Ditch is a complex structure, begun in the Iron Age and enlarged up to late Roman times.[164]

Stukeley's ideas are, I think, in no way discreditable, and contain, in their muddled way, a perception of certain basic archaeological principles. The first, as I have said, is the recognition of a long pre-Roman period over which the field antiquities could be distributed, a second is the appreciation of the possibility that various prehistoric cultures might arrive in southern England by means of invasions or immigrations from the Continent, and a third is the application of the geographical and topographical method to the study of a group of related structures (the linear earthworks) in order to interpret them as a coherent whole in the light of such historical knowledge as was available. The observation of the relative dating of two contiguous earthworks such as the barrows and the Roman road is, of course, as fundamental to archaeological fieldwork today as it was in the eighteenth century.

Stukeley made one very interesting comment with regard to Bronze Age barrows in Wiltshire, and recorded it among his miscellaneous Avebury notes. 'I observe', he wrote, 'the barrows upon Hakpen Hill and others are set with great art not upon the very highest part of the hills but upon so much of the declivity or edge as that they make app[earance] as above to those in the valley.'[165] This siting of barrows upon 'false crests', which is frequent in many parts of Britain, was, it seems, not noticed again until modern times, when Sir Cyril Fox brought the evidence of archaeology and geology to show 'that barrows sited on false crest lines were intended to be seen from some point below them, and that the position of a barrow thus gives an indication of the direction in which the homes of its builders should be sought'. In discussing this phenomenon, Sir Cyril pays a tribute to Stukeley's remarkable percipience in noticing this detail: it is indeed a first-rate example of his soundness as a field archaeologist.[166]

At the hillfort of Figsbury, near Salisbury (now known from excavation to be in the main of the Iron Age), Stukeley was again able to make some interesting comments based on sound observation. True, he christened the site Chloridunum (from Constantius Chlorus, whom he imagined to be its builder), but he noticed that the rampart seemed to be too high to be satisfactorily accounted for by its ditch, and suggested that it had been heightened by material taken from an inner ditch some distance within the circuit of the main defences.[167]

This comes near to the sequence proposed as the result of excavation in 1924 and subsequent interpretation, with the inner enclosure a Late Neolithic henge monument, later quarried to provide additional material for the rampart of the Iron Age fort.[168]

In his travels over the Wiltshire and Dorset downs he could not fail to observe the constant traces of ancient grass-grown field-systems with numerous small square fields defined by baulks or, on the slopes, terraces. These he noted inside the hillfort of Ogbury, between Amesbury and Salisbury:

within it are many little banks, carry'd strait and meeting one another at right angles, square, oblong parallels and some oblique, as the meres and divisions between plow'd lands; yet it seems never to have been plow'd.[169]

and again on Cranborne Chase he writes:

I frequently observed on the sides of hills long divisions very strait crossing one another with all kinds of angle; they look like the baulks or meres of plow'd lands, and are really made of flint oregrown with turf: they are too small for plow'd lands, unless of the most ancient Britons, who dealt little that way.[170]

What Stukeley had described are now recognized as the prehistoric field-systems of agriculturists ploughing small fields on the chalk uplands in the long period ranging from the Late Bronze Age (about the eighth century BC) up to and during the Roman occupation in the first four centuries AD. The type persists throughout this long time relatively unchanged, and excavation is the only method of providing a date within these broad limits. At Ogbury the fields are fitted into the circuit of the ramparts of the Iron Age hillfort,[171] and are therefore later, probably dating from the years when the Pax Romana had rendered the old fortifications, built in the days of insecurity and inter-tribal wars, obsolete. When the ploughing took place on a slope there was a constant creep of loosened plough-soil downhill, to pile up on the lower edge of the field and to form there a terrace or lynchet. The flints noted by Stukeley as occurring in the field divisions are, of course, stones collected off the fields during their cultivation and dumped conveniently on the boundary. His reluctance to accept these as ancient field-systems was perhaps in part the result of thinking of Ancient Britons as hunters ignorant of agriculture and in part of familiarity with a landscape in which the large open fields of pre-enclosure days were still the normal units of farming, and had he been a Cornishman or Welshman he might have had more acquaintance with the small square fields which still remained in these regions.

In the west he looked at Bath, and at Exeter visited Dr Musgrave, the author of treatises on rheumatism and the *Antiquitates Britanno-Belgicae* (1719). Turning then towards Dorset he came to Dorchester, where he found an antiquity much to his taste in the Roman amphitheatre known as Maumbury Rings. Stukeley had become a Freemason in January 1721, and by 1723 was Master of the Lodge meeting at the Fountain Tavern in the Strand – the same inn at which the early meetings of the Society of Antiquaries were held – and he wrote a full account of the Dorchester amphitheatre which he read to this Lodge in October 1723 and subsequently had printed as a pamphlet, *Of the Roman Amphitheater at Dorchester*, illustrated with a ground-plan of the monument.[172] This account is also included in the *Iter Dumnoniense* as a separate essay. The site of Maumbury Rings has been excavated, and was found to consist of a Late Neolithic henge monument which had been altered and adapted in Roman times to serve as an amphitheatre for the adjoining town of Dorchester (Durnovaria). It was later further adapted as a gun position during the Civil Wars.[173] Stukeley's plan is a very schematic and 'reconstructed' rendering of the monument.

The tour continued eastward, Stukeley inquiring and noting anything he thought of interest on the way. 'It pleases me to inquire the names of these old things, however aukward', he writes in defence of his record of the name of a barrow as Bols Turret, and he gives us a glimpse of his gossiping about the local antiquities to the landlady of the Rose Inn at Gussage All Saints in Cranborne Chase who, 'after some discourse preparatory', told him a muddled tale about Roman remains and the legend of the seven churches of Knowlton, and ended by pointing to the tale of Troy 'described in the ballad upon her wall, where she showed me these passionate verses,

> Waste lie those walls that were so good
> And corn now grows where Troy towers stood'.

It is pleasant to think of this echo of *iam seges ubi Troia fuit* in an eighteenth-century Dorset ale-house: the ballad is *The Wandering Prince of Troy*, the earliest text being *c*.1620.

Passing through Portsmouth, where he gives a very enthusiastic but quite non-archaeological description of the British line-of-battle fleet,[174] he came to Chichester, and inserts a dissertation on the *Cogidubnus* inscription by Roger Gale. He returns through Midhurst and Farnham to Staines and London. Near Staines he recorded a rectangular earthwork (of uncertain date) which was later to be obliterated by ploughing and 'lost' until rediscovered by air photography two centuries later.[175]

In the intervals of those tours he had not been without his archaeological life in London. He introduced Lord Hertford and Lord Winchelsea to the Society of Antiquaries in January 1723,[176] and may have taken part in those remarkable book-hunting expeditions in Paternoster Row in which Lord Winchelsea joined the Duke of Devonshire and the Earls of Oxford, Pembroke, and Sutherland in a search for rare books and manuscripts.[177] Stukeley was now Secretary of the Antiquaries,[178] and was becoming interested in the pre-Roman British coinage. In 1721–2 a series of Committees of the Society had been set up to collect material for a *Metallographia Britannica*, with Stukeley and Lord Winchelsea responsible for the British coins, Roger Gale on the Roman committee, Humphrey Wanley solely responsible for the Saxon coins, and Samuel Gale for Danish, while Lord Hertford sat on the larger Committee for English coins.[179] We have seen that in 1722 the 'Roman Knights' had been founded to study Roman Britain.

The Royal Society still included much antiquarian material within its scope, and even Freemasonry was approached by Stukeley from its archaeological aspect, 'suspecting it to be remains of the mysterys of the antients'.[180] Apart from these more or less formal meetings there was learned gossip about antiquities to be had on informal occasions, such as in the Grecian Coffee-house with the grave Ralph Thoresby, who on one occasion, when Stukeley was laid up with the gout, came with Samuel Gale to visit him in his house and to be shown drawings made during the tours of the preceding summers.[181]

In 1724 he made several tours, of which little survives save the dated drawings, or the engravings from them published posthumously in the second edition of the *Itinerarium Curiosum* in 1776.[182] There was another visit to Avebury and Stonehenge, returning by Ringwood and Romsey in June, and a month later he went to Lincoln via Stevenage, Stamford, and Ancaster, and in October to Kent. In September he made a visit to Oxford, the first since 1710, and there met Thomas Hearne. For some years before this meeting Hearne had been fretting and fuming in his diary about Stukeley, and doubtless complaining still more querulously to his Oxford cronies. Stukeley in 1722 'is a very fancifull Man and the Things he hath published are built upon fancy. He is looked upon as a Man of no great Authority, and his Reputation dwindles every day, as I have learn'd from very good hands.'[183] The decline in Stukeley's reputation seems entirely wishful thinking on Hearne's part – it was at this time steadily on the rise – but every few months he felt impelled to put in another charge of 'fancifullness' – his drawings are inaccurate, he is hypothetical and conceited, he cannot copy inscriptions accurately. Small wonder then that the interview in 1724 was not a success, and the next day Hearne wrote in his best cross-grained style about the visit:

This Dr. S. is a mighty conceited man, and 'tis observed by all that I have talked with that what he does hath no manner of likeness to the original. He goes all by fancy. Hence his cut of Waltham Cross is not one bit like it; nor indeed is the print of old Verulam any thing but meer fancy. In short as he addicts himself to fancy altogether what he does must have no regard among judicious and truly ingenious men. He told me he had been at Thame thinking it was a Roman City. Good God! This is nothing but idle dreaming. How is it possible to think at this rate? . . . Though he be a Physician, yet I am informed he knows very little or nothing of the matter.[184]

The Waltham Cross drawing does as a matter of fact seem to have been a perfectly good representation of the structure, but Hearne also noted that Stukeley showed him a plan of the walls of the Roman town of Silchester which bore little resemblance to the original, and here it must be confessed Hearne is absolutely right. Stukeley's plan of Silchester[185] makes it into a regular oblong with rounded corners, whereas the actual site is an irregular polygon. There is little excuse to be made, for the remains are conspicuous and complete on the ground even though their polygonal plan is not immediately apparent, and Stukeley visited Silchester more than once. Nor does the plan as he erroneously gives it support any theories or assist an argument. It is quite inexplicable except as sheer carelessness. Hearne's judgment of Stukeley as 'fanciful' is curiously prophetic when one remembers that, though now in the 1720s he was doing excellent objective work, in later years he was to merit Hearne's criticisms to the fullest degree. Stukeley's conversation at least must at all times have been imaginative and rather fantastic.

It is interesting to note that when Sir John Clerk in his *Memoirs* records his friendship with Roger Gale and Stukeley, he adds, 'Both were Authors of several good things, particularly the last, tho' not so learned and judicious a Man as the first.'[186] By the 1750s quite vigorous criticism was being expressed by careful local observers such as Hutchins, the historian of Dorset, and Richard Willis of Andover, who wrote to Stukeley taking him to task for errors in the *Itinerarium* where the local antiquities are concerned (such as the line of the Silchester–Sarum Roman road).[187] No reply was received to his letter, but ten years later he returned to the attack with specific criticism of the Silchester plan – 'How could you publish the plate in your Itineraria', Willis writes, 'inscribed Stukeley designavit, make it a Parallelogram (as it is a Nonagon of nine unequal sides and angles) and say (pag. 170) "tis a parallelogram".'[188]

In 1724 Stukeley published a collection of seven of his tours made between 1710 and 1723 as *Itinerarium Curiosum Centuria I*, with a sub-title *An Account of the Antiquities and remarkable Curiosities in Nature or Art observed in Travels through Great Britain*.[189] The tours were illustrated with engravings made by Vandergucht and others, and adorned with an emblematical frontispiece of classical design with a bust of Stukeley superimposed in a rather surrealist manner on the plinth of a broken Ionic pillar.

We have in the foregoing pages examined the content of these tours, and noted their faults as well as their virtues, but Hearne was not the man to admit that they could have any merit at all. It was a wonderful opportunity, not to be missed; he must have cackled with glee as he told Whiteside of the Ashmolean and West of Balliol of the book 'wch some very deservedly call Dr. Stukeley's hundred Fancies' and which was 'universally condemn'd as strange, weak, ridiculous stuff'.[190] He had not seen the book himself, and did not want to; it did not sell well, he was glad to say, but a review he had read showed him it was as bad as he had anticipated. By devious inquiries he found that the review had been written by Stukeley himself, which only made it worse.[191] Best of all, he had discovered that Stukeley was friendly with a man in Oxford he disliked, which gave a chance for a passage in the diary in the finest Hearne manner:

One of the Dr.'s Acquaintance is one Turner of Merton College (at least, he was very lately of that College), a Clergyman, a great Pretender to Antiquities, but most certainly a very impudent, debauch'd, drunken, lying, lewd Wretch, a Buffoon, and a very great Crony of that impudent, saucy, brazen-faced Rascall, Bowles. Both these Fellows are Scandals to their Profession and their Gowns.[192]

Hearne was as painstaking in the cultivation of his dislikes as in his editing of medieval texts.

The summer of 1725 saw Stukeley and Roger Gale setting out on what was to be the last of the great series of antiquarian journeys the former was to make.[193] It was also the longest, and took Stukeley to new regions in North Britain, but it does not contain very much of moment save for descriptions of several stone circles and allied monuments, and an account of their journey along the Roman Wall. They went by Dunstable up into the Midlands – Coventry, Birmingham, Derby, Buxton – and so westwards to Chester, and then striking north made for Liverpool and the Cumberland hills. It is interesting to read Stukeley's notes on the Lake District written fifty years before the popular discovery of the picturesque excitements of mountains and wild country: Windermere is noticed principally for its potted char and the rain – 'This country is exceedingly obnoxious to rain, and some of the hill-tops on one side or other are perpetually covered with cloud.'[194] But Ullswater appealed to the latent romantic in Stukeley – 'When one stands at the end of these lakes', he writes, 'the prospect is exceeding delightful; the mountains on each side rising to a great height, one behind another the whole length, and broke off into short ones, like the scenes at a playhouse: nor need a painter go to Italy for variety and grandeur of prospects.'[195]

In Cumberland and Westmorland (now part of Cumbria) he was able to examine several stone circles and allied monuments – at Shap he thought he could trace a system of avenues in the Avebury manner, and he made notes and drawings of Long Meg and her Daughters ('A great Celtic temple')[196] and the Keswick stone circle, as well as the Bronze Age circular monuments at Mayborough and Arthur's Round Table, that had already been noted by Dugdale. Thence via Whitehaven they came to the Wall, and made their way along it past Housesteads to Newcastle, returning southwards through Durham to the country seat of the Gales at Scruton in Yorkshire, and then past the Devil's Arrows at Boroughbridge to Doncaster, where the tour ended.

The Roman Wall, as might be expected, made a deep impression on Stukeley. He and Gale enthusiastically copied inscriptions and recorded sites, but never had the majesty of the Empire made itself so overshadowingly apparent to him. The Wall dominated his thoughts and he was to conclude his *Iter Boreale* with a passage which has a dual significance as a piece of excellent and dignified prose and as in some sense a valedictory postscript to his real archaeological studies:

The amazing scene of Roman grandeur in Britain which I beheld this journey, the more it occurred with pleasure to my own imagination, the more I despaired of conveying it to the reader in a proper light by a rehearsal. It is easy for some nations to magnify trifles, and in words gild over inconsiderable transactions till they swell to the appearance of an history; and some moderns have gone great lengths that way; but if in any people action has outdone the capacity of rhetoric, or in any place they have left historians far behind in their valour and military performances, it was in our own country; and we are as much surprised in finding such infinite reliques of theirs here, as that we have no history of them that speaks with any particularity of the last 300 years that the Romans dwelt in Britain, and rendered it perfectly provincial. The learned memoirs are very short; and it is well they were guided with such a spirit, as left monuments sufficient to supply that defect, when handled as they deserve; though I have no hope of coming up to that, yet I hold myself obliged to preserve, as well as I can, the memory of such things as I saw; which, added to what future times will discover, will revive the Roman glory among us, and may serve to invite noble minds to endeavour to that merit and public-spiritedness which shine through all their actions. This tribute at least we owe them, and they deserve it at our hands, to preserve their remains.[197]

He was to make no more archaeological tours,[198] and the antiquarian researches he carried on for the remainder of his life were to be a sad falling-off from his work of earlier years. Already some curious restlessness was touching him: by the end of the year he had decided to leave London for the country and by the early summer of 1726 he had taken a house in Grantham, in his native Lincolnshire.

The reasons behind Stukeley's decision to move from London into the country are obscure.[199] The impulse seems to have been a sudden one, to judge from a long letter he wrote to Samuel Gale in February 1726/7, but his enthusiasm and delight in his new house and garden is no less apparent. He is planting 'greens, flowers, alcoves, herbs, fruit trees and what not', fitting up his study indoors, fixing 'four bustos, after the antique, on termini between doric pillasters' in his hall, riding round to visit his neighbours on his horse, Squire Dick,[200] and looking forward to the amenities of a 'monthly assembly for dancing among the fair sex, and a weekly meeting for conversation among the gentlemen'. Throughout his lifetime his enthusiasm for gardening came second only to that for his antiquarian studies – he tells Gale, 'I have worked so hard in my garden as to sweat out all the London fog, am become vastly athletic . . . my antient country complexion is returned to my cheeks . . . my lips recover their pristin red, and my own locks, moderately curled, resemble the Egyptian picture of Orus Apollo, or the emblem of rejuvenescence.'[201] Sir John Clerk of Penicuik, the Scottish antiquary, paid him an unexpected visit one day when he was settling in at Grantham and recorded the visit in his journal.[202]

We came to Grantham to dinner [he writes] and for the Sake of seeing my Learned Correspondent Dr. Stukeley. I stayed there all the afternoon. So soon as I lighted I went to find out the Doctor at his owne house. He was at home and as rough and dirty as a bear. He would not dine with me but invited me to dine with him which I cou'd not comply with because of my fellowe Travellers. I return'd to the Doctor in the afternoon drank coffee and took a turn with him about his Gardens. At night he suped with me and my friends at our Inn and we rose all much delighted with his company.

The Doctor is a very Learned Physitian Phylosopher Mathematician Poet and Antiquarian. He designs very well and in the afternoon when I stayed with him he took a Scetch of my face which every body said was very like. He was written several things but not meeting with the encouragement he expected from the publick he has withdrawen himself from London to live privately at Grantham having a Little Estate of 150 lb. per ann with no Family and little business in his profession.

Stukeley had been gardening on this occasion, as Sir John makes clear when he reported the meeting to Roger Gale later, and this was why 'never rural god appeared so rough and dirty'; it is interesting to learn of one reason at least for his retirement from London. He seems to have been disappointed in his hopes of establishing himself as a leading antiquary, though characteristically he never admits this in his own writings, and Sir John felt that it 'is a pity he does not meet with some public encouragement, he would make an excellent geographer'.[203] His appreciation of Stukeley's geographical approach to problems of antiquity is interesting and percipient.

Sir John Clerk was not his only visitor in these early days of his country retirement. In May the Duke of Bedford breakfasted with him, and Isaac Whood, the portrait painter to whom the duke was patron and who had accompanied him on the visit, drew a convincing pencil profile of Stukeley with an ivy wreath in his hair;[204] later in the summer the Earl of Oxford and George Vertue came to see him.[205] But towards the end of the year, and perhaps as a result of those monthly dances for the fair sex, we suddenly find Stukeley married to a local gentleman's daughter, Frances Williamson of Allington. Little is known of the circumstances of this affair: Roger Gale had, it seems, predicted marriage to Stukeley when hearing his decision to live in the country 'though your aversion to it at that time made it almost incredible', and it also appears from Gale's congratulatory letter on the marriage that Frances was a woman of some intellectual attainments and had once been a pupil of Mattaire, the classical scholar.[206]

Frances had two miscarriages soon after the marriage, and on the second occasion Stukeley conducted a very odd ceremony in the garden which had now been laid out as a sort of Druidic grove:

The embrio, about as big as a filberd, I buryd under the high altar in the chapel of my hermitage vineyard; for there I built a niche in a ragged wall oregrown with ivy, in which I placed my Roman altar, a brick from Verulam, and a waterpipe sent me by my Lord Colrain from Marshland. Underneath is a camomile bed for greater ease of the bended knee, and there we enterred it, present my wifes mother, and aunt, with ceremonys proper to the occasion.[207]

This was in October 1728 and it is a little surprising after this semi-pagan performance to find him only six months later deciding on ordination in the Church of England.

This decision forms the essential turning-point in his whole life, and comes as the culmination of a series of impulsive moves – leaving London and getting married, both unexpected to his friends – and all three events must surely be related to some psychological disturbance which profoundly affected his life from 1726–9. The intellectual processes which can be traced linking his antiquarian studies with a desire to take orders and enter the field of religious controversy will be discussed in the next chapter, but there are hints that the momentous decision was partly motivated by quite worldly considerations. He hints somewhat broadly in a letter to Sir Hans Sloane in September 1729 that he makes only £50 a year from his medical practice and that a comfortable living in the Church would be very desirable – what could Sir Hans do about the living of All Saints, Stamford?[208] And before that, writing to an unnamed correspondent in 1728, he talks of Horsley's work on Roman coins progressing well, 'but when I had set myself to look over such things, a rap comes to the door for me to go perhaps a mile off, and my fortune will not support me handsomely without some little business, and that makes me at present very remiss in these affairs'.[209] Marriage, an impending family, and the calls on a country GP were going to make inroads on his small private means and on his leisure for antiquarian studies, but in the comfortable circumstances of a Church living under eighteenth-century conditions a scholar might have ample means and time to turn his attention to philosophical pursuits. And since he already meditated on turning his archaeological knowledge to controversial ends, what more valuable champion could the Church of England acquire in a time of dangerous free-thinking than one who was convinced not only of his own orthodoxy but of that of the Druids?

The substance of the letters interchanged between Stukeley and his friend, the Archbishop of Canterbury, William Wake, will be given in the next chapter in the course of an examination of the development of his ideas on Druidism between 1719 and 1740: here it is sufficient to say that he was accepted as a candidate for ordination by the archbishop in June 1729, and by February 1730 was installed in the living of All Saints, Stamford. His friends had been hoping from 1725 onwards that he would publish the results of his Avebury and Stonehenge fieldwork, and inquiries as to the progress of the work occur in the letters from the Gales and others from time to time.[210] He had started working on the papers connected with Avebury soon after he settled at Grantham, and hoped in 1727 to publish in a year or two.[211] In October 1730 Samuel Gale wrote to Hearne, telling him that antiquities were a little on the decline in London, 'but they are waiting with Impatience for a Curious Dissertation upon Abery and Stonehenge, from Dr. Stukeley, in which . . . there will appear some amazing discoverys'. 'N.B.', adds Hearne, 'This is Dr. Stukeley, whom I have formerly mentioned. He was a Physician, but is now in Orders and hath a Living. He is a fancifull man and looked upon as beside himself.'[212] *Stonehenge* was not, however, to appear until 1740, and *Abury* three years later. By then his mental temper had vastly altered from that of twenty years before – it was no longer Doctor Stukeley writing, but the Reverend William Stukeley, a divine engaged in religious controversy, and Hearne's splenetic criticisms were in a fair way to becoming justified.

IV

Avebury, Stonehenge, and the Druids

IN THE LAST CHAPTER we have followed the course of Stukeley's life from his arrival in London in 1717 to his return to the country in 1726, his ordination in 1729, and his publication of his two books on Stonehenge and Avebury in 1740 and 1743 respectively. While discussing the fieldwork he carried out during the first ten years of this period we have put on one side a consideration of his most important contribution to archaeology, that at the great stone circles which form the subject of these two folios. The intrinsic value of this work makes it no less significant than the information it gives us on the growth of certain ideas in Stukeley's mind. These ideas were to become the theories about Druids and Druidism assiduously propagated by him in the later years of his life and which had so powerful an effect on later eighteenth-century imaginative literature as well as on antiquarian studies even a hundred years later.

We can consider here, in very brief outline, the present state of knowledge with regard to the Druids and their relationship to stone circles and other prehistoric monuments in Britain. Archaeological evidence is consistent in showing that the circles of standing stones, sometimes (as henge monuments) accompanied by enclosing banks and ditches, which John Aubrey first claimed, in the most tentative manner, as temples of the Druids, first appear in the Late Neolithic Age of Britain (that is, from about 2500 BC), and that though in certain regions analogous monuments probably continued to be built well into the Bronze Age, the great majority of these circles date from the beginning of that period. At Stonehenge considerable structural alteration took place during the Middle Bronze Age phase, round about 1550 BC, but this is exceptional.

The Druids appear in a number of scattered and often ambiguous references in the classical writers from the first few centuries BC as a priesthood of the Celts, at that time occupying territories from Galatia to Gaul and in a well-developed iron-using state of culture. We cannot here examine the Druid cult so far as it is recoverable from these relatively scrappy references, but we note in passing that it appears to have been a religion allied to others associated with those people who spoke Indo-European languages from the second millennium BC at least. There is nowhere in the classical writers any association made between the Druids and stone circles and similar monuments, though there is explicit reference made to their using sacred groves and, by implication at least, no form of built temples.

Druidism was regarded by its priests as already ancient at the time when their views were recorded in writing by Greeks or Romans, and there is no reason to think that it had preserved a state of pristine purity for untold centuries rather than that it had absorbed and incorporated many elements from earlier and alien religious systems. There is little doubt of the strength of the Late Neolithic tradition of circular sanctuaries in the British Isles up to the Early Iron Age.

The association of the Druids with the stone circles is therefore no more than an occasional adoption by the Iron Age priesthood of ancient, native elements. So long as one retains the word 'Celt' for these people who spoke Celtic tongues in classical antiquity, and regards the Druids as essentially the priesthood of these folk, the connection between Druidism and stone circles can only be regarded as secondary.[213]

Before discussing Stukeley's views on the subject it will be well to clear the ground by estimating as well as we are able the information on Druids, stone circles, and other megalithic monuments that would have been available to him around 1717–19, before he started any intensive fieldwork at either of the Wiltshire monuments. Much of this material has been dealt with by the writer and others in studies of the growth of ideas about Druids in England during the seventeenth and eighteenth centuries,[214] but in our detailed examination of Stukeley's individual share in this we can add from internal evidence certain important facts about his direct or indirect indebtedness to specific books or individuals. He had, of course, the classical writers' testimony on Druidism as his basis and, in an age when a fair acquaintance with at least the Latin authors formed part of an educated gentleman's intellectual background to a degree unknown today, the acquisition of the main literary sources cannot have presented any difficulty.

STONEHENGE

17 A typical engraving from a drawing by Stukeley in his *Stonehenge* of 1740, with a gentleman demonstrating the site to two ladies, one of whom has lost interest.

18 A page of Stukeley's field-notes at Stonehenge, 7 August 1723. Above, section of the composition of a barrow excavated by him near Stonehenge, the first such record in British archaeology; and below, the barrow-studded landscape around Amesbury.

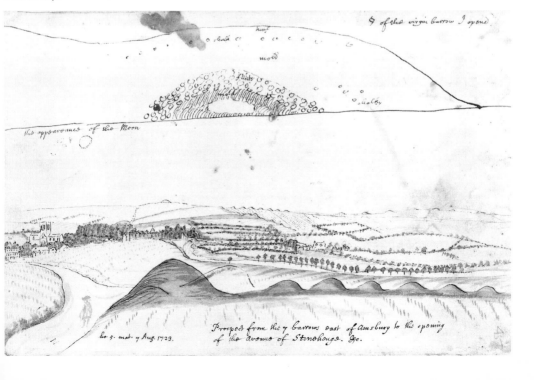

THE HISTORY OF
THE TEMPLES
OF THE ANTIENT
CELTS.

O qui me gelidis in vallib Hæmi
Sistat; ingenti ramorum protegat umbra!
Fœlix qui potuit Rerum cognoscere causas!

Atq; metus Omnes & inexorabile Fatum
Subjecit pedibus, strepitumq Acherontis
avari. Virg.

19 Decorative title-page drawn by Stukeley for the unpublished book on Avebury and Stonehenge written at Avebury in July 1723, as descriptive of the temples of the ancient Celts, with his favourite quotation from Virgil, *Georgics* II, 488–92.

The history of the Temples &
religion of the Druids.

The history of the religion and
temples of the DRVIDS.

20 Alternative title-page, later than that of 1723, where the Druids have ominously replaced the Celts.

A Druid

Dna A: M Delin.   The Chief Druid   from a Statue

A British Druid

Stukeley delineavit   G. V. Gucht Sculpsit

THE EVOLUTION OF THE DRUID

21 (*above left*) The wholly imaginary
figure with staff, book and flowing
beard, portrayed by Aylett Sammes
from a description of an unattributed
sculpture in his *Britannia Antiqua
Illustrata*, 1676.

22 (*above right*) The version of
Sammes' invention 'from a Statue'
given by Henry Rowlands in his *Mona
Antiqua Restaurata*, 1723, with
sandals, and the book replaced by an
oak branch.

23 (*right*) Stukeley's drawing of 1724
published in his *Stonehenge*, 1740,
adapted from Rowlands with shortened
beard, the oak branch removed, and a
Bronze Age axe-blade slung at the
Druid's waist.

24 Portrait in oil of William Warburton (1698–1779), Bishop of Gloucester from 1759, clerical controversialist and a friend of Stukeley, appearing as 'Panagrius' in Stukeley's unpublished dialogue on the history of Stamford.

25 (*below*) Design by Stukeley for an elaborate Gothick bridge for the Duke of Montagu's park at Boughton, Northants.

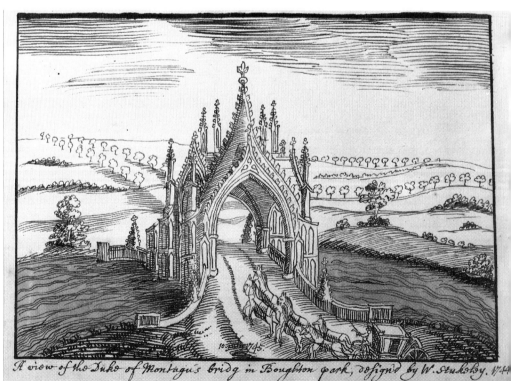

A view of the Duke of Montagu's bridg in Boughton park, design'd by W. Stukeley. 1744

26 The drawings published by Stukeley in 1736 of the pieces of the Roman rectangular silver dish or *lanx* from Risley Park in Derbyshire, the only record of this now lost antiquity.

W. Stukeley del.   J. Mynde sc.

27 (*above*) Engraving from a drawing by Stukeley, 19 October 1742, of sculptures in the chalk-cut structure at Royston, Herts, published in his *Origines Roystonianae*, 1743.   **28** (*below*) Photograph of part of the Royston sculptures as they exist today.

29 (*opposite*) Page of a letter from Charles Bertram to Stukeley, written from Copenhagen 10 November 1747, and giving an account of Danish barrows and chambered tombs.

in Falster. N.° 4 like the first, but w.th the adition of a Basis & Eight large Stones, facing the 8 Chief Winds, & resembles the affixed figure. N. of Onslov in the above-said Island Falster.

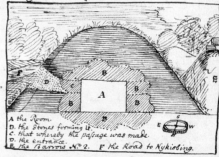

N.° 5 not very common, & resembling the Crown of a hat; such a one of a prodigious largeness, above 8 Yards high, occupies the Church-Yard at Carise, a Village in Zealand; this is said to be one of the primitive Danish Kings Sepulchers, & is therefore left unmolested by the inhabitants. N.° 6. is not very much unlike our modern Graves in form, being twice its bredth in length; these, by the Country-people, are stiled Kiämper-Gravè, Giants-graves, and esteemed the primitive & antidiluvian Graves of the Antient Giants. they are hemmed in on all sides by huge Stones of 500 to 2300 ℔ weight, to prevent being plowed up, as they say. (please to observe that none of the Stones, I have hitherto seen, exceed four Yards in length & are almost as thick as they are long;) toward the West end, for they lye due W. & E. is an oblong Square trough, about 6 foot long, & 4 wide, the sides cased with large course Stones, very flat, as tho' cut with an instrument, what these contained I cannot as yet say; I have dug 4 or 5, foot deep in one of them N of Onslov Church, & about 50 pades from it, but could find nothing, please to see the rude draught of it, as follows.

A. the Square Trough.

These Giant-like graves, are one with another 30. Yards long & 10 broad, the hight proportionable to the bredth. Thus, Great Sir, have I briefly described the Barrows in this Country, & before I leave this Discourse, for Your greater Satisfaction, give You the profile of one I have been in, since my last writing to You, standing at the edge of a Forrest, by the side of the road going from Onslov to Nykiöbing in Falster, & 1½ mile from the said pleasant town; the place of 3 such (tho' there be many more in the adjacent Forrest) is called Trè höyÿ three-hills. it contains a Room (the Boors say, there be such in them all) some 15 or 18 foot long, 5 broad & 4 high, formed by huge massy Stones adapted to it as You may see in the Subjoined Figure.

[Figure]

A the Room.
B. the Stones forming it
C. that whereby the passage was made.
D. the entrance.
E. the Barrow N.° 2.   F. the Road to Nykiöbing.

The South end, supposed to have been the right entrance, was made up with flat ...... wedged one on another; in it I was told, was found an Iron Sword, some knives of Flint, an Urn with ashes & some antient Coins (of latten) but I could not procure a sight of any of them; Yet I have seen of the urns dug up in Jutland in such Barrows, & have also here subjoined th

BRITANNICARUM
GENTIUM
HISTORIÆ ANTIQUÆ
SCRIPTORES TRES:

RICARDUS CORINENSIS,
GILDAS BADONICUS,
NENNIUS BANCHORENSIS.
Recensuit NOTISQUE & INDICE auxit

CAROLUS BERTRAMUS
SOCIETATIS ANTIQUARIORUM LONDINENSIS SOCIUS. &c.

verus divitias eripit nemo.

HAVNIÆ:
Impensis EDITORIS, MDCCLVII.

30 (*above*) The Richard of Cirencester forgery as published in Copenhagen in 1757, together with texts of the genuine Gildas *De excidio Britanniae* and Nennius *Historia Britonum*. Bertram as editor appears as a Fellow of the Society of Antiquaries, and the remarkable frontispiece appears to show the three authors in conference.

31, 32 (*left*) Bronze medallion struck to commemorate Stukeley after his death in 1765 and before the fall of one of the Stonehenge trilithons in 1797, shown as still upright in the view on the reverse. The unknown engraver gives the wrong age for Stukeley at his death, which was seventy-eight and not eighty-four.

There were also available certain works by Continental and British scholars on the subject of the Druids, and on Celtic and Germanic gods. Of these books, we may notice the *De Dis Germanis* of Elias Schedius (Amsterdam 1648) and the *Dissertatio de Druidis* of Esias Pufendorf of Chemnitz (1650) among the European works, and in England there were such works as the *De origine Druidum* of Henry Jacob, published in Dickenson's *Delphi Phoenicizantes* (1655), and the *Syntagma de Druidum moribus ac institutis* of Thomas Smith (1664). As an appendix to William Sacheverell's *Account of the Isle of Man* (1702) there had been printed a dissertation on the identification of the *Mona insula* of Caesar and Tacitus, together with *An Account of the Antient Druids* by Thomas Brown. We know from the sale catalogue of Stukeley's library published the year after his death (1766) that he possessed Schedius, Jacob, and Smith, as well as Guenebault's little monograph on Chyndonax to which we have already referred, but there is, of course, no evidence for the dates on which he acquired them.[215]

In addition to these books which specifically dealt with Druids, there were a number of works available at the beginning of the eighteenth century which dealt with pre-Roman antiquities and particularly with megalithic monuments. Stonehenge had already acquired a literature of its own, which included the works of Inigo Jones (1655), Charleton (1663), and Webb (1665), and these had been summarized by Gibson in his 1695 edition of the *Britannia*, together with extracts from Aubrey's *Monumenta* describing, among other sites, Avebury.[216] Plot had described Rollright in his *Natural History of Oxfordshire* (1677). Stone circles in the Hebrides had been described and illustrated by Martin Martin in his *Description of the Western Islands of Scotland* (1703), and those of Orkney by James Wallace in *An Account of the Islands of Orkney* (1693). General books on British antiquities included Aylett Sammes' *Britannia Antiqua Illustrata* (1676), while for the foreign megalithic monuments, about the only available book, and one to which constant reference is made by every writer who touches on such things in late seventeenth and eighteenth centuries, was the *Danicorum Monumentorum Libri Sex* of Ole Worm (Copenhagen 1643), with its *Additamenta* printed at the end of the same author's *Danica Literatura Antiquissima* of 1651.

Among unpublished material we can identify several sources used by Stukeley before 1719. The use he made of Gale's transcript of the *Monumenta Britannica* we have already commented upon and, in the same folio commonplace book as he made his notes from this manuscript, we find numerous extracts and sketches relating to Welsh and Cornish megalithic monuments taken from the notes of Edward Lhuyd, some of which were then in the possession of John Anstis, Garter King of Arms. He may have seen the manuscript of *A Fools Bolt soon shott at Stonage* which had been in the hands of Andrew Paschal of Chedzoy in Somerset at the end of the seventeenth century[217] and which was to be printed by Hearne as one of his incongruous additions to a medieval chronicle – in this case to *Langtoft's Chronicle* (1725). He had Somerset contacts in John Strachey and it is probable that he obtained from him or from William Musgrave of Exeter a plan of the Stanton Drew stone circles in advance of its publication in the latter's *Antiquitates Britanno-Belgicae* which was actually published in 1719.[218]

It is, of course, more difficult to assess his indebtedness to personal contacts and conversation with his friends and colleagues. Since he knew Anstis, and was lent by him Lhuyd's notes to transcribe, he is likely to have obtained further details from him about Cornish megaliths, for Anstis was a Cornishman and sufficiently interested in prehistoric antiquities to make up two manuscript books of notes on Cornish and other field monuments.[219] Lhuyd's manuscript notes on antiquities, some drawings from which Stukeley copied into his commonplace book, and which were subsequently engraved and published posthumously in the second part of the *Itinerarium Curiosum*, now appear to be mostly lost, or at least irreparably scattered.[220]

Stukeley had also made the acquaintance of a German, Johann Georg Keysler, who had been in England since 1716, during which time he had been elected a Fellow of the Royal Society, and who was interested in the megalithic monuments which he had encountered in the course of extensive travels on the Continent. Keysler published an account of the northern megaliths in his *Antiquitates Selectae Septentrionales et Celticae* at Hanover in 1720, after this return from England, and later (1728) produced an edition of Schedius with an appendix by himself, *De Cultu Solis, Freji et Othini*.[221] Discussions between Keysler and Stukeley on Druids and megaliths would have been inevitable.

But by far the most intriguing figure among those whose interests lay in things Druidical, and with whom Stukeley could have come in contact, was John Toland.[222] Born in Ireland in 1670, he had spent a disjointed life at the universities of Glasgow and Edinburgh, as a tutor to Protestant families, and in periods of residence on the Continent.

Returning to England he published in 1696 the pamphlet *Christianity not Mysterious*, which brought him from obscurity to an unenviable fame as one of the best-known and most-hated men of this time. No book on the religious thought of the eighteenth century can avoid mention of Toland and a discussion of his importance: he is as insistent a figure today as he was in his lifetime when an irate Irish peer ceased to attend church on the grounds that formerly he used to hear something about Jesus Christ from the pulpit, but now it was nothing but John Toland.[223] He is usually claimed as the main spokesman of the rationalists and free-thinkers whose very miscellaneous views were grouped together as 'Deism', and when we come to discuss Stukeley's religious attitude when he set out to 'Combat the deists from an unexpected quarter'[224] in the 1730s, we shall have to examine the views of Toland and the Deistical writers at greater length. But at the moment we are concerned with a period in Stukeley's life when he was untroubled with thoughts of religious controversy, and must examine a neglected aspect of Toland, that of the student of comparative religion and of the Druids and their antiquities.

Toland returned to England some time before 1694, and in that year came for a period of residence in Oxford, though not as a member of the university, 'where he read in the libraries'. [225] Edmund Gibson had just gone down from Queen's College and was in London working on his edition of Camden's *Britannia* and keeping up an entertaining correspondence with his friend Thomas Tanner, who was still at Oxford.[226] From this interchange of letters between two young men in their early twenties we see how an informal committee was being formed to help in the various portions of the revised *Britannia*, which in its published form the following year was to print the names of these gentlemen with due acknowledgment of the sections for which they had been responsible. In Oxford in 1694 was old Mr Aubrey with the *Monumenta* manuscript from which excerpts were to be included by Gibson in his work (though he was horrified at the chaotic state of the manuscript when he finally received it),[227] and also, by the end of April, young Mr Toland. His reputation had preceded him – Gibson had written a note to Dr Arthur Charlett with the scandalous story of how 'Monsieur Toland was arraign'd and convicted, in the Coffee-house, of burning a Common Prayer book',[228] and the Master of University is hardly likely to have kept such a titbit of gossip to himself. But Gibson had evidently some respect for Toland as an antiquary, for twice within a week he writes to Tanner to ask whether he has sounded the Irishman about helping with the account of the

antiquities of his country in the *Britannia*.[229] Then there was trouble –
Toland, though brilliant, must have been an intolerable young man,
and his 'insolent conceited way of talking' made Gibson break off
relations,[230] and in the published work we look in vain for mention of
Toland, and find Sir Richard Cox alone responsible for Ireland.

But Toland had made friends with Aubrey in Oxford (Aubrey
would have befriended anyone, even the most objectionable youth)
and was later to write that the older man 'was the only person I ever
then met, who had a right notion of the temples of the Druids, or
indeed any notion that the circles so often mentioned were such
temples at all'.[231] The study of Druid temples was, however, to be put
on one side, and after 1696 Toland lived the uneasy life of a penurious
literary hack, in debt and denounced from every pulpit, but
unrepentantly writing his often brilliant and always incisive
pamphlets questioning the accepted doctrines of the Church of
England. In later life, however, we find him under the patronage of an
Irish peer, Lord Molesworth, living in Putney and again interesting
himself in Druids. He died in March 1721/2 and his essays on
Druidism were published posthumously in 1726.

A remarkable document exists in the form of a copy of Martin
Martin's *Description of the Western Isles* with the marginal
annotations of Toland and his patron made in 1720, many of these
notes relating to stone circles or similar monuments and their
connection with Druids.[232] This brings us to a point that is worth
while examining in some detail, for it has an important bearing on
Stukeley's views about Avebury and his relationship with Toland
himself. In his account of the ancient monuments of Orkney Martin
describes the Stenness and Brodgar stone circles, saying that they 'are
believed to have been Places design'd to offer Sacrifice in time of *Pagan*
Idolatry; and for this reason the People called them the Ancient
Temples of the Gods', and then adds that 'Several of the Inhabitants
have a Tradition, that the Sun was worshipped in the larger, and the
Moon in the lesser Circle'.[233] This idea seems to have attracted
Toland: he has written a marginal note against Martin's account of
Callanish in the Hebrides to claim that here, too, were two circles to
the Sun and Moon respectively, and he repeats the idea in his
posthumously published essays on the Druids.[234] These did not appear
until 1726, and Stukeley does not seem to have possessed them until
they were given him by Warburton in 1729,[235] but nevertheless when
Stukeley was at Avebury in 1721 he made a plan on which he labelled
the two inner circles of the monument as 'Solar' and 'Lunar'

temples,[236] and these same attributions reappear in several other Avebury drawings of 1721-3. While he may have discovered the Orkney entry in Martin's book for himself, and been attracted by the idea independently of Toland, it is surely more likely that there had been some form of contact between the two men in about 1720, when stone circles and Druids were discussed, and the Solar and Lunar attribution given by Martin was pointed out by Toland to Stukeley.

It is difficult to find definite evidence that Stukeley and Toland actually knew one another in 1717-20. In a letter to his old school friend, Ambrose Pimlow, in 1729, Stukeley says, in reply to a question, 'Indeed I know my Lord Molesworth, and if he . . . were in town, I would wait on him'[237]: if his acquaintance were more than very recent at this time the possibility of a connection with Toland is much enhanced. In his MS draft of a book on Avebury, Stonehenge and other stone circles written in July 1723 and discussed below, Stukeley made a note 'Mr Tolands history of the druids in Ld Molesworths hands', but with no indication as to whether he consulted it.[238] The great interest of such a connection, of course, lies in the fact that Stukeley was by 1729 taking up a militant anti-Deistical position and would be at pains to conceal any friendship with the heresiarch which may have existed in his unregenerate youth. The only evidence I can trace for his views on religion in the 1717-20 period is contained in an undated and unaddressed letter which may be to Samuel Gale and was certainly written about 1729.[239] In this letter he defends his decision to take Holy Orders, and then goes on:

Though London conversation, and being laughed out of going to church on account of my profession, and a thoughtlessness about religious matters, made me talk in a loose way. . . . ·

This sounds very like a pricking of conscience over his past reputation among his friends. With this might be taken the less definite evidence of a number of *The Freethinker*, dated 5 June 1719, and dealing in scathing terms with the tendency of the medical faculty to desert the scientific path of freethinking for the 'spirit of orthodoxy' which is pasted, without any disapproving comment, into the commonplace book Stukeley was using at that time for archaeological notes.[240] If Toland and the young freethinking doctor did in fact meet and discuss stone circles and Druids (and I think the evidence is all in favour of this) it must have meant a direct personal link with Aubrey himself. And what a piquancy it gives to the righteous indignation against freethinkers and Deists of Stukeley's middle years, with the very hints and ideas derived from the sinful Toland now turned and used against him by the antiquarian champion of orthodoxy!

What impression is Stukeley likely to have gathered from the reading and conversation outlined above? The classical writers would have given him a number of scrappy, disjointed, and often contradictory pieces of information about Druids and Celtic religious beliefs. Even today these texts[241] form source material that must be used with the utmost discretion, and in Stukeley's rather uncritical mind a vague conception must have formed itself of a priesthood not wholly barbarous (despite the awkward references to sacrifices and holocausts) and having in a form of reincarnation doctrines something akin to Pythagorean ideas. He could not avoid the terrible groves of Lucan, nor the unanimous acceptance of these as the Druidic temples by such as Schedius and Pufendorf, but what he had read in Aubrey's notes and what may have been reiterated in conversations with Toland would provide something much more exciting: Druidic temples which still stood as tangible structures built of great stones.

The seventeenth-century writers had managed to suggest between them almost every conceivable claimant for the building of Stonehenge except the Druids. Inigo Jones made it Roman, Charleton Danish (and Plot thought Rollright Danish, too); Edmund Bolton certainly thought it British – 'that STONAGE was a works of the BRITANNS, the rudenesse it selfe perswades' – but it was the tomb of Boadicea and the Druids are there only by inference.[242] Plot, too, considered it 'some British forum or Temple'.[243] Mr Gibbons, who wrote the *Fools Bolt*, also thought it British, and said so in a splendid passage of nonsense, in which Stonehenge becomes

an old *British* Triumphal Trophical Temple, erected to *Anaraith*, their Goddess of Victory, in a bloody Field there won by Illustrious *Stunings* and his *Cangick* Giants, from *Divitiacus* and his *Belgae*: in which Temple the Captives and Spoils were sacrificed to the said Idol *Anaraith*.

Keysler takes up an interesting position in his little book, stressing the occurrence of the great stone chambered tombs in north Germany and Scandinavia – regions which he felt could not be called Druidic by any stretch of the imagination. He notes the varying views held about Stonehenge and other stone circles in England, and makes especial reference to the idea that they were Druidical temples; a view evidently discussed with him when in England. But he must dissent, despite the fact that this view is held in England among scholars to whom he owes a debt of gratitude. He concludes in fact that Stonehenge is not a temple, nor is it British or Roman, but it is an ancient Anglo-Saxon monument, and a tomb such as the structures he knows in Holstein.

Keysler's error, as we can now see it to be, was that he confused two types of prehistoric structures in north Europe both built of great stones, but otherwise distinct. The chambered tombs under cairns or barrows which he knew so well in north Germany may belong ultimately to the same family as the similar structures in west and north Britain and other parts of the Atlantic seaboard, and are collective burial vaults of Neolithic folk of *c.*4500–3000 B C, but the stone circles (such as Avebury or Stonehenge) belong to a class of open sanctuaries mainly dating from the beginnings of the Bronze Age (*c.*2000 B C) and practically confined to the British Isles. However, one must give Keysler credit for being one of the very few antiquaries of his day who were able to approach the problem from more than an insular viewpoint, and he did at least recognize, however dimly, that there was a large class of allied megalithic monuments in northern Europe which, though scattered over a large geographical area, had some sort of underlying homogeneity.

I think, then, that Stukeley began his work at Stonehenge and Avebury with a muddled but relatively unprejudiced mind. He had collected enough data to know that the two great stone circles were representatives of a large class of similar smaller monuments scattered over west and north Britain, and from Keysler and Ole Worm he would have known something of megalithic monuments in north Europe comparable at least to the chambered tombs which he would encounter in the Avebury district and elsewhere (such as Kits Coty House in Kent). His primary concern at both the Wiltshire circles was to make an exhaustive examination of them and the immediately surrounding country, and to prepare plans and 'prospects' of them. Unfortunately we know little of his survey methods in the field, but he certainly used a theodolite at Stonehenge, and Gunter's standard chain of sixty feet was in use from the early seventeenth century. Aubrey used a plane-table for his Avebury survey. His reading of Aubrey's notes, probably reinforced by conversations with Toland, would incline him to the view that the circles were to be attributed to the Druids, but there is no evidence that this or any other theory was of dominant importance in his mind when he began work in 1719 on a purely objective record.

Two MSS available since the first edition of this study, now in the Bodleian and Cardiff Public Library[244], together comprise a draft in two parts of such a projected book, begun at Avebury in early July 1723 and finished probably in that year, entitled *The History of the Temples of the Antient Celts*. The plan and content of this book was in effect what in modern terms would constitute a study of henge monuments and circles in Britain, with detailed new surveys made in the field of Avebury and Stonehenge. Behind it lies a wholesale plundering of Aubrey's *Templa Druidum* section of the *Monumenta Britannica*, based on the notes contained in the Devizes commonplace book; other items were added from MSS of Lhuyd to which Stukeley had access, and his own field-notes of Rollright, Stanton Drew, Kits Coty House and the long barrow of Julaber's Grave in Kent. Among published sources he uses the 1695 Camden, James Wallace for the Orkneys, Martin Martin for Callanish, and Keysler for the Continent. By 1725, had he not published by then, he could have incorporated his first-hand notes on the circles of Long Meg and near Keswick, and the henges of Mayborough and Arthur's Round Table near Penrith. The Avebury and Stonehenge descriptions that form the bulk of the 1723 draft were of course entirely original fieldwork set out in objective detail. There are some miscellaneous sections on, for instance, ritual dances and processions, and quotations from the Bible and classical authors where thought appropriate. At the end of Part II, the Stonehenge section, the Druids make their only appearance on a single page, as a Celtic priesthood in Britain to whom the megalithic monuments under discussion might reasonably be assigned.

Stukeley spends much time in the Stonehenge section in reasoned refutation of the Roman origin championed by Inigo Jones and Webb. Throughout he is at pains to demonstrate an indigenous, pre-Roman context for his stone circles and henges, using in default of the concept or the word 'prehistoric', the adjective 'Celtic' as he was to in the *Itinerarium*. He sets out the recurrent features which he sees as characterizing his Celtic Temples, beginning with their setting – they have an 'area or plain before or around 'em' and lie near rivers or springs – and many are approached by an avenue of stones or earthworks. The main feature is the circular temple, usually in the form of rings of standing stones which may be multiple. They may contain a *cella* or 'cove' of three uprights, or incorporate an 'altar' within or adjacent to them, and here he admits confusion with chambered tombs – ''tis so hard to distinguish absolutely the Celtic temples always from sepulchres & frequently they are so conjoined undoubtedly as the burials gave first occasion to the temples'. At the end of his Stonehenge section he has, under the heading 'Enginry', an extremely sensible and practical (if in detail impracticable) discussion of the transport and erection of large stone blocks by sledges, timber cradles, rollers and levers, an enquiry so far as I know unique in early antiquarian studies, long anticipating the famous address by King Frederik VII of Denmark on the subject in 1857.

The style of the draft is clear and almost colloquial, and invariably fresh, lively and enthusiastic. 'I shall take the reader a fine tour along with me quite round the verge of the temple' he writes of Avebury, 'but how much more agreeable upon the spot, tho' accompany'd with the trouble of climbing over the hedges'. At Stonehenge we are again given a conducted tour, first of the surrounding landscape and its barrows, and then the monument approached from the Avenue. Large parts of these objective descriptions were later incorporated in the published versions of *Stonehenge* (1740) and *Abury* (1743), but by this time embedded in the elaborate fantasies of Druids, ancient mythology and patriarchal religion which he had so unfortunately evolved over the intervening years. At Stonehenge as at Avebury he was conscious that his fieldwork was a record before impending destruction, 'to perpetuate the vestiges of this celebrated wonder & of the barrows avenues cursus &c for I forsee that it will in few years be universally plowd over & consequently defacd'.

The story of the transformation of this 1723 book into those of the 1740s can be followed in part. By the time he was writing the preface to *Itinerarium Curiosum I* over Christmas 1724 it had become in his mind 'the history of the ancient Celts, particularly the first inhabitants of Great Britain' in four parts. The first was to deal with the 'history of the origin and passage of the Celts from Asia into the west of Europe, particularly into Britain; of their manners, languages, etc.'; the second with Celtic religion and temples, and the third and fourth were monographs on Avebury and Stonehenge. Druids are not here mentioned by name, but in 1733 Sir John Clerk, visiting Stukeley at Stamford, found him writing a book on 'the Religion of the Druids and all their Temples and monuments', and at some date after 1723 he drew a new version of his original decorative title-page, altering the wording to *The History of the Religion and Temples of the Druids*.[245] The Druids had come, and come to stay.

Before we examine his work in detail, first at Stonehenge and then at Avebury, there is one stage in his investigations which is common to both sites. Inigo Jones, as we have seen, had claimed Stonehenge as a Roman structure, and in 1723 Twining was to make a like claim for Avebury[246] – a view also held by Hearne and by members of the non-antiquarian public, to judge from a poem of 1733, which in quintessentially eighteenth-century heroic couplets describes

> Where *Kennet* rises with a pregnant Rill
> And glides thro' fatt'ning Meads serenely still
> Old *Avebury's* Relicks feed the curious Eye
> And great in Ruins *Roman* Structures lie.[247]

This view Stukeley had to combat at the outset of his work, for Druids or no Druids, he rightly enough held that these circles must be pre-Roman. When investigating the monument known as Arthur's O'on in Scotland (as described in the last chapter), he had worked out for himself the length of the Roman foot, basing his deductions on the statement in Pliny[248] that the brick used by the Romans was one foot wide by a foot-and-a-half long, and applying this statement to actual Roman bricks he had picked up at St Albans and in the City of London, with the result that he ascertained the Roman 'foot' to be in fact eleven and a half English inches – a good enough approximation to the true value of 11.65 inches. Using this unit of measurement he found that the dimensions of Arthur's O'on worked out in even multiples of about 11.5 inches, and took this reasonably enough as support of a Roman date.[249]

Turning to Stonehenge, he felt that the same arguments should apply, 'for', as he sensibly said, 'whoever makes any eminent building, most certainly forms it upon the common measure in use, among the people of that place',[250] and if Inigo Jones and the others were right the unit of measurement there and in other stone circles should be the Roman foot which he had already determined. He therefore measured Stonehenge carefully – there is a charming account of how he and Lord Winchelsea and others 'took I believe among us 2000 measures' and how 'Lord Winchelsea has workt very hard, and was ravisht with Stonehenge, it was a great strife between us, which should talk of leaving it first'.[251] From these measurements he thought he could reconstruct the unit on which the Stonehenge plan was laid out, which in the unfortunately romantic name of a 'Druid's Cubit' is thus abruptly brandished before the reader: 'Take a staff 10 foot 4 inches and $\frac{3}{4}$ long. Divide it into six equal parts. These are the cubits of the ancients. Each cubit is divided into six parts. These are palms.'[252] Using then a unit of 20.8 inches he showed that the circle was laid out in equal multiples of this, and was therefore not Roman. Sir Isaac Newton, in a posthumously published treatise, had independently worked out 'the Sacred Cubit of the Jews and the Cubits of the several Nations', using in part the measurements of the Great Pyramid.[253]

The search for an accurate unit of measurement used by prehistoric man in the layout of megalithic monuments, initiated by Stukeley, was continued a century ago by Flinders Petrie at Stonehenge, who on the basis of his own measurements concluded that the monument had been planned in terms of the very 'Roman' foot his predecessor had rejected: unfortunately both were mistaken. More recently, with the work of Alexander Thom and others, a new unit, the 'megalithic yard' of 2.72 feet, has been put forward, with every appearance of mathematical rigour, as a unit adhered to with precision over large geographical areas. This has in turn been questioned not only by archaeologists but by mathematicians and statisticians, and in its place a unit not of such high accuracy and 'related to some measure of the human body' has been proposed as a reasonable alternative.[254]

The monument of Stonehenge emerges today, as the result of excavation, as a composite structure whose building and rebuilding extended over many centuries. Three constructional phases emerge, the third itself capable of further subdivision, and radiocarbon dates confirm the sequence. The first, Late Neolithic, phase, about 2800–2300 BC, comprises the circular bank and ditch, the fifty-six 'Aubrey Holes' (see below) and the outlying Heel Stone. In the second phase, the axis was shifted to approximate to the summer solstice sunrise, an incomplete double circle of bluestones brought from Pembrokeshire set up, and the first stretch of an axial Avenue marked by banks and ditches laid out, all by about 2000 BC. In Phase III the monument we see today was brought into being with alterations over three sub-stages, with the huge North Wiltshire sarsen uprights and lintels set up and tooled to shape, and the bluestones arranged and re-arranged, all about 1500 BC. The Avenue was finally extended to the River Avon about 1000 BC.[255]

The positive achievements of Stukeley's work at Stonehenge are considerable, despite the failure of his 'Druid's Cubit'. The manuscript documentation for this site is less detailed than for Avebury, but he does not seem to have produced any sequence of theories as he did for the North Wiltshire site. The unique character of the structure, with its dressed stones and lintelled architrave, marked it off to his mind as it does to us today as an exceptional site, and his conception of it in the broadest terms as a great prehistoric sanctuary of southern Britain is one on which we cannot very much improve. His plan, though failing by modern standards of accuracy, was nevertheless a very much better achievement than anything that had been produced before, and many of the subsequent versions of the Stonehenge plan in the later eighteenth and the nineteenth century are considerably worse. Aubrey had made a plan in his *Monumenta* which is chiefly memorable for its inclusion of a series of slight depressions immediately inside the enclosing earthwork, which were found during the 1921–5 excavations of the Society of Antiquaries to have been on the site of a ring of holes cut in the chalk, belonging to the first phase of the monument, into the primary filling of which human cremations were inserted. There was no sign of these on the ground when the excavations were carried out exactly two centuries after Stukeley's own years of work, and he himself does not record them. They have been named the Aubrey Holes in honour of John Aubrey's observation: possibly the increasing number of visitors to the site between his day and Stukeley's might account for their obliteration by the 1720s, for it is hard to believe that, if still recognizable, they would have escaped Stukeley's keen eye.

Aubrey, however, missed a feature that Stukeley was the first to record, and which was scarcely more obvious than the Aubrey Holes must have been. This was the Avenue leading from the entrance of Stonehenge towards the Avon, and already referred to. He introduces it to his readers with an additional observation which has had repercussions up to today. Chapter VIII of his *Stonehenge* (1740) opens:

> The Avenue of *Stonehenge* was never observ'd by any one who have wrote of it, tho' a very elegant part of it, and very apparent. It answers . . . to the principal line of the whole work, the north-east, where abouts the sun rises, when the days are longest.

The Avenue, so named by Stukeley, and like his *trilithon* for the uprights-and-lintel elements, an apt designation still in use today, runs straight on the axis for about 580 yards and belongs to Phase II, with a curved prolongation to the River Avon of about 1000 BC. In recording its course for the first time Stukeley hoped he might 'perhaps preserve the memory of it hereafter, when the traces of this mighty work are obliterated by the plough, which is to be fear'd, will be its fate'.[256] He was right, and his record was not vindicated until 1920, as an early triumph of archaeological air photography.[257] In his observation that Stonehenge had an approximate astronomical orientation on the sunrise at the summer solstice is the germ of all subsequent astro-archaeological investigations up to the present day.

Another field observation, not directly related to Stonehenge itself, was of the elongated earthwork enclosure which he named the Cursus, and thought to be a prehistoric racecourse of some kind. Again the name has stuck, and the Stonehenge Cursus can now be seen as a member of a large group of such enclosures widely distributed in Britain and of Late Neolithic date.[258]

In addition to field observation and record Stukeley excavated some of the very numerous Bronze Age barrows that, as he rightly observed, cluster round Stonehenge in such a manner as to indicate an almost certain grouping round a ritual focus. Lord Pembroke provided the finances and labour for these investigations, and one would not have expected that in the eighteenth century archaeological excavation would be more than hole-digging for loot. But in actual fact, Stukeley's observations and record of his barrow digging are far superior to anything normally undertaken before at all events, the middle of the last century, when the relic-seekers were all too likely to sink a shaft down to the grave beneath the mound and extract as best they might an ancient urn to adorn the library mantelpiece. Today, when we appreciate the importance of studying the entire structure of the barrow and the sequence of its formation during the funeral ceremonies we see quite a modern note in Stukeley's detailed record:

The manner of composition of the barrow was good earth, quite thro', except a coat of chalk of about two foot thickness, covering it quite over, under the turf. Hence it appears, that the method of making these barrows was to dig up the turf for a great space round, till the barrow was brought to its intended bulk. Then with the chalk, dug out of the environing ditch, they powder'd it all over.

Or, again:

After the turf taken off, we came to the layer of chalk, as before, then fine garden mould. About three foot below the surface, a layer of flints, humouring the convexity of the barrow. . . . This being about a foot thick, rested on a layer of soft mould another foot; in which was inclos'd an urn full of bones.[259]

And not only did he write these precise notes, but among his Stonehenge manuscripts there survives a drawn section of the make-up of the mound of the barrow, which must be by far the earliest example in British archaeology of this essential form of visual record.[260]

At Avebury Stukeley was dealing with a monument which spread out over a large tract of downland instead of forming a relatively compact unit, and its very stones were being broken up and destroyed before his eyes. Avebury appears to have had two main periods of destruction, the first being in the Middle Ages, when the great stones were levered into pits and buried with an anxious care which suggests religious zeal in removing the conspicuous elements of a pagan monument that it did not quite dare to destroy outright.[261] But in the early eighteenth century no superstitious prejudices were going to stand in the way of those who saw a ready market for building stone in the new houses of the expanding village. With a novel method of destruction in heating the recumbent stones in a great fire (mainly of straw) and then cracking them by pouring cold water upon them, the 'Stone-Killer' Tom Robinson and his accomplices were getting merrily to work on what Stukeley called in his spirited drawing of the event an 'Abury Atto de Fe'.[262] Stukeley's description of this stone-breaking is worth quoting:

The barbarous massacre of a stone here with leavers and hammers, sledges and fire, is as terrible a sight as a Spanish Atto de fe. The vast cave they dig around it, the hollow under the stone like a glasshouse furnace or baker's oven, the huge chasms made through the body of the stone, the straw, the faggots, the smoak, the prongs, and squallor of the fellows looks like a knot of devils grilling the soul of a sinner.[263]

He could not stop the work of destruction, but he could at least record what still existed (though less every year) or mark the sites of stones from the information of Reuben Horsall or other local inhabitants. His 'great frontispiece plate', a plan of the circles showing in detail all this information, is a magnificent production and before the 1934–8 excavations was the only clue to the layout as it existed in his time.[264]

The sequence of Stukeley's work at Avebury can be reconstructed in some detail from the extant dated drawings. Already in 1721 he was making a plan with the two inner circles entitled 'Solar' and 'Lunar', respectively,[265] and, as I have pointed out, this suggests a connection with Toland's then unpublished ideas. In 1722 is another drawing of the 'Temple of the Moon', and in the next year the solar and lunar pair are well established. One may also note the word 'Obelisk' which he uses for the single upright stone in the centre of the south Inner Circle – this is used for standing stones in Wallace's book of 1693 on Orkney, and also by Toland.[266]

Stukeley had now made plans and drawings not only of the main group of stone circles within the great bank and ditch, but also of the avenue leading towards the village of West Kennet, where it terminated in a small double circle of standing stones which was to be destroyed within a year or two of Stukeley's record and only rediscovered by excavation in 1930.[267] This circle, known to the country people, he says, as The Sanctuary, he drew on 8 July 1723 and labelled it 'Temple of Ertha'.[268] This name is Stukeley's version of 'Hertha', itself a misreading of the 'Nerthus' of Tacitus (*Germ.* 40), a deity of the underworld.[269] The form Hertha was current in the seventeenth and eighteenth centuries, and apart from the Tacitus reference Stukeley may have been influenced by the woodcut in Ole Worm's book on ancient Danish monuments which shows various megalithic chambered tombs with stone peristaliths and a place labelled '*Erdetal in luco, amaena vallis Herthae Deae, ut putatur, olim dicatur*'.[270] Stukeley, accepting the earth-goddess interpretation of Hertha-Nerthus, anglicized the name of the circles into 'Temple of Earth', for it appears in this form in two drawings[271] and is referred to by Lord Winchelsea.[272]

Lord Winchelsea, Cingetorix of the Roman Knights, deserves further mention. As we saw, in July 1723 he had been hard at work measuring Stonehenge with Stukeley, and about a week earlier had taken part in a field day at Avebury. 'Lord Winchelsea, Lord Hartford, and the ladys', Stukeley reported to Roger Gale, 'came one day to visit the Druid as they called me: I treated them on the top of Silbury with a bowl of punch. Lord Winchelsea was with me the whole day and helpt me measure till he was tired to the last degree'[273]. Poor Cingetorix! He certainly deserved his drink, especially when we remember that whereas Stukeley was only in his mid thirties, he was not far off seventy at the time. It is a tribute not only to his own stamina and kindness, but to the Druid's infectious enthusiasm.

In addition to the Kennet Avenue of two parallel lines of standing stones, I have already mentioned that Stukeley claimed to have found another similar double line stretching westward from the great circle towards the modern village of Beckhampton. It was to play an important part in Stukeley's later theories as to the symbolism of the Avebury plan, and the modern view is that 'the grounds for accepting the former existence of the Beckhampton Avenue seem to be strong'.[274] Stukeley could not trace its end (it is possible, in fact, that it never did run farther than the Beckhampton 'Long Stones'), but he felt that it should have had a circle to balance The Sanctuary, and on a great drawing which is undated but probably was made in 1723,[275] and shows the whole Avebury complex in detail, he has dotted in a

hypothetical circle which he labelled 'Temple of the Infernal Regions'
– an unfortunate identification which he subsequently scored out so
heavily that the original words can only be read with great difficulty.

In his last year's fieldwork at Avebury, in 1724, Stukeley seems to
have been in a remarkably clear state of mind, for from his dated
alterations we find him changing the 'Temple of Ertha' to the sensibly
non-committal 'Temple on Overton Hill' on 18 May of this year,[276]
and it is presumably to the same period that we may attribute the
elimination of the Infernal Regions and of the words 'of the Earth'
from his field surveys of The Sanctuary.[277] Probably, too, the ideas
about Solar and Lunar Temples were also discarded at this time, for
they do not appear in the final version of the plan. His mood of sane,
scientific, accurate observation and record was not to be recovered for
the rest of his long life. Had he published in 1724 the book on Avebury,
Stonehenge and related stone circles which he announced in his
preface to the *Itinerarium Curiosum* of that year, and which as we
have seen was virtually complete in draft, his subsequent
archaeological reputation might have been very different.

An interesting parallel to the sequence of ideas as we can trace them
in the Avebury drawings is provided by a page in the Devizes
commonplace book.[278] This contains an oblique projection of the plan
of the 'Classerness' stone circle and avenues (Callanish in the
Hebrides). The original title written in is 'The Form of the Heathen
Temple . . .', but the word 'Heathen' is crossed out and 'Druid'
substituted, and a note in handwriting characteristic of Stukeley about
1730–40 then adds: 'It was part of a Dracontium or serpentine temple,
but very ill drawn.' Doubts then seem to have occurred, for the words
'but quaere' are added to this in the same hand, but with a different
pen and ink. The original scale to the drawing was in feet, but the later
hand adds one in cubits.

Stukeley's intellectual life was about to be profoundly altered by a
decision to which reference has already been made. William Wake,
formerly Bishop of Lincoln, had been appointed to the Primacy of all
England in 1725. He, like his contemporary, Edmund Gibson, was an
historian and antiquary and was one of the last representatives of the
great tradition of ecclesiastical historical learning belonging properly
to the Restoration period. Stukeley was friendly with him – the
Lincolnshire connection as well as a common interest in antiquities
would have brought them together – and in May 1729 Wake had
apparently written to Stukeley inquiring about medieval English
coins. Replying on 3 June,[279] Stukeley gives the first intimation which

can be traced in his papers of his decision to take orders in the Church of England. His recommendations for ordination were perhaps unusual even in those days of Latitudinarian churchmen, tolerant of a very wide range of beliefs, and of clerics more concerned with polemics than piety.

I have ever been studious in divinity [he writes] especially in the most abstruse and sublime parts of it; and my disquisitions into the history of our Celtic ancestors and their religion, have led me into them, and given me the opportunity of discovering some notions about the Doctrine of the Trinity which I think are not common.

Far from being contrary to reason, he goes on, he thinks he can prove the doctrine 'deducible from reason its self', and demonstrate that the 'antient Egyptians, Plato, our old Druids, and all the heathen philosophers' had a true, Church-of-England, appreciation of the Doctrine of the Trinity. With these, and other mysterious hints of new interpretations of the Old Testament, and a pointed reference to the inconvenience of his medical practice, he begs Wake to consider him as a candidate for ordination.

The Primate replied by return in a letter[280] which is of some interest. It seems reasonable to regard it not merely as an expression of Wake's private opinion but representative of the views of the higher clergy at this time on the circumstances in which they would welcome a layman into Holy Orders.[281] He is immediately encouraging, and seems undeterred by the uncommon notions about the Trinity. He sees in Stukeley a welcome recruit to the ranks of clerical controversialists so badly needed to defend the Church of England against freethinking:

Never was there a time in which we wanted all the assistance we can get against the prevailing infidelity of the present wicked age; and as our adversaries are men pretending to reason superior to others, so nothing can more abate their pride, and stop their prevalance, than to see Christianity defended by those who are in all respects as eminent in naturall knowledge, and philosophical enquiries, as they can pretend to be. I am persuaded your education and practice as a Physician, will for this reason enable you to do God and Christianity better service than one brought up to Divinity from the beginning could do. . . .

The correspondence continues: Stukeley decides to take Orders and agrees with his Grace about the 'growing infidelity of the present age'.[282] Wake advises him as to reading in preparation, and agrees to ordain him Deacon at Croydon on 20 July;[283] Stukeley replies with renewed zeal quickened with a resentment of that deluge of profaneness and infidelity that prevails so much at present, and threatens an utter subversion of religion in general . . . nor have I any expectations, nor have I made my intentions known to any person but your Grace; it is a thing that has not enter'd my thought. I can only say about it, that I shall neither seek for preferment nor refuse it, in an undecent way. God has blest me with a competent fortune; the dignity of a clergyman will not, I hope, suffer from my wearing it.[284]

There is a statement not strictly true in this letter – he had in fact told Roger Gale about his intentions by the middle of June, for that worthy gentleman was thoroughly alarmed and wrote in reply a letter urging caution lest precipitate action might result in a doctor without a practice and an unbeneficed clergyman. 'Your reconciling Plato and Moses', wrote Gale, 'and the Druid and Christian religion may gain you applause, and perhaps a Patron, but it is good to be sure of the latter upon firmer motives than that scheme may inspire people with at present.'[285] Hearne's comment is terse and characteristic. On 10 August 1729 he writes: 'Dr. Stukeley, to the surprise of everybody, has taken orders. His friends think him crazy.'[286]

But Stukeley, by no means a fool in worldly matters, had already a living in mind, that of All Saints, Stamford. He wrote to Wake about this in September,[287] and at the same time solicited Sir Hans Sloane's help in the matter:[288] in October he went up to London himself, 'making interest for All Saints Living' as he blandly records in his diary.[289] The intrigues were successful, and on 16 of October the Lord Chancellor granted him the living, apparently in the teeth of High Church opposition,[290] and he took up residence at the beginning of 1730.

We must consider briefly the situation in the Church of England in the early eighteenth century which could give rise to excited phrases like a 'deluge of profaneness and infidelity' and cause Stukeley to write later that his aim was 'to combat the deists from an unexpected quarter'. We are not dealing with atheism: very few denied the existence of God or of a providential universe created for man's benefit. The philosophers of the Enlightenment had developed two novel and accommodating concepts, that of the state of nature and that of man as an innately reasonable being, both unquestionably good because divinely ordained as part of the design, order and law that the mathematicians had demonstrated in the Universe. If (as Pope put it) 'the State of Nature was the reign of God', it followed, said Deists such as Matthew Tindal in 1730, that the Creator must from the first have 'given mankind some rule or law for their conduct', which was the original and true religion of 'Adam, Seth and Noah' in Voltaire's words. Such a belief must be universal, and so include Christians and heathens, Hurons and Hottentots. The most disturbing consequence arising from such a belief was that the Christian doctrine of Revelation, and the attendant mysteries of its faith administered by a priesthood, could be regarded as an irrelevance compared with a 'Christianity as Old as the Creation' proclaimed in the title of Tindal's book. Deism could only be subversive to the Established Church of England of which William Wake was Primate and in which William Stukeley was seeking ordination.[291]

It is difficult to discover what Stukeley's religious position really was, and what he conceived as being 'Deistic' doctrines. His appeals to a reasonable basis for Christianity bring him into the normal Latitudinarian attitude so well exemplified by Tillotson, and the Christian revelation seems to have carried less weight with him than a strong sense of a 'natural' religion which extended back into primitive times, before the Deluge (and so the primeval religion of the Deists), but given a specifically Christian tinge by asserting that the doctrine of the Trinity was known to the ancients. We must turn to the ideas put forward in Stukeley's published works, especially in *Stonehenge* and *Abury*, for a clue to his complicated beliefs about the Druids and Christianity which he had begun to hold soon after the completion of his Avebury fieldwork and which were to remain with him for the rest of his life.

From Stukeley's two books mentioned above, and from the posthumously published essays *The Brill, Caesar's Camp at Pancras,* and *The Weddings* (a description of the stone circles at Stanton Drew) we may piece together his picture of the British Druids. They had come to England as part of 'an oriental colony' of Phoenicians, 'in the very earliest times, even as soon as Tyre was founded: during the life of Abraham, or very soon after', indeed, 'soon after Noah's flood'. These Druids were 'of *Abraham's* religion intirely', and while he is careful to write that 'we cannot say that Jehovah appeared personally to them', yet he thinks they could by their own reasoning have reached 'a knowledge of the plurality of persons in the Deity' and so become at least not Unitarians, but in a fair way to claim themselves good churchmen. Isolated in Britain ('left in the extremest west to the improvement of their thoughts', as he puts it), they had preserved the patriarchal traditions intact – 'the true religion has chiefly, since the repeopling of mankind after the flood, subsisted in our island'. This religion 'is so extremely like Christianity, that in effect it differ'd from it only in this; they believed in a Messiah who was to come into this world, as we believe in him that is come'. The leader of the Druidic immigrants Stukeley conceived as being the Tyrian Hercules, 'a worthy scholar of Abraham' and 'in the same generation as Noah's great grandsons'. He had landed in west Britain and probably, as one of his new labours, had built the stone circle of Boscawen-Un, in Cornwall.[292]

As we read them today, these ideas of Stukeley's seem, at first, a fantastic invention, hatched in his own brain while he pored over the drawings of Stonehenge and Avebury in the seclusion of his country vicarage. But when we come to examine them critically, we find that few of them are original, and, granting certain premisses that every learned man of the early eighteenth century would accept, that they are not really so fantastic as they seem at a remove of two centuries. It must be remembered at the outset that any discussion of antiquity had to be fitted into a Biblical framework which not only governed the broad principles of chronology by setting (in the widely accepted scheme) the date of the Creation at 4004 B C, but which also included one decisive and cataclysmic event of worldwide magnitude, the Deluge. The Tower of Babel, the Flood, and the re-peopling of the world by 'the arkite ogdoad' (the eight persons in the Ark – Noah, Shem, Ham, and Japhet, and their wives) were inescapable facts in the mind of Stukeley, and in the minds of all his contemporaries, while with these was linked the necessary belief that the primitive language of original humanity must have been Hebrew.

It is this philological assumption that gives us our first clue in distinguishing the sources of Stukeley's Druidic ideas. The seventeenth-century French scholar, Samuel Bochart,[293] had searched for the remnants of the pre-Diluvian, pre-Babel, language of mankind, and had, with a wealth of misplaced erudition, found this in Phoenician. Following this by the observation of genuine, though misunderstood, affinities between the various Indo-European languages, including the Celtic tongues, Bochart had concluded that Gaul had been peopled after the Flood by Phoenician voyagers, and he further demonstrated to his own satisfaction, and in common with many scholars of his time, that the classical myths were also derived from Old Testament sources – Bacchus and Noah were linked by a common liking for the wine-skin, while Moses and the Muses were an obvious assonance.

Now Stukeley certainly used this work; and indeed refers respectfully to 'the great *Bochart*', but before his day another English antiquary had drunk deeply at the same well. Aylett Sammes, whose *Britannia Antiqua Illustrata*, published in 1676, was in Stukeley's library, freely acknowledges that his work was based on that of Bochart – 'I do not arrogate to my self the first discovery of these Antiquities', he writes in his preface. He then goes on to say that, as Bochart had demonstrated the Phoenician peopling of Gaul, so he hopes to take this a stage farther, 'making use of the same method in laying open the Original and Commerce of the Primitive Inhabitants of this Island'. The Druids make a conspicuous appearance in the pages of Sammes's work, with illustrations of the wicker image full of victims for the holocaust, and of a Druid himself, venerably bearded, with mantle and hood, bare-footed and with staff, scrip, and book. But they are in no sense patriarchal Christians, for Sammes makes sensible use of the classical authorities with their references to Celtic gods, sacrifices, holocausts, and other idolatrous and heathenish practices, from which he makes no attempt to exculpate the British Druids. An important contribution of his own to the Phoenician myth, however, is none other than the Tyrian Hercules – Hercules, 'the Son of *Demarus* King of *Tyra*', who landed in Devonshire at Hartland Point. Here, then, is the germ of Stukeley's ideas about Hercules, and an introduction to Bochart if he had not already met with that writer.

In 1723, when Stukeley was nearly at the end of his work at Avebury, a book was published that owed much to Sammes. The Reverend Henry Rowlands was the scholarly vicar of an Anglesey parish, who was interested in the local antiquities of the island, and wrote an account of these which shows its debt to Sammes, *Mona Antiqua Restaurata*. Although not published until 1723, a MS version was in circulation as early as 1708.[294] Rowlands, of course, accepts the post-Diluvial peopling of Europe – 'Antiquity recordeth, and the Consent of Nations celebrateth the Sons of *Japhet* to have been the first Planters of *Europe*', he writes, and then, assuming Welsh (an 'ancient *Celtish* or *British* Tongue') to be that of the first 'planters' of Anglesey after the Flood, he accepts Bochart's view that Welsh is really Hebrew, and that it preserves, nearest of all surviving languages, the original speech of mankind before Babel.[295] It follows from this

that some of the first Planters of this Island, being so near in descent, to the Fountains of true Religion and Worship, as to have one of *Noah's* sons for Grandsire or Great-grandsire, may be well imagin'd, to have carried and convey'd some of the Rites and Usages of that true Religion here, pure and

untainted, in their first propagating of them; tho' I must confess they soon
after became, as well here as in other Countries, abominably corrupted, and
perverted into the grossest heathenish Fictions and Barbarities.

The first part of this proposition seems to have been eagerly accepted
by Stukeley, though the wiser conclusion of Rowlands is ignored.
Later in the book Rowlands appears to have abandoned his ideas
about the implanting of 'true Religion' by Phoenician Druids in
Anglesey, for they become 'insinuating priests' who

had Charms enough in their Skill and Knowledge, in their address and
Conversation, to obtain to themselves the chief Posts of Management
wherever they resided; and when obtain'd, to secure their Credit and
Reputation, and there-upon, to bear up a Port and Authority (no hard thing
for them to do in that easy obsequious Age).

In Anglesey, Rowlands had excuse enough to discuss the Druids,
since the reference in Tacitus to this priesthood and its sanctuaries in
the island in the first century A D are detailed and explicit. Anglesey
also contains a large number of megalithic chambered tombs dating
from Neolithic times, as well as standing stones of unknown age, and
Rowlands is at pains to find an origin for these. He knows from the
classical writers that the Druids worshipped in groves, and though
those of Anglesey would have vanished long ago, yet he can find
enough groves of oaks in the Old Testament to exclaim with the
seventeenth-century writer Dickenson, '*En primos sacerdotes
quernos! En patriarchas Druidas!*'[296] Altars of stone have also a
scriptural warrant, so the ruined chambered tombs become Druid
altars, with the ritual of sacrifice performed on top of the denuded
capstones of the burial chambers: standing stones are unhewn idols.
He is therefore able neatly to account for all the more conspicuous
local antiquities, and as there are no stone circles in Anglesey
recognizable as such, he is not troubled by seeking an explanation for
these. He refers in passing to English stone circles, however, implying
that the prevailing view was that they were of Danish origin; though,
as he asks, 'Might not Stonehenge and Roll-rick Coronets be very well
the Relicks of antient *Druidism*' re-used by the Danes, and he quotes
Martin Martin in support of a Druidical origin for stone circles in
Scotland.

From Bochart, Sammes, and Rowlands, therefore, Stukeley appears
to have derived his ideas of the Phoenician colonization of Britain, led
by the Tyrian Hercules (who was also championed by Toland), and
including Druids who were likely to have inherited something of the

religion of the Old Testament patriarchs – the last hypothesis dependent, of course, on the current beliefs about the re-peopling of the world after the Deluge by the sons of Noah. To understand his conception of the Druids as a nearly Christian priesthood, however, we must turn to other views about them which had been vaguely held for over a century.

In parenthesis, though, we see how Stukeley's visual idea of a Druid was built up. Sammes had depicted a Druid in a fancy drawing of a bearded sage, venerable and barefoot, holding a staff and an open book, with a bag slung at his side. This portrayal was concocted by Sammes from the verbal description of statues found at the foot of the Fichtelberg Mountain in Germany (with no attribution to Druids or anyone else), as recorded by Conrad Celtes and, following him, John Selden. This was copied by Rowlands with certain alterations – the bare feet were shod with sandals, an oak-branch substituted for the book in the left hand, and fantastic versions of prehistoric circular huts were introduced into the background. Stukeley puts as a frontispiece to his *Stonehenge* a representation of 'A British Druid', drawn in February 1723/4 (presumably therefore just after the publication of Rowlands's book), in which the figure, recognizably the same in general stance and dress to that in Rowlands's, has a shortened beard and a Bronze Age axe hung at his belt, and though nothing is held in his left hand he stands under an oak tree. In the background are barrows and a hillfort appropriate to the Wiltshire downland.

The idealization of the Druids which made possible their claim, in Stukeley's imagination, to be the enlightened priests of a religion by no means unlike that of the eighteenth-century Church of England, had begun early in the seventeenth century.[297] Drayton in his *Polyolbion* (1612) pictures the Druids as 'sacred Bards' and sages 'like whom great Nature's depths no man yet ever knew', sublime philosophers in Britain before the advent of Caesar, and monotheists at that. Selden, in his notes to the poem, takes the matter farther, and suggests that the Pythagorean ideas of metempsychosis may be of Druid origin, and this point was taken up eagerly by Toland, who identified the mysterious Abaris the Hyperborean as a Celtic Druid, who, wrapped in his native plaid, disputed in perfect Greek with Pythagoras himself. Toland's enthusiasm was that of the Irishman eager to defend the Celt, but his general opinion of Druids was worse than that of Rowlands, and delivered with elaborate irony:

To arrive at perfection in sophistry requires a long habit, as well as in juggling, in which last they were very expert: but to be masters of both, and withal to learn the art of managing the mob, which is vulgarly called *leading the people by the nose*, demands abundant study and exercise.[298]

But the belief in noble Druids was fed partly by patriotic feeling and partly by that sense of liberty which was to find its political expression in the French Revolution at the end of the century. The Druids are regarded as leaders of a resistance movement against the oppression of Roman rule – a feeling that finds overt expression in Thomson's poem *Liberty* (1735) and Collins's *Ode to Liberty* (1747), in both of which Druids have a place as the apostles of freedom.

With such a background, then, with Druids already associated in the literary world with liberty, virtue, and culture, Stukeley could find a ready acceptance of his own individual contributions to the Druid myth. He could claim for them as temples not the memory of long-vanished groves, but the still extant ruins of magnificent circular sanctuaries of great stones, and, as a Church of England parson distressed by the prevalent rationalism, he could show these same Druids to be the inheritors of the true patriarchal religion, with which 'the christian, is but one and the same'.[299]

To this end the archaeological fieldwork of the previous years, still unpublished, could be used as ammunition in a holy war against the Deists. The new vicar of All Saints, Stamford, with misguided enthusiasm, set about the task of converting his archaeological notes into religious tracts. By the end of June 1730 he was able to reveal to Roger Gale the real nature of Avebury:

The form of that stupendous work [he wrote] is a picture of the Deity, more particularly of the Trinity, but most particularly what they anciently called the Father and the Word, who created all things. . . . A snake proceeding from a circle is the eternal procession of the Son, from the first cause. . . . My main motive in pursuing this subject is to combat the deists from an unexpected quarter, and to preserve so noble a monument of our ancestors' piety, I may add, orthodoxy.[300]

As Miss Tompkins has remarked, Stukeley felt it necessary that the ceremonies of the Druids at Avebury should closely resemble the services in his own parish church at Stamford.[301]

The 'snake proceeding from a circle' was an idea evolved by Stukeley from his simplified restoration of what he imagined was the original plan of the Avebury complex. The problematical Beckhampton Avenue on the west formed the tail of the serpent, which passed through the main circles and emerged on the south as the Kennet Avenue, with the Overton Hill stone circles as its head to the east. On this 'hieroglyphic figure' he expended much thought, and believed that all other stone circles with avenues known to him (for instance that of Callanish in the Outer Hebrides) belonged to a class of temples for which he invented the name *Dracontia*: serpent or dragon temples. There seems no warrant for such a word, as *dracontium* in classical antiquity was used only for a plant described by Pliny, but Stukeley uses it throughout in his own peculiar meaning.

The quarter from which the Deists were to be combated was so unexpected that it is very doubtful whether they recognized as an opponent the antiquarian clergyman with his two folios on stone circles. But he took care to make his intention clear enough in his prefatory remarks to *Stonehenge*, first to be published in 1740, which explain that this volume, and the forthcoming *Abury*, were to be considered as two parts only of a great work on 'Patriarchal Christianity, or a Chronological History of the Origin and Progress of true Religion, and of Idolatry'. This was planned in seven sections dealing respectively with (1) A Mosaic Chronology from the Creation to Exodus, (2) 'Melchisedec, or a delineation of the first and patriarchal religion', (3) Of the mysteries of the ancients, and of idolatry (based apparently mainly on the *Tabula Isiaca*, a Roman forgery to which Dr. Mead had drawn attention but which he, and the rest of the learned world of the time, took to be genuine),[302] (4) A dissertation on writing and the origin of the alphabet, (5) The patriarchal history of Abraham and the Phoenician colonization of Britain, (6) Of the temples of the Druids in Britain, especially Avebury, and (7) A description of Stonehenge. 'I propose', he continues, 'to publish these two first, and proceed to the speculative parts afterwards; reserving them, God willing, to the maturer time of my life.' Then follows a declaration of faith:

My intent is (besides preserving the memory of these extraordinary monuments, so much to the honour of our country, now in great danger of ruin) to promote, as much as I am able, the knowledge and practice of ancient and true Religion; to revive in the minds of the learned the spirit of Christianity . . . to warm our hearts into that true sense of Religion, which keeps the medium between ignorant superstition and learned free-thinking, between enthusiasm and the rational worship of God, which is no where upon earth done, in my judgement, better than in the Church of *England*.[303]

The scheme is plain: the learned would read about stone circles, and thence would be gently drawn to the Druids, and before they knew where they were the beauties of the ancient patriarchal religion, foreshadowing the whole doctrine of the Church of England, would be presented so persuasively that any freethinking ideas would be put to rout. He was intent to attract a wide public – 'the method of writing, which I have chose is a diffusive one, not pretending to a formal and stiff scholastic proof of everything I say, which would be odious and irksome to the reader, as well as myself', he writes rather ingenuously, but 'to one that has proper sagacity and judgment, conviction will steal upon him insensibly, if I am not mistaken'.[304] We have travelled a long way from the accurate scholarship of the Restoration historians, in the last decade of which tradition Stukeley began his work, and are already in the age in which Bolingbroke could express his 'thorough contempt for the whole business' of the great historical achievements of the earlier scholars, and not far from that of Gibbon, when the antiquary 'blushes at his alliance with Hearne'.[305] Indeed, we are a long way from Stukeley's own excellent intentions of 1724, when he was planning an objective work on stone circles and British Celtic prehistory. It even seems that as late as 1733 his work on Druid religion and temples was not conceived as a religious tract – at least Sir John Clerk gives no hint that it was.[306]

The two last sections alone of the ambitious work he finally projected were published, though much of the remainder was written and remains in deservedly obscure manuscript form. In earlier pages we have examined the real archaeological contribution contained in the eccentric pages of *Stonehenge* and *Abury*, where it is entangled with the most curious mixture of Biblical and classical allusions and flights of the wildest etymological fancies. The Stonehenge book is the less diffuse, and comes nearer to an objective report on fieldwork and excavation, but in the three years which elapsed between its appearance and that of *Abury*, Stukeley's mind seems to have become perceptibly more obsessed with theory, and in the second book the sound fieldwork only peeps out here and there among the nonsense. And when 'PHUT son of CHAM' begins to dominate the scene ('a person of eminence, tho' not taken notice of so much as he deserves'),[307] Druids, Phoenicians, Chaldeans, and the Tyrian Hercules are all confusedly worshipping in a Dracontium in imminent expectation of the Messiah. It is time to stop.

However much words might be altered to fit theories, one would think that drawings at least were records preserving their objectivity from the better days of the 1720s. This is true of nearly all the numerous plates which adorn the two books and which give them today much of their value to the archaeologist. But there is evidence of one grave and deliberate falsification which can be traced by means of the assembled Stukeley papers. His published plan of the stone circles at The Sanctuary, mentioned above, shows them as ovals, not true circles. But the 1930 excavations of the site showed them to be in fact accurately circular, and we find that Stukeley's original field-surveys of the site, which survive, show true circles and minor features completely in accordance with the facts as recovered by excavation. An intermediate link is an original drawing of *c.*1740 in which the positions of the stones are arranged as ovals in grey wash, but are superimposed on a faint pencil outline showing them as circles, while in one of the original plans an oval outline has been roughly sketched in. It appears that by 1740 the mystic serpent had to be given a more naturalistic head than that afforded by true circles, and the original survey was altered accordingly.[308]

Between 1725 and 1730 Stukeley's life was marked with changes, as we have seen. 'The last of my expeditions', he wrote on a Kentish sketch, and he was in Kent in late May and early June 1725, later in the year making however his northern tour with Roger Gale between July and December. Thereafter there were to be no more tours or visits to Avebury or Stonehenge, and though in retrospect he thought London had not been good for his health, and that his gout had increased, this could have hardly been a reason for a young single man of 38 giving up pleasant and salutary holidays on horseback. In 1726 he suddenly decided to leave London and live as a country physician at Grantham in Lincolnshire, as we have seen, an action he felt necessary to justify to himself more than once in the autobiographical fragments he wrote in later life – 'an irresistible impulse seiz'd my mind to leave the Town'; 'I was stir'd up to a resolution of leaving the Town by an excessive love to nature & simplicity, which is only to be indulg'd in perfection in the Country'.[309] These conventional protestations of rural bliss may however be thought to carry less weight than another admission written at the same time. In London, he writes, he had been 'hoping to better my fortune first some way or other' and 'expected my great friends, who encouraged me in the pursuit of Antiquarian Studys, would have made some provision for me otherwise. But seeing no probability of that after 7 years waiting' he left London for Grantham.[310] He must have said something of this kind to Sir John Clerk when he visited him there in the following year, for as we saw Sir

John wrote of Stukeley in his journal 'not meeting with the encouragement he expected from the publick he has withdrawn himself from London'.

If then Stukeley left London partly in pique at not having his antiquarian achievements sufficiently recognized (particularly financially), we may perhaps look further in this direction. His *Itinerarium Curiosum* of 1724 was published by subscription, and at the end of the preface he announces, and solicits subscriptions to, his next work, a History of the Ancient Celts, evidently the book he had first drafted at Avebury in July 1723. He stresses that it will contain over 300 engraved plates, some already made, and so owing to 'the vast expence attending this work, I shall print no more than are subscribed for'. Perhaps he hoped that his 'great friends' in London would come forward with a subvention, but in the event it is clear that adequate subscriptions were not forthcoming, and the book did not go to press.

By 1725 the climate of thought was changing, and any public demand for factual antiquarian studies in the manner of Plot or Aubrey was on the wane. And we may wonder whether Stukeley's reputation had been really enhanced by the *Itinerarium*: do Hearne's malicious comments reflect a more widespread critical attitude towards a book which after all does contain egregious blunders (as with Silchester) and some rather lightweight topography and speculation? If the publication of such tours was not going to bring him praise or profit, there might be little incentive to continue them. Stukeley was determined to publish his Stonehenge and Avebury work in some form, but this form was to be dictated by the last of the dislocations of his life at this time, his ordination in 1729.

In the first edition of this study, in 1950, I interpreted Stukeley's actions in 1726–9 as the result of a 'psychological disturbance' marked too by a change in his attitude towards his archaeological data from a neutral empiricism to an often wildly speculative religious interpretation, and suggested comparison with what at that time was held to be an intellectual change in Sir Isaac Newton after his nervous crisis in 1693. This view of Newton is hardly tenable today, as recent studies show there was no essential difference in his thinking on Biblical chronology, prophecy and eschatology, and his strangely passionate devotion to these studies, throughout his working life, and no shift from a 'scientific' to a 'religious' phase.[311] But we may remember that Stukeley had known Newton personally since 1720, and discussed the details of Solomon's Temple with him six years later, and was concerned, as an antiquary would be, with a chronology of the ancient world into which he could fit his stone circles and, increasingly, his Druids. Stukeley's 'Druid Cubit' may have been prompted by Newton's work on Solomon's mensuration. With a genuine love of the country and its antiquities, the only career really open to him as an alternative to medicine was the Church: to become a parson-antiquary rather than a physician-antiquary. Here at least indirect influences from conversations with the pious Newton are possible, and conceivably Stukeley's 'scientific' attempt to date Stonehenge to 480 B C by the magnetic variation of the compass (which he believed the Druids possessed) may echo Newton's use of the precession of the equinox to assign the voyage of the Argonauts (which he believed to be a strictly historical event) to the equally implausible date of 937 B C, as a key date in his own ancient chronology.[312] At all events, encouraged by the personal approbation of the Archbishop of Canterbury, ordination presented no problems, a gentlemanly livelihood was assured, and like his combat with the Deists, the Druids too could be approached 'from an unexpected quarter'.

V

The Country Parson

AT STAMFORD, the new Vicar of All Saints settled down with some enjoyment to his cure of souls. The medieval associations of the town, with its still extant remains of the college buildings which had been made as the result of the migration of students from Oxford in the fourteenth century, appealed to the antiquarian in Stukeley – he was childishly delighted when he was greeted by Mr Peck, the local antiquary, not only as the Vicar, but with a string of titles derived from establishments within the parish which has a Puginesque ring of unreality – 'Warden of the Augustin Fryers; Capellan of Bradecroft Chappel; St. Mary's Chantry; President of Black Hall, Peterborough Hall, Sempringham Hall, Durham and Vaudy',[313] to select from an even longer list. No more was the busy antiquarian to be called out to visit a country patient, but could sit securely and cogitate uninterruptedly on Mosaic Chronology, of which a book in three parts was composed in 1731 and was presumably one of the sections of the work on Patriarchal Christianity of which only the Stonehenge and Avebury portions were in fact published.

But there was more practical archaeology, too; a large silver dish or lanx of fourth century Roman workmanship had been found at Risley Park in Derbyshire and Stukeley had been in communication about this as early as 1729, though it was not until seven years later that he read an account of it to the Society of Antiquaries. He was prompted to do so by the discovery in 1735 of the silver lanx from Corbridge, a complete piece comparable to the Risley find, which was broken into fragments which it is uncertain whether Stukeley saw himself. But he had them drawn, and engraved by Vandergucht, together with the inscription the lanx had borne recording its gift to an early Christian church, and his publication in 1736 is now the only record of this important document of late Roman Christianity in Britain, since the original fragments are lost.[314]

He had at this time also formed a friendship with William Warburton, later to become Bishop of Gloucester and famous as a clerical controversialist with his *Divine Legation of Moses* (1738), but now incumbent of the living of Brent Broughton near Newark.[315] Stukeley composed a History of Stamford in the form of a dialogue between himself and Warburton, who appear disguised as 'Panagius' and 'Palaephatus'.[316]

This document contains an amusing example of Stukeley's ingenuous vanity. The protagonists in the dialogue are introduced each with a brief character-sketch, and that of 'Palaephatus', who is Stukeley himself, describes him as:

a person of curiosity, who had spent a series of years in the metropolis, to cultivate his mind in the circle of sciences: and who avoyding the allurements which Fortune there threw in his way, to accumulate wealth; thro' an irrisistible fondness to nature, and the country-life, he by a resolution which amaz'd all his acquaintances when his reputation was not a little, now in the prime of life, he quitted the Town in 1726.... He secreted himself for a while, from the great, the learned and the noble of his acquaintance, for the serene pleasures of solitude, and contemplation. There the inbred seeds of religion blosom'd with fresh vigour, and formed in him a resolution of betaking himself to the sacred function: that by inoculating the knowledge of secular, upon divine learning, he might produce fruits more useful to the world.

There is a simplicity in this self-satisfied autobiographical entry that is disarming: we cannot dislike anyone who could write so absurdly and unaffectedly in his own praise.

In 1733 he received a visit from the Scottish antiquary, Sir John Clerk of Penicuik, who had found him working in his garden when he had made an unexpected call at Grantham some years before. Sir John put up at the Bull at Stamford and immediately went to visit Stukeley. 'I found the Doctor in possession of the chief Living at Stamford and parsone of the great Church,' wrote Sir John in his diary.[317]

'He has turn'd a little Enthusiastick but as a Divine it became him well. He entertain'd me with a view of all his Studies and Lucubrations, many of which were very learn'd and Laborious. I found him busy on a book in which he was to describe the Religion of the Druids and all their Temples and monuments, particularly Stonehenge in Wiltshire, near Salisbury. The Doctor draws very accurately and had made very neat drawings on these subjects.

They talked of Roman coins; Sir John 'carried the Doctor to the Tavern to sup with me', and next morning he breakfasted early with Stukeley and they set off to see Tickencote Church ('very old and by

Northeast prospect of Tickencourt church.
H: Serkeley delin.

8 *Drawing by Stukeley in July 1731 of Tickencote church
(formerly Rutland, now Leicestershire), showing the fine twelfth-
century chancel before its restoration in 1792. Stukeley, who
thought it 'very old and by the Gothick manner', took Sir John
Clerk to see it in 1733.*

the Gothick manner') and 'went a Hunting of a Roman city about
which the Doctor had not been well inform'd' and so was not
discoverable. Stukeley seems to have been enjoying his incumbency –
he 'look'd very smug and canonical', Sir John reported to Roger Gale
after the visit.[318]

To the year 1736 belongs the first of what were to be the oddest of
Stukeley's serial publications, *Palaeographia Sacra No. 1*. The subtitle
of this is sufficiently surprising – *A Comment on an Ode of Horace,
shewing the Bacchus of the Heathen to be the Jehovah of the Jews* –
nor are we disappointed when we read further beyond the short
preface, in which Stukeley states he will print the original Ode
(Horace, *Carm*. ii. 19) together with a parallel interpretation – 'I will
leave it to the reader's judgment, in short, and would not apall his
gusto too much with a novel entertainment.' The Ode and its
'Paraphrastic Translation' open thus:

> *In Bacchum*
>
> Bacchum in remotis carmina rupibus
> vidi docentem (credite posteri)
> nymphasque discentes et aures
> capripedum Satyrorum acutas.

> *A Hymn to Jehovah*
> I saw the Lord (let future times believe)
> teaching to Israel's god-like race, a song
> of triumph; from Mount Sinai's rocky cliff
> eccho'd by Miriam and her female throng.

The Messianic interpretation of Virgil's *Pollio* eclogue seems really
quite reasonable when compared with this delicious flight of fancy,
which continues no less astonishingly through the entire Ode.
Basically, of course, it was in the tradition of Bochart, Huet and even
Rowlands to equate Biblical and classical characters in this reckless
manner.[319]

Until the end of the last century there remained at Stamford an
amusing relic of the medieval Oxford migration in the form of the
brass knocker which gives its name to Brasenose College and which
had been wrenched off its original door in the college and carried as a
trophy to Stamford, there to become the emblem and talisman of a
new Brasenose. In the summer of 1736 Stukeley was founding a
literary and antiquarian society in the town, and, casting about for an

appropriate name, decided on that of The Brazen Nose Society 'in memory of that antient College of the once flourishing University here'. The Society was to be 'a weekly conference for the promoting of useful learning sacred and civil, the knowledg of antiquitys and nature and for preserving the memorials of persons and things fit to be transmitted to posterity'. There were six founder-members as well as Stukeley, and a number of subscribing members by correspondence, bringing up the total number to about thirty.[320] The Spalding Gentlemen's Society was the obvious model for that at Stamford. In 1728/9 he had tried to found a similar club at Ancaster.[321]

The first meeting was to be typical in its range of subjects – astronomy and the latitude of Stamford, lunar maps, a remarkable wasps' nest, a 'stone as big as a walnut, taken out of the bladder of a little Dutch dog', and a medieval seal were all discussed, and at later meetings we find experiments with an air pump and a microscope and, a great excitement, pictures projected by 'the Italian shades or magic lanthorn'. Stukeley kept the minutes assiduously for a short time, but the little square, vellum-bound minute-books, all labelled hopefully BRAZEN NOSE XII and so on, soon became the receptacle for his personal diary, and the Society lapses. We shall see how ten years later he tried to revive it without success.[322]

In the winter of 1737 his wife, Frances Stukeley, died at the age of forty. By February 1737/8 he was considering the situation in a very practical light, and he is concerned, he says in a letter to Samuel Gale, 'to study how I may best improve this dispensation of Providence for His Glory and my own comfort', and as he is not yet fifty 'and think 'tis too soon to retire into a black box', he suggests that he and Gale should set up a joint ménage with 'a house, a maid and a man, some little distance from town, at Totenham Cross, or Hampsted, or the like; where you are to repose when you sally out of fumopolis, whilst I make use of your urban palazzo in return'.[323] But although things seemed to Roger Gale to have been settled by May of that year,[324] the projected move did not take place, for Stukeley remained at Stamford, and in the next year married the sister of the two Gales, returning with her to Stamford. The new Mrs Stukeley's marriage-portion of £10,000, and the addition of the living at Somerby in Lincolnshire in the same year, helped his financial position to the extent of his being able to maintain two establishments from 1740 onwards, when for several successive years he spent the summer in the country at Stamford, but the winter months in London with his wife and family at a house in Gloucester Street. Later gossip was not favourable to the second Mrs Stukeley. In 1823 Whitaker, the Yorkshire historian, thought that at the Gales's country seat of Scruton Stukeley found 'more enjoyment in the company of a brother-in-law than in the charms of a wife. Stukeley, it is well known, married Discord, personified in the sister of his friend.'[325]

In Stamford Stukeley had shown his customary enthusiasm in gardening, and had, as at Grantham, spent much enjoyable time in laying out and beautifying his grounds. His new wife was also a keen gardener, we gather from incidental correspondence, and it is in keeping with the dawning romanticism of the age that he should build a 'Hermitage' in the garden in 1738. A drawing survives[326] of this charmingly whimsical structure, with niches, pointed windows and a fountain, and surmounted by a very rustic stone arch insecurely carrying a pillar and globe, and we see it must have been very similar to the contemporary Hermitage at Richmond 'the Architecture of which is . . . very Gothique, being a Heap of Stones thrown into a very artful Disorder, and curiously embellished with Moss, and Shrubs, to represent *rude Nature*'.[327]

During these years the forces of destruction and restoration were remarkably active among the churches of Stamford, and stained glass in particular was being removed and thrown away. Mr Popple of St Martin's had removed the stained glass from his church so that he should not need to wear spectacles, and Stukeley was delighted to note soon afterwards that blinds had to be fitted to the new clear-glass windows to cut out the overpowering glare from the sun.[328] He was himself rescuing such glass as he could, bargaining with the glaziers as they carted it away on their barrows, and this was used to adorn the windows of his house and the garden 'temples' he was later to build.

From the time of Newton's death in 1727 until 1741 the Presidency of the Royal Society had been held by Sir Hans Sloane, who, while he had valiantly tried to carry on the great Newtonian tradition and had instituted certain important reforms in the Society, was by 1740 over eighty years of age, and for many years his duties had mainly been performed by proxy. It is characteristic of the changing intellectual temper of the time that the next president was one under whose administration the Society became a laughing-stock to the critics, and who was responsible for printing in the Transactions 'a much greater proportion of trifling and puerile papers than are any where else to be found'.[329] Martin Folkes, elected president in 1741, had no pretensions to being a profound scholar or scientist, and it is inconceivable that a dilettante of this kind could have been elected to a position of such

The Hermitage Stamford 1738.

9 *Drawing by Stukeley in 1738 of 'The Hermitage', with grotto, fountain and mock ruin folly created by him in his garden at Stamford.*

outstanding eminence in the world of learning thirty years before. Stukeley was to quarrel with him about the publication of communications to the Society that even Folkes felt should not be printed in the Transactions, but Folkes stands pilloried to posterity in a passage in Stukeley's commonplace book that combines the epigrammatic unexpectedness of Aubrey with the vitriolic malice of Hearne:

Martin Folkes has an estate of near £3000 got by his Father in the Law. He is a man of no aeconomy. Before at age he married Mrs. Bracegirdle off the stage. His mother grievd at it so much that she threw her self out of a window and broke her arm. His only son broke his neck off a horse back at Paris. His eldest daughter ran away with a book keeper and who used her very ill. Quarrelling with Sir Hans Sloan about the Presidentship of the Royal Society, and being baffled, he went to Rome with his wife, daughters, dog, cat, parrot and monkey. There his wife grew religiously mad. He went to Venice and got a dangerous hurt upon his leg. Returning he was Successor to Sir Hans, president of the R.S. Losing his teeth, he speaks so as not to be understood. He constantly refuses all papers that treat of longitude. He chuses the Councel and Officers out of his junto of Sycophants that meet him every night at Rawthmills coffee house, or that dine with him on thursdays at the Miter, fleet street. He has a great deal of learning, philosophy, astronomy: but knows nothing of natural history. In matters of religion an errant infidel and loud scoffer. Professes himself a godfather to all monkeys, believes nothing of a future state, of the Scriptures, of revelation. . . . He has been propagating the infidel system with great assiduity, and made it even fashionable in the Royal Society, so that when any mention is made of Moses, of the deluge, of religion, scriptures, etc. it generally is received with a loud laugh. . . . He dyed in a deplorable manner. Two years after, his daughters both married to indigent persons.[330]

It is clear that there could be little in common between Stukeley, with his growing preoccupation with the mysteries of Revelation, Solomon's Temple, Isis and the Druids, and Folkes, grinning toothlessly whenever he brought up these matters at the Royal Society's meetings. But he seems to have attended regularly during the winter months he now spent in London, and his journal becomes for half the year an abstract of their proceedings. These abstracts only serve to underline the impression of the low level to which the debates of this august body had sunk, which one gathers from the published Transactions and Sir John Hill's entertaining squib dedicated to Folkes in 1751.[331]

As well as the Royal Society and the Antiquaries, from 1741 yet another antiquarian society was holding meetings in London.[332] On 11

December of that year Stukeley was invited by Lord Sandwich to meet him and some other gentlemen at the Lebeck's Head tavern in Chandos Street, where were gathered Dr Perry, Dr Pocock, and a Danish traveller, Capt. Norden. All had travelled in the Near East and Egypt, and Norden was later to publish a handsome volume of Egyptian engravings. These four were constituted Founder Members of an Egyptian Society, and they then nominated Associate Members which included Stukeley, Folkes, and Milles, later to become known as the antiquarian Dean at whom Horace Walpole poked fun in letter after letter. Lord Sandwich was elected President under the oriental title of 'Sheich', and among other names brought up for future membership was the Duke of Montagu. Meetings were to be held every Friday fortnight from November to April.[333]

At one of these meetings of the Egyptian Society, in January 1741/2, the Duke of Montagu was admitted a member, and seeing the sistrum that had been made and laid before the Sheikh as an emblem of office, he asked Stukeley the meaning of 'the so famous Egyptian rattle'. This elicited an impromptu discourse with an appropriate reference to Abraham and Genesis xv, which was later written out and sent to his Grace. It was the beginning of an odd friendship which was to have important consequences in Stukeley's later life.

John, second Duke of Montagu, was at this time, like Stukeley, in his early fifties, had succeeded to the Dukedom in 1709, and, after a youth employed in various Court appointments and with Marl-borough in Flanders, had become chiefly known as the leader of the disastrous expedition to St Lucia and St Vincent on his appointment as Deputy-Governor in 1722.[334] He had a vein of eccentricity which puzzled his contemporaries but which must have found an answering chord in Stukeley's own curious character. He was passionately devoted to animals, and on his great estate of Boughton in Northants would have no cattle or horses killed, but brought to end their days peacefully in a special paddock, while he was surrounded by dogs, the ugliest of which he favoured because no one else would be kind to it.[335] There is a sort of odd simplicity in all this which strikes one as very much akin to Stukeley's – less congenial perhaps were his practical jokes, which so exasperated his termagant mother-in-law, old Sarah Duchess of Marlborough, whose youngest daughter he had married. 'All his talents', she wrote in 1740,

lie in things only natural in boys of fifteen years old, and he is about two and fifty. To get people into his gardens and wet them with squirts, and to invite people to his country houses, and put things into their beds to make them itch, and twenty such pretty fancies like these.[336]

But Lord Hailes, commenting on this, found himself bound in fairness to add:

He had other pretty fancies, not mentioned in the memoranda of his mother-in-law; he did good without ostentation. His vast benevolence of soul is not recorded by Pope; but it will be remembered while there is any tradition of human kindness and charity in England.[337]

Horace Walpole has also left on record his appreciation of the duke's good qualities. 'My father had a great opinion of his understanding', he writes to Mann in 1749, '. . . in short, with some foibles, he was a most amiable man, and one of the most feeling I ever knew.'[338] This use of the word 'feeling' is significant: it is the quality later to be merged in 'sensibility' as one of the most esteemed emotional states of the Romantic Revival in the second half of the century. Stukeley and the duke were both Men of Feeling before the sentiment had become fashionable, and before Sterne's *Sentimental Journey* (1768) and Mackenzie's *Man of Feeling* (1771) had set a literary seal upon this desirable emotion.

Stukeley, in a character sketch of the duke among his papers, mentions how he 'often observed a strange similarity of disposition' between himself and Montagu; how they shared 'that tenderness toward and love of animals as takes great pleasure in doing kind things to 'em' and how both had the same taste 'in the Gothic architecture, in painted glass, in the open-hearted, candid, undesigning and free manner of conversation'.[339] He was soon a welcome and frequent visitor at Boughton, and for him no doubt the squirts were quelled and the itching powder unsprinkled. They went riding in the grounds, and Stukeley, fearful of the freethinking tendencies his host might develop from contact with such as Folkes, would take the opportunity to say a word in season. 'And with this', he concludes a description of such a conversation in his diary, 'we arrived at the end of his Grace's territorys, in the wood south of Weldon. I took my leave of him and he, in returning, will meditate on my discourse.'[340] On another occasion they

rode in his phaeton round the serpentine ridings in his woods, which I persuaded him to make, as a contrast to the straight ones. A flock of sheep happened to cross us, the Duke admired the prettiness, the simplicity, the innocence of the animal and how sorry he was when by chance he saw 'em killing one, he turn'd away his head, and could not bear to look at it.

Stukeley hereupon preached a short sermon on sacrifice and Adam and Eve – 'and are we strictly and literally to believe this? Yes, says I, 'tis literally true. . . .' 'These sort of discourses', Stukeley goes on, 'which I have often snatch'd opportunity of introducing to his Grace, had the desired effect, and he contemplated upon the matter seriously.'[341]

In the intervals of these delightful visits to Boughton life ran uneventfully at Stamford and in London in the winter. But in October 1742 he received a letter badly written, ill spelt, and containing an account of a new antiquarian discovery made accidentally in the course of digging. 'You being a Person very Curious in Things of Antiquity', the correspondent begins, 'I thought it would Oblige you to give you a short Account of a Place thought to be a very Grate Curiosity Latly discovered in this Town.' The town was Royston in Hertfordshire, and in removing a stone the workmen 'found it was Hollor' and that there was in fact a large 'Cavaty' beneath the street. 'So they then emadgind that som very Grate Trashur was hid in that Place', but only found a 'Scull and som Hewman bones', and conjecture was rife in Royston as to the nature of the discovery, for 'som think it was for a place of Worship in the Earliest times of Chrestyanaty . . . but all think it a Grate Curiosity.' This is a type of letter known to most British archaeologists when a find has been made in accidental digging, but it must have come as a surprise to Stukeley, as it does to us, to discover that his illiterate correspondent was in fact the local Member of Parliament, Mr William Goodhall.[342]

With characteristic impetuosity Stukeley immediately rode to Royston to see this 'Grate Curiosity' – Mr Goodhall had written his letter on 15 October, and Stukeley was there on the 19th, examining and drawing the discovery. The site still exists and is still something of a mystery. It consists of a large beehive-shaped underground chamber, cut in the solid chalk sub-soil of Royston. It is over 25 feet deep and 17 feet in diameter, and is decorated with a series of low relief sculptures on the chalk walls which include figures of St Christopher, St Katherine and St Laurence, and Crucifixion scenes, haphazardly disposed and crudely executed by several hands. Association with the Knights Templar of Baldock has been suggested, and the carvings appear to be of thirteenth-century date. The cell, or hermitage, or place of pilgrimage seems to have been filled up after the Dissolution of the Monasteries.[343]

Stukeley was not unnaturally intrigued by this strange discovery, and set to work to write an account of the cell and what seemed to him the probable circumstances of its construction. In 1743 he published a pamphlet entitled *Palaeographia Britannica No. 1*, with a subtitle *Origines Roystonianae, or an Account of the Oratory of Lady Roisia de Vere, Foundress of Royston . . .* , in which he set out to show that the underground chamber was a hermitage or oratory made for a Lady Roisia de Vere in about 1170, and that the carvings on the walls represented (very allegorically) historical scenes which could be identified and related to events in the twelfth and thirteenth centuries. There is much bogus philology and history in the pamphlet, although it is a fact that the name of Royston does show in its earlier forms (e.g. Crux Roaisie, 1184) that it is connected with some figure of the name of Rohesia.[344] However, Stukeley was by no means so far wide of the mark as he well might have been, except in going out of his way to interpret the straightforward sculpture in an allegorical manner.

But a brother clergyman, the Rev. Charles Parkin, Rector of Oxburgh in Norfolk, could not accept these views, and in 1744 produced a pamphlet of his own (though adorned with Stukeley's engravings) entitled *An Answer to, or Remarks upon Dr. Stukeley's Origines Roystonianae*, in which he demonstrated to his own entire satisfaction that the Royston oratory and cross were both Saxon. Stukeley felt that he had been affronted, and the memory of Lady Roisia slighted, by this, and in 1746 retaliated with *Origines Roystonianae II or a Defence of Lady ROISIA de Vere Foundress of Roiston, against the calumny of Mr. Parkin. . . .* A vast amount of irrelevant and inaccurate erudition on historical and antiquarian matters was here brought to confute Mr Parkin, who in April 1747 was visited by a friend of Stukeley's, who reported that:

> I reduced him at last to a very absurd behaviour in desiring me to acquaint you he had no personal pique against you. But with a great Horse laugh said that as you had called his Faith, Charity and Divinity into question it was incumbent on him to clear it up. . . . In short I have chagrined and confounded him plaguily and he was obliged to stand the Roast for six hours . . . but his Laugh was so loud and incessant at the conceit of his escape that I had no opportunity of saying anything. . . .[345]

Despite the six hours' roasting, Parkin produced in 1748 *A Reply To the Peevish, Weak and Malevolent Objections brought by Dr. Stukeley . . .* to his previous pamphlet, and in a cloud of acrimony and historical fantasies the pamphlet war ceases.

In the intervals of compiling his essays on Lady Roisia, Stukeley was concerning himself in quite another activity, that of designing buildings in the Gothic style. As we have seen, since boyhood the practical approach to architecture had appealed to him, and in later years had come a growing interest in, and love for, Gothic. As a young man he had decried Hawksmoor's work at All Souls and had been enthusiastic for the classical mode of building, and as a Roman Knight he had denounced the Goths, but antiquarianism had led him by association to admire the work of the Middle Ages and to see no wrong in using it for modern ornamental purposes. His religious views, too, may have carried some weight, with a feeling for the historical continuity in English churches and cathedrals. At York in 1740 he thus describes the Minster:

> The cathedral is an astonishing beauty, and produces an effect superior (in my opinion) to any building upon earth. I cannot persuade myself to except even St. Peter's at Rome. Beside the general proportions, wherein I think it exceeds all other cathedrals, and the delicate whiteness and fine texture of the stone contributes much to its elegance. Add the painting of the windows, which is very intire, a little excepted. But after you have seen and contemplated this most magnificent structure, nothing can give you a new pleasure, but going into the chapter-house; grand and beautiful beyond imagination. I must needs prefer it to the Pantheon itself.[346]

In the dim religious light of York Minster Stukeley may well have felt, as a minor poet was to express it some years later, that here was an answer to Folkes and the infidels:

> *Gothic* the style, and tending to excite
> Free-thinkers to a sense of what is right.[347]

A contemporary enthusiast for Gothic was the architect Batty Langley, whose *Gothic Architecture improved by Rules and Proportions in many Grand Designs* was published in 1742 and whose fantastic umbrellos, pavilions, and chimney-pieces were to become a byword for a rococo style as irresponsible as its rival, the Chinese mode, and which was to be ancestor to Horace Walpole's Strawberry Hill in the 1750s.[348] But Stukeley, setting out as he did in 1744 to design a Gothic bridge for the Duke of Montagu's park at Boughton, approached the problem from the viewpoint of an antiquary who had personally examined and drawn Gothic buildings since boyhood, and was far from the Batty Langley frippery or the theatrical romanticism of Sanderson Miller and the builders of mock ruins. We may recall the equally solid approach made by the antiquary Browne Willis, who as early as 1713 had collected subscriptions and discreetly gothicized the designs for a plain classic church at Fenny Stratford. In the field of actual buildings and not merely in the designs of the inventive architect, we may mention Nicholas Revett's work in 1745 for the Hell Fire Club at Medmenham Abbey, though here the screen of ruined arches and the ivy-clad tower are hardly more authentically Gothic than Miller's ruins at Radway and Edgehill.[349]

The Boughton bridge was unfortunately never built, though Stukeley's drawings survive and there was a model made which still remains at the house. The bridge was to have been of three spans, over the central arch there being a sort of tabernacle with buttresses and crocketed arches in a fourteenth-century manner, surmounted with pinnacles, and it has a singular structural integrity as well as architectural originality. It seems that one Thomas Eayre, a builder and bell-founder, was called in to construct the bridge from Stukeley's designs, and thought after seeing the model that it would be 'a prodigus, curios and fine thing', and though he was not sure that the design as it stood would bear the weight of the central mass, he felt that a slight modification would make it practicable.[350]

There also remains among Stukeley's papers a design for the duke's mausoleum (also never built) drawn in the same year as that of the bridge. It was to be built as a chapel in the south-east angle of Weekley Church, and is a fan-vaulted square, with the duke's arms in the Garter forming a central roof-boss, and is lighted by two three-light windows with four-centred arches. The only monument to the duke was to be a plain inscribed marble slab in the centre of the floor and, consonant with his Grace's eccentric ideas, there was apparently intended to be provision for 'a young man and woman to be married over his grave on may day morning, with £100 portion'.[351]

In addition to these serious constructional problems, Stukeley had produced a fantastic building more in the Batty Langley manner in his garden at Stamford, in the form of a Temple of Flora in which Mrs Stukeley might keep her pot-plants. 'The work is gothic that suits the place best', he writes to Samuel Gale, and an elevation of the entrance survives,[352] showing a far less satisfactory interpretation of Gothic elements than does the bridge. 'The building is theatrical', he goes on, and it seems with some justice; inside there are 'bustos' and other curiosities, the windows have stained glass rescued from the destruction in the Stamford churches, and there is a cupola with a bell 'which I ring every morning, a most agreeable exercise'.[353]

But despite these amusements he was beginning to tire of the provinciality of Stamford. In December 1745 he had attempted to revive the Brazen Nose Society, which seems to have become moribund soon after its original foundation. A new minute-book was started, with a page made out for the list of subscribers, with the words at the head 'We whose names are subscribed . . .', but the only name on the page is his own. Later pages contain the name of one honorary member and, rather pathetically, those of 'three carpenters, subscribers to the society'.[354] There was the Clergyman's Book Club, too, that he had founded seventeen years before 'with intent of making it a Vertuoso Club, but it prov'd absolutely abortive: for they had no taste for anything but wine and tobacco', and in 1743 he could hardly tolerate his fellow members there.[355] One of his periodical moods of restlessness seems to have come upon him: he was curiously affected by small happenings, such as the death of Tit, the cat – 'an uncommon creature and of all I ever knew the most sensible most loving and indeed with many other engaging qualitys'.[356] He returned to this little event again in his diary – the gardener had buried the cat 'under the mulberry tree going into Rosamund's Bower' without his knowledge, and on finding this out, 'I have almost taken a dislike to the garden: never car'd to come near that delightful place: nor so much as to look toward it.' The cat then receives a eulogy which deserves quotation:

> The creature had a sense so far superior to her kind; had such inimitable ways of testifying her love to her master and mistress, that she was as a companion, especially so to me when according to custom, I smoak'd my contemplative pipe, in the evening at 6 o'clock. From the admirable endowments of the cat I took a great liking to her, which gave me so much pleasure, without trouble. Her death I griev'd for exceedingly.[357]

In this unsettled state of mind he heard of the vacancy of the living of St George's, Queen's Square, Bloomsbury, at the end of October 1747 – a living in the Duke of Montagu's gift. He decided not to mention it to the duke, and in his diary tries to reassure himself that he loves the country, is nearly sixty, and is not ambitious. But in the middle of November he received a letter from the duke offering him the living. His diary now becomes very full and very agitated, and he was clearly faced with what seemed to him an impossible decision one way or the other. But a cousin visiting the town urged Stukeley to write 'accepting without reserve, and pressed me to set out instantly for London which I did after dinner'. He seems to have accepted his cousin's advice without demur. Probably he was glad to have his mind made up for him.

He received the presentation to the living and returned home on 2 December having reacted against the scheme and 'not at all resolved in my mind to accept my Patron's great favour'. He conferred with his friends Warburton and Bernard, and finally decided to abide by his decision to move to London.

The final pages of his diary for 1747 contain a long sustained self-justification for his action which reads oddly when we cannot see that the step from Stamford to a London living entailed such a drastic uprooting as Stukeley seems to have dreaded. He sees the Hand of Providence in every triviality of the past few years, which are enumerated in detail. 'When I collated all these occurrences and some more', he concludes, 'I discovered not obscurely the finger of Providence pointing to my removal.' His mind was at last made up, and he followed where Providence pointed, to the Rectory of St George's, Queen's Square.

VI

Last Days in London

WHILE HE WAS STILL resident in Stamford, in June 1747, Stukeley received a letter from a stranger, an Englishman resident in Denmark.

> I receiv'd a letter [Stukeley wrote later] from *Charles Julius Bertram*, professor of the *English* tongue in the Royal marine Academy, *Copenhagen*, a person unknown to me. The letter was polite, full of compliments, as usual with foreigners, expressing much candor and respect to me; being only acquainted with some works of mine published.

Stukeley seems to have been not unnaturally surprised at this letter: he wondered how Bertram could have heard of him, and why he had written thus politely to a stranger in another country. As I have already mentioned, a fellow member with Stukeley of the Egyptian Society founded in 1741 had been a Dane, Captain Norden, and it is possible that he may have mentioned Stukeley to Bertram. At all events, Stukeley was delighted to enter into a learned correspondence with Denmark: he replied to Bertram in suitable terms, and this

> produced another letter, with a prolix and elaborate *latin* epistle inclos'd, from the famous Mr. *Gramm*, privy-counsellor, and chief librarian to his *Danish* Majesty: a learned gentleman, who had been in England and visited our universities . . . he was Mr. *Bertram's* great friend and patron.

Stukeley's narrative of events is contained in a publication of ten years later, comprising two papers read to the Society of Antiquaries in 1756 on a remarkable discovery communicated to him by Charles Bertram; no less than an account, itinerary and map of Roman Britain by a fourteenth-century monk of Westminster named Richard of Cirencester, contained in a medieval manuscript which Bertram, with access to the original, had copied and transmitted to Stukeley. It should be said before going any further that no such manuscript ever existed, and we are entering on the story of one of the most audacious and successful literary forgeries of the eighteenth century. Manuscript material that has become available since the first edition of this book enables us to trace the strange events in greater detail than hitherto.[358]

We have some thirty letters from Bertram to Stukeley but the other side of the correspondence is lost. The opening letter, received by Stukeley at Stamford on 11 June 1747, was in fact dated a year previously, 23 August 1746, a fact noted by him in his published account. It begins without superscription and in a large flourished script, '*Nemo sine crimine vivit* says the great Horace, and mine is to love antiquities, a fault which in itself would easily be pardoned by You Great Sir'. (In the circumstances it is at least interesting that the quotation cannot be traced in Horace or indeed any classical Latin source.)[359] The writer has read the *Itinerarium Curiosum* and would like to embark on an antiquarian correspondence, and is especially interested in the History of the Celts mentioned by Stukeley in his *Itinerarium* preface. He signs himself Charles Julius Bertram, from the Royal Marine Academy in Copenhagen, and adds that letters should be addressed to him as 'Proff. linguae Anglicanae' in that institution. The impression of seniority given here is in fact spurious: Charles Bertram, son of an English silk dyer in Copenhagen, was a young man of twenty-three who was giving English lessons in the Academy. Stukeley, having received this letter a year later, replied with a 'civil answer' for which Bertram thanks him in a reply enclosing a letter of recommendation in Latin from the distinguished Danish privy councillor Hans Gram, scholar and historian, and keeper of the Royal Library, Stukeley's formal reply to which survives. Bertram, in his letter, after a brief note on Danish megalithic monuments, goes on

I have at present in my possession, a copy of an old Manuscript Fragment (and in hope of getting the original) called Richardi Monachi Westmonasteriensis Commentariolum Geographicum de situ Britanniae & Stationum quas Romani ipsi in ea Insula aedificaverunt. it seems to me to have been part of a greater Treatise, beginning with Folio xxiii Sequitur: I therefore humbly beg your opinion of it, and whether it stands in any of the Manuscript Collections in Britain.

It comprises, he adds, 'four sheets & a half in Quarto', the half sheet being a coloured map of Roman Britain. Whether at this time already complete or only in the course of composition, the forgery had been gently launched on its dubious career.

10 Part of the 'transcript' of the forged 'Richard of Cirencester'
text sent by Charles Bertram to Stukeley in 1749, with
chronological notes by the latter.

Later in 1747 Bertram wrote a long reply to a letter from Stukeley, giving him an account of Danish barrows, megalithic monuments and other antiquities with pen and wash sketches, and a 'transcript' of the first chapter of 'My fragment of Ricardi Westm:', with further extracts and the colophon (as eventually printed). Stukeley had urged him to publish, but he demurs, 'except I were beforehand assured of your assistance in dubious passages or places where I might be quite to seek'. Stukeley, as we saw, had accepted the London living in November 1747 and moved there in February of the following year, putting his correspondence with Bertram to one side, but 'when I became fix'd in *London*, I thought it proper to cultivate my *Copenhagen* correspondence' and 'began to think of the manuscript'. In the meantime Bertram waited anxiously for a reply to his letter and in August 1748 wrote again, but by October he was able to thank Stukeley for a reply and for 'a Chest of Your works', and to return to the Richard of Westminster manuscript (as the forgery was referred to until, as we shall see, Stukeley identified Richard as 'of Cirencester'), of which Stukeley had evidently asked for a copy and had made some comments causing Bertram to expostulate 'here I must own, I am very sorry to see you imagine I retain'd y^t author incognito, out of views of gain', and to explain that he had in fact made an arrangement with a printer and bought a copper plate for an engraving of the map, though he has little hopes of sales in Denmark. He sends a transcript of the 'first 8 chapters' ('pardon the Errors') and leaves it to Stukeley to decide whether to print it himself or to raise subscriptions on Bertram's behalf.

The correspondence now rests for six months. But on 25 February 1749 Bertram replies to a letter of Stukeley's which had again pressed for publication in Denmark, and pleads his financial straits: he sends however a copy of the map and a complete transcript of the text, though 'by Reasons of the Multiplicity of my affairs [I] could not write it myself, nor is it as I would wish it; Yet I have endeavoured to correct all the Errors.' This transcript must be Bodleian MS Top.gen.g.1, and the fiction of an amanuensis would have given Bertram a chance of emending the original if need arose. 'And now you have the whole before you, I intreat you to consider well of it, and inform me what is best to be done therewith.'

Most of us in the past have tended to think of Stukeley as an easy and credulous dupe in the Richard of Cirencester affair, but in fact we now see him exercising commendable caution. On 12 May 1749 Bertram had to write what must have been the most difficult letter of his whole disingenuous correspondence, in response to a dozen specific and numbered queries from Stukeley on the detailed nature and provenance of the alleged original manuscript. As no such document of course existed, all the answers had to be prevarications of various degrees of complexity. The first query, on size and material, was easily disposed of – 'between an Octavo and a Quarto', and on vellum with the map on fine parchment – and the second by 'some viij Lines, of the fifth Page, as exactly copied as was possible' enclosed with the letter and no longer surviving. To the third question Bertram answered that the initials and their 'flourishes' were in blue or red; to the fourth, that he had come on it 'fortuitously, as I have several choice Pieces' of MSS or early printed books. Then came the worst, crucial couple of queries, evidently on the precise origin and present location of the original: here nothing short of a blatant and direct lie was possible. The questions

are not in my Power to inform you of, more than that the Gentleman who had it before, won't be named, nor can I in justice do it, if I relate to you what follows: For upon strict Enquiry how and where he had the MS he answered; that, as to that, it could be but of little Satisfaction either to me, or the Public, if he told me; besides, added he, if so be I do, you shall never, upon Breach of our Friendship, and Your Honour, name me by Name, either directly, or Indirectly. This I promised to perform, and then he told me, he & another Gentleman, when they were wild, and Young, pirated it out of a Volume of Treatises in a Public Library, and that was the Real Cause why the Book begins with p.xxiii.

The gentleman, 'now fully ashamed of the Fact' added that no further pages of Richard's text were present in the volume, 'the rest being Grants, &c, all belonging to the Law'. As to Stukeley's seventh query on provenance, 'the gentleman was from England, and so I suppose was the MS too'.

The remaining questions were less embarrassing – the likely period of the manuscript, the Westminster connection, Bertram's own projected commentary. It must have been with some relief that he followed this piece of fiction with a long discussion of Stukeley's cure for the gout. For his part, Stukeley clearly remained unhappy about the manuscript, for six years later, in December 1756 and on the eve of publication, Bertram writes 'But what shall I do to satisfy your entreaties of placing the MS in the *British Musaeum*?' Stukeley had apparently offered to buy it for five guineas, but 'nor dare I as things stand make too great a stir about it, the Gentleman is sufficiently

Sequit̃ Coſtanos geographieũ de ſitu Brizaſiæ tationũ
ꝗ Roam ipſi ĩ ea inſta ediſicauerũt.

Lib. I **C. I.**

a ſpecimen of the original manuſcript of Richard of weſtminſter, on velum. a large ſized quarto.
the map is on the fineſt ſort of vellum. there was
another volume containing 22 pages, before it;
which is loſt. I ſuppoſe, it was that other work
which he wrote, the hiſtory of Brittain before
the Roman times. ~~which is loſt~~. it was not wrote
in the manner of geoffry of monmouth, but fro
authentic memoirs. & therefore, its loſs is the
more to be lamented.

11 *One of the fake 'facsimiles' by Charles Bertram of the opening
paragraphs of the Richard of Cirencester forgery sent to Stukeley,
and engraved in his* Account of Richard of Cirencester, 1757.
Stukeley has added his own notes.

alarm'd already', but 'our common Friend the Great *Gram* saw the Original of *Richard*, had it in his hands above 4 weeks, and never once breathed the least Accent of its being fictitious'. Gram had conveniently died in 1748: Stukeley had evidently bluntly hinted at fraud.

To return to earlier events, on 13 January 1752 Bertram breaks a 'profound silence' and sends Stukeley, from whom he had not heard, a set of short replies to the queries just described, a new 'facsimile', this time of the opening 'Sequitur' paragraph of which a second copy survives and which was eventually engraved for Stukeley's 1757 *Account*, and a preface to the proposed publication in Latin. If Bertram were not to publish it himself, would Stukeley like to, in a second volume of the *Itinerarium Curiosum*? If so, 'I am willing to send you a *correct* copy'. Meanwhile, Stukeley had actively pursued the matter of Richard, the monk of Westminster, in London, by consulting his 'learned friend, the reverend Mr *Widmore*, librarian to *Westminster-Abby*' who 'in perusing the *Abby* rolls diligently', identified a late fourteenth century Richard of Cirencester, who was the author of a *Speculum Historiale de gestis Regum Angliae* and so, being historically minded, was an obvious candidate as the author of the *De Situ* as well. The new 'facsimile' now became available to him, 'which I shewed to my late friend Mr Casley, keeper in the *Cotton* library, who immediately pronounced it to be 400 years old'. The foundling manuscript could now claim a respectable paternity. One odd point emerges from the subsequent correspondence; though Stukeley must have conveyed to Bertram with some elation the news of Richard of Cirencester, there is no reference to this event in Bertram's letters, and 'Richard' or 'Richard of Westminster' continues to be used except on one occasion, on 28 July 1756, on the eve of Bertram's publication of Richard of Cirencester under that name. As Stukeley recorded in his diary that he saw a (genuine) Richard of Cirencester MS in Lambeth Palace Library in May 1751, he must have had Widmore's identification before then.[360]

The correspondence continues in 1753, when in a letter of 28 April on miscellaneous antiquarian topics Bertram writes 'Several of my Welwishers here have perswaded me to break to you their opinion, that were I a Member of the *Antiquarian* or *Royal Societies*, such a Thing, they fancy, would give my Affairs here a sudden Turn and make my Patrons at Court more active'. In response to this blatant canvassing Stukeley may have approached the Royal Society without success, but on 31 October 1754 Bertram is thanking him effusively for unspecified 'fresh and great Proofs of the Love and Affection you bear me' and 'I really believe it will, in Time, make a vast Alteration in my Affairs'. On 28 July 1756 he transmits his formal thanks on election as a Fellow of the Society of Antiquaries of London, 'especially seeing it is against their received Custom'. Stukeley had certainly done all he could on behalf of his protegé, and in March and April 1756 had read a paper in two parts to the Society, published in the following year as *An Account of Richard of Cirencester, Monk of Westminster, and of his WORKS*, a commentary reproducing the famous map but not the text, which was published by Bertram at his own cost in Copenhagen in the same year, in a little volume entitled *Britannicarum Gentium Historiae Antiquae Scriptores Tres*, and containing the texts of Gildas, Nennius, and Richard of Cirencester, who thus appeared for the first time in print in the most respectable company. Bertram as editor appears on the title-page as a Fellow of the Society of Antiquaries of London, and the book is dedicated to this learned body: it further bears the *imprimatur* of the Rector of the Queen's University at Copenhagen. Opposite the title-page is a curious engraving in which, within a Gothic architectural setting of a medieval scriptorium, the *scriptores tres* are unexpectedly met together over the centuries and seem to be comparing notes. The nervous, rather scratchy technique is quite unlike the usual engraving of the period, and, unattributed, one's first guess would be a work of A. W. Pugin a century later. It is the work of an amateur, and as the signature shows was engraved by Bertam himself. He was a talented young man.

It was a document calculated to excite any British antiquarian. Purporting to have been written in the fourteenth century by a monk of Westminster, it contained an account of Roman Britain which, in addition to the known classical sources, apparently utilized hitherto unknown documents which rendered possible a far fuller account of the Roman province than any based on the texts extant in the eighteenth century. Indeed, Richard, the monk, expressly stated at one point that the Itinerary he copied (one of the most exciting things in the manuscript) was derived from a Roman general's memoirs – '*ex Fragmentis quibusdam a Duce quodam Romano consignatis et posteritati relictis sequens collectum est itinerarium*', his text runs. As well as the written text, there was a map of Roman Britain, again giving far more detail than those previously compiled from available sources.

Before dealing in detail with this remarkable document, it will be well to review briefly the manuscript sources for the topography of Roman Britain as Stukeley would have known them (and as indeed we know them today, the only significant additions being derived from place-names recorded on inscriptions). Apart from scattered references in the Greek and Roman geographers and historians from Pytheas in the mid-fourth century BC to Procopius in the sixth century AD, and the explicit historical material in Caesar, Tacitus, Dio, and Ammianus Marcellinus (to mention the more important), the essential documents are five in number. Earliest are the latitude and longitude lists of Ptolemy (about AD 140–150); there follows the Antonine Itinerary, a road book covering the whole Roman Empire and probably compiled in the early third century; the next document is an actual map of the Empire, compiled in the third century and copied in the thirteenth, known as the Peutinger Map. The *Notitia Dignitatum* is in effect an Imperial Army List, compiled at the beginning of the fifth century, and the last document is the list of place-names compiled at Ravenna by an unknown geographer in the early eighth century.[361]

All these sources were conveniently available, with comments, in Book III of Horsley's *Britannia Romana* of 1732: Ptolemy had never been entirely lost sight of throughout the Middle Ages, and maps were compiled from his data by Renaissance geographers such as Mercator, and were common knowledge by the eighteenth century. The Antonine Itinerary for Britain had been published with commentaries since Camden's day and, as we have seen, Roger Gale published his father's elaborate work on it in 1709. In addition to Horsley's text, three editions of the *Notitia* had been published in Europe between 1552 and 1729 and it was known to Camden. The Ravenna List had been published not only on the Continent, but by Roger Gale with his edition of the Antonine Itinerary.

Bertram's 'discovery' of an additional source, previously unknown, was obviously of first-class importance. The work, entitled *De Situ Britanniae et stationum quas Romani ipsi in Insula aedificaverunt*, was in two books, the second unfinished but apparently planned to be considerably shorter than the first. Book I had eight chapters, beginning with a geographical account of Britain as known to the ancients, continuing with the manner and customs of the aboriginal British, their religion, and the Druids. Then followed an enumeration of the natural resources of Britain and, in Chapter VI, a detailed account of the Roman administration of the country, the separate provinces, the Celtic tribal areas, and the towns. Following this, and forming Chapter VII, was an Itinerary on the lines of the Antonine road-book, but with many additional names, or the known ones in different positions. The map accompanying this contained at least 250 names of which 100 were, in Stukeley's words, 'wholly new or ill-placed by former writers', and the concluding Chapter VIII gave an account of Ireland and of the islands around the British coasts. Book II, which comes to an abrupt end, has a Chapter I of British chronology from the Creation to the fifth century AD, and the incomplete Chapter II listed the Roman emperors and governors of Britain.

From the time of Bertram's and Stukeley's two publications Richard occupied an honoured place in the literature of Roman Britain until the nineteenth century. But already in 1795 Thomas Reynolds, four years later to publish an edition of the Antonine Itinerary and a reprint of Richard of Cirencester's text, openly declared his belief that the remarkable document was nothing more nor less than a fabrication. This was not a popular view: the authenticity of the *De Situ* was championed by the antiquaries of the late eighteenth and early nineteenth centuries such as Hutchins, Whitaker, Colt Hoare and Roy; Gough expresses some doubts, but on the whole accepts it; Gibbon accepts the list of ninety-two Roman *municipiae, coloniae,* &c., given by Richard, though elsewhere he seems wary, and refers to the work as 'feeble evidence'. In 1827 the great Northumberland historian, John Hodgson, uncompromisingly denounced it as a forgery, and by the middle of the century German scholars at least (e.g. Wex in 1845) were able to show by searching textual criticism that this was undoubtedly the case. By 1847–67 the English scholar Bernard Woodward had followed this lead and the inevitable conclusions to which it brought him, and with J. E. B. Mayor's monumental treatment of 1869, with an annihilating *apparatus criticus* brought to bear on the *De Situ*, Richard of Cirencester was finally discredited as an authority on Roman Britain. Yet the rejection of the *De Situ* as in any way an original work of the Middle Ages, let alone having a Roman basis, is founded on inescapable facts brought to light by patient textual criticism, in itself of such interest that it is worth while summarizing Mayor's elaborate arguments.

The issue is confused at the outset by the fact that Richard of Cirencester, a monk of Westminster in the fourteenth century and the author of an historical work which still survives, is an authentic enough character. As we have seen in following the sequence of the Bertram–Stukeley correspondence, the author of the *De Situ* is first

referred to by Bertram merely as 'Richard, a monk of Westminster' –
'a perfectly safe shot', as Randall remarks in commenting on this
episode. Fortune played into his hands when Widmore's researches
actually produced good documentary evidence not only for a monk of
this name (which would be likely enough), but one who was known as
the author of the genuine *Speculum Historiale*. Bertram does not seem
to have known that the correct form of Richard's name in medieval
latin was *de Cirencestria*, and so invented the bogus form *Corinensis*
(otherwise unknown) from the Latin *Corinium*, when changing
Richard of Westminster into Richard of Cirencester. But despite this
slip, it is obvious that his case was enormously strengthened by the
lucky accident arising from his choice of the name Richard.

However, the existence of the genuine *Speculum* provided the
nineteenth-century critics with a means whereby the latinity and style
of the *De Situ* could be tested. The sentence construction and phrasing
were soon seen to be that of eighteenth-century scholars, and not that
of the fourteenth century; the forms of place-names which occurred
both in the *De Situ* and the *Speculum* did not agree, and whereas in the
former work quotations from many classical writers, often obscure
(and twice from the Greek), occur, in the genuine *Speculum* there is
not even a quotation from a major Latin poet at first hand. The
famous map can be shown to have been influenced not only by that of
Ortelius in the sixteenth century, but by those of Bertram's
contemporaries, such as Herman Moll and Morden.

The text can be analysed to show the source of every statement
(except where names of places are sheer inventions of Bertram's own,
like *Ad Fines*, *Ad Murum*, or *Ad Vallum*), and here we find Bertram
making mistakes. He uses, for instance, readings which occur only in
the earlier printed texts of Tacitus, he includes an editor's inserted
clause in a passage of Caesar, he is misled by an error of Horsley's,
and, relying on Camden for a quotation from Lucan, makes a false
quantity by copying Camden's *Thetis* instead of the genuine *Tethys*.
Some information may even have come from Stukeley's own works,
such as the identification of *Sorbiodunum* as a *praesidium*, while
Camden, Horsley, and Baxter are extensively used throughout.
'Writers are not wanting, who assert that Hercules came hither and
established a sovreignty', the bogus Richard is made to remark, but
the only relevant classical source for the legend (Ammianus
Marcellinus, quoting Timagenes) takes Hercules no farther than the
coast of Gaul. This was, however, eagerly followed up by Aylett
Sammes in his book of 1676, in which the coming of Hercules to

Devonshire is confidently asserted (on no evidence at all), and this idea was enthusiastically adopted by Stukeley in *Stonehenge* and *Abury*. Bertram must have known how delighted Stukeley would be to have authority for this coming of Hercules, and inserted the statement accordingly, though it is interesting that he is very careful in his chapter on Celtic religion and the Druids not to go beyond the limits of the classical authorities, and so in no way to encourage Stukeley's peculiar ideas about the priesthood.

The 'facsimile' of the opening paragraphs of the *De Situ* is as spurious as anything else connected with the work, but it shares something of the ingenious quality of the rest. It was not easy for Bertram to come by a knowledge of palaeography, but he does seem to have consulted some manuscript specimens. The late Dr Richard Hunt very kindly gave me his views on the 'facsimile':[362]

At first glance it looks quite plausible, the heading 'Sequitur . . .' especially so. The formula has a genuine ring, and I should think he was following a MS pretty closely. The text is not so good, but hardly worse than some published engraved facsimiles of the period. Where it does go wrong is in the abbreviations. . . . These are suspensions of a type never found in genuine medieval MSS, and, if Casley had tried to read the text, and not just gone on the general impression made by the specimen, I find it hard to see how he could have thought it genuine.

I should have thought this script on which Bertram was modelling his hand was 13th century rather than 14th.

Charles Bertram emerges from his correspondence as an enigmatic and eventually rather sad figure. He was to die in 1765, aged forty-two, having to his credit several books on English grammar and one on the uniforms of the Danish regiments, but apparently with no particular financial or academic benefit derived from his Fellowship of the Society of Antiquaries or his Richard of Cirencester. In his last letter to Stukeley, of 16 September 1763, he writes despondently of his lack of preferment and financial straits: he is selling up his library 'to carry on my Printing and clear off my Debts'. His earlier letters however show him as a keen field archaeologist, and as we saw he wrote out a classification of Danish barrows and megaliths in a letter of 1747; in 1753 he sends a pen and wash drawing of a chambered long barrow at Tjäreby near Korsör, and in June 1758 wrote up an able account of an archaeological field trip he made two years previously between Copenhagen and Roskilde, illustrated with good and charming pen and watercolour plans and views, which he sent to Stukeley on 14

June.[363] And yet he takes his unenviable place among the other forgers, half-forgers and fabricators of the eighteenth century, with Chatterton and Ireland, Iolo Morganwg and Macpherson. Mayor found him 'a forger alike contemptible as penman, Latinist, historian, geographer, critic'; Henry Bradley, however, writing in the *Dictionary of National Biography*, felt that 'the ingenuity and learning in Bertram's forgery are really extraordinary, and fully account for the unparalleled success the imposture obtained', and perhaps Bradley comes nearer the truth. One can only speculate at the psychology behind Bertram's falsifications: was it an undergraduate joke that went too far, past the point where it was possible to confess to an innocent hoax? Or was it more likely the attempt of an unknown and lonely young man to call attention to himself by a spectacular discovery in the world of learning and so advance his academic and financial status? Whatever the real and perhaps complex motivation, Richard the monk of Westminster does not seem to have contributed much happiness to his creator's subsequent life.

Bertram was a shrewd enough judge of the standards of contemporary scholarship. It was not only Stukeley who was deceived, but the whole learned world, and this affords a startling commentary on the decay of historical studies by the middle of the eighteenth century. It is surely inconceivable that such a forgery could have succeeded sixty years earlier, when the palaeographical acumen of Wanley and his colleagues, and the vast knowledge of medieval Latin texts of the whole great fraternity of historical learning, would have been brought to bear upon it.

In the intervals of the agreeable archaeological excitements afforded by the Bertram correspondence, Stukeley was settling down to enjoy his life in London. The difficult decision, and the regrets for leaving the country, seem to have been soon forgotten: he had a disposition which made him able to take pleasure in whatever circumstance he found himself, once the worry of the actual move was over. His patron, the Duke of Montagu, died in 1749, and in the same year he was concerned with the application to George II for a Royal Charter for the Society of Antiquaries, which was granted in 1749/50, with Martin Folkes as 'the First and Modern President'.[364] Apart from his official duties as Secretary, from the foundation of the Society until his removal to the country in 1727, he seems to have taken little part in the business of the Society, and in his Journals it is the Royal Society which appears as the main focus of his intellectual interests in later life, though after his re-admission in 1754 he still continued to read papers to the Antiquaries until the end of his life, latterly, alas, raising a laugh among the more irreverent Fellows present.[365]

At this time there was a topical London scandal which formed the subject of much comment and amusement.

> I sing not of Battles, nor do I much chuse
> With too many vict'ries to burden my Muse,
> I sing not of Actions that rise to Renown
> But I sing of a monstrous huge *Bridge* tumbling down.

Thus the popular broadsheet ballad.[366] The Westminster Bridge controversy dated back to the 1720s, when the pamphlet-war began which was to last intermittently for twenty years.[367] Mr Price, the 'late ingenious Mr Hawksmoor', and Mr Batty Langley had all produced designs for the projected structure,[368] and though an Act was passed in 1736, it was not until 1738/9 that Lord Pembroke laid the first stone of the western middle pier of a bridge designed by a Swiss engineer, Labelye.[369] The work continued slowly, with Stukeley's friend Andrews Jelfe as one of the two masons in charge, and the bridge was brought to some sort of completion by 1748.

But it was now perceived that Labelye's design was faulty, and one of the piers of the bridge, built on insufficient foundations, was sinking. Batty Langley was delighted, and immediately published a pamphlet shrill with abuse of the Commissioners who had agreed that 'the *Honour* of the Invention and the Profits of the Imployment should be violently, if not villainously risqued from me (an *Englishman*) by an INSOLVENT IGNORANT, ARROGATING *Swiss*' but triumphant that the bridge was collapsing. An engraved frontispiece gives Langley's rejected design for the bridge and in one corner is a gallows with a dangling figure labelled 'The Swiss Imposter rewarded, as his Ignorance justly deserves'.[370]

Stukeley's architectural zeal was fired by this, and he immediately produced his own design to remedy the sinking pier by some sort of relieving arch, and brought this to the notice of the authorities.[371] According to his own statement this was adopted with success, but as the bridge at Westminster was itself replaced by another in the nineteenth century, we cannot today examine the structure and trace in it Stukeley's work.

During these years Stukeley's attention was turning more and more to the Emperor Carausius and his coins, and he was eventually to publish several works on this subject, and to write still more that remain in manuscript.[372] Other people were interested in the same subject – the Frenchman Genebrier had produced a History of Carausius in 1740,[373] and in England, Dr John Kennedy was also collecting Carausius coins and was later to write on them. And now the great Dr Mead comes back into the picture, having purchased a silver coin of Carausius (found at Silchester) which struck him as such a rarity that he presented it to the King of France. Kennedy obtained a sketch of the coin and showed it to Stukeley in August 1750,[374] and both seem to have agreed that the legend on the reverse, which showed a female bust, was not FORTVNA, but ORIVNA. It is extraordinary to think that such a remarkable reading should have been preferred to the obvious conclusion that the letters of Fortuna were incompletely visible, but even more astonishing that this confident misinterpretation should have been made, not from the actual coin, but from a drawing. From first to last in the not very edifying 'Oriuna' controversy neither Kennedy nor Stukeley saw or handled the original coin, which remained in the Cabinet of Medals in France. (The coin survives, and it can be seen that Brunet's drawing published by Stukeley is in fact 'extremely accurate except in one telling detail', the horizontal stroke of the 'T' of [F]ORTUNA, detectable on the original coin.)[375]

Kennedy was the first to publish this momentous discovery in a *Dissertation on Oriuna* (1751), in which he claimed 'her' to be the guardian goddess of Carausius, though he mentions in passing not only the suggestion that the legend really read *Fortuna* but that others had thought 'her' the wife of Carausius. Neither possibility could, he felt, be entertained seriously. This latter idea was, in fact, the view of Stukeley, who wrote an essay to prove this point in the following year, published as *Palaeographia Britannica, No. III* in 1752 (the earlier numbers having dealt with the underground cell at Royston). Kennedy answered with *Further Observations . . .* in 1756, Stukeley's *History of Carausius* appeared in 1757, and was followed up by two acrimonious pamphlets by Kennedy.

The whole affair reflects no credit on either of the participants, or on the contemporary standards of numismatics and allied studies. While one cannot exonerate Stukeley from what amounts to credulous stupidity, one must remember that Dr Kennedy was no better, and that no individual antiquary nor any organized body such as the Society of Antiquaries so much as suggested that the whole matter could effectually be cleared up by common sense and a critical examination of the coin in question.

Stukeley's work on the coins of Carausius, as we can judge it today, contains little 'beyond a handful of brilliant guesses', to quote a modern numismatic authority.[376] In one or two attributions of Carausian coins to British mints, Stukeley (probably accidentally) seems to have made really correct identifications – with regard to the *Clausentum* mint Mattingly says 'it is one of those few cases in which his intuition was triumphantly right'. But, beyond this, there is little to his credit in the voluminous books of notes and drafts of Histories of Carausius that he so laboriously compiled in the later years of his life.

Stukeley's interest in coins, and especially those of the pre-Roman British princes, had continued since those early days when the Antiquaries set up their Committee to examine the whole problem of the coins of Britain from the remotest times. His notebooks on British coins go back to 1720,[377] and contain much valuable information: as with his Avebury and Stonehenge work, had he published his objective observations earlier his reputation would have been much enhanced. But he continued to collect drawings and notes on British coins until his death, and made drafts of a work on *The Medallic History of the Most Antient Kings of Britain*[378] which was never published, though his son-in-law, Richard Fleming, published after his death twenty-three of the engraved plates prepared for this work.[379] The attribution of coins of this type to the pre-Roman Britons had been made by Camden, and in the eighteenth century there were many curious essays towards their interpretation. There was that of Pettingal which, said Sir John Evans, 'shows a considerable amount of learning, but an insufficient acquaintance with facts and the usual course of events', or Samuel Pegge's ideas that could only be stigmatized as 'supremely ridiculous'. The coins published by Fleming from Stukeley's drawings are unfortunately inaccurately depicted, but (to quote Evans again) the plates 'have the redeeming feature of occasionally presenting, side by side with the coins of Cunobeline, Roman coins, from which Dr. Stukeley thought, and occasionally with much show of reason, the types to have been derived'.[380]

In one instance modern research on British coins has shown Stukeley to be correct. It should be explained that, of the pre-Roman inscribed coinage of Britain, certain coins can be connected by their abbreviated inscriptions with Belgic princes and dynasties whose names are known in their full romanized forms in the pages of classical writers. There are other individuals striking coins, however, whose names, in the shortened form in which they appear on the coins, are known from no other sources. When Evans wrote in 1864, a coin of a class with the inscription ANDOC, drawn by Stukeley in his Plate IV,

No. 7, had the name with one extra letter, reading ANDOCO, but no actual example of the coin was known, and Stukeley's drawing was the sole authority for this fuller version of a name otherwise unknown. But by 1940, three specimens had been found, 'showing that Stukeley's drawing was substantially correct', so by a cipher, at least, he can claim to be the first to add a little substance to this rather shadowy relative of Tasciovanus.[381]

It is interesting, in connection with the representation of horses in a distinctive Celtic art-style on many British coins, to find that one of Stukeley's daughters, Anna, had acquired sufficient familiarity with her father's drawings and coin cabinet to recognize the White Horse of Uffington as essentially in the same art tradition. In 1758, when she had become a Mrs Fairchild, she went on a visit to Berkshire and sent back to her father an account of White Horse Hill and the chambered tomb of Wayland Smith's Cave: 'The figure of the horse on the side of the hill is poorly drawn, though of immense bulk: but', she says, 'very much in the scheme of the Brittish horses on the reverse of their coins.'[382] Anna was an acute observer, and it was not until the end of the nineteenth century that the White Horse was once again claimed as an Iron Age monument rather than an alleged Saxon memorial of the Battle of Ashdown.

In the 1750s Stukeley was not without his usual wide range of interests. There was the 'Oriuna' controversy in the field of archaeology; the great Lisbon earthquake gave an opportunity for a telling sermon, papers to the Royal Society, and a little book on the *Philosophy of Earthquakes, Natural and Religious*, in 1750. He claimed that the phenomena associated with earthquakes were the result of electrical disturbances in the air, the actual movement of the earth being a secondary effect of these. Horace Walpole liked this idea – he writes to Mann of the earthquake – 'one Stukeley, a parson, has accounted for it, and I think prettily, by electricity – but that is the fashionable cause, and everything is resolved into electrical appearances.'[383]

In 1753 the work of landscape gardening in progress in the grounds of Kew House, the residence of the Princess Dowager, brought to light what can now be recognized as a Late Bronze Age hoard of socketed axes and other tools, broken for use by a founder. Who better qualified to explain these curious antiquities than Dr Stukeley? His advice was sought, and in the summer of 1754 he visited Kew, was shown the site and the find, and returned home to write up an account of the 'Druid celts' to present to the Princess. In early October an audience was arranged, and Stukeley was to be found waiting at the garden door for the approach of the royal party who were walking in the grounds. As they drew near he eagerly stepped forward, to be recalled to a proper sense of decorum by a gentleman usher, but the Princess called to him by name 'and after many kind expressions of thanks for my letter, conducted me to her apartment, where she pulled off her bonnet, and we conversed face to face for about half an hour'.[384]

It was a memorable conversation. They talked – or perhaps it was mostly Stukeley who talked – of the Druids, patriarchal religion, oaks, acorns, and mistletoe; of the bronze hoard, of Stonehenge (the Princess assured Stukeley that she had read his book), and of the Royal Society. The royal condescension, the informal tête-à-tête, the interest in antiquarian studies – all these must have raised Stukeley to a luminous Druidic heaven. He returned home carrying a branch of oak picked up in the garden, acorn-heavy, symbolic. Passing the house of Mrs Peirson, to whom at that time he professed a platonic though sentimental devotion, he saw the servant come out and sent her the oak bough as 'a present from the royal Archdruidess, to her sister Druidess'. His Journal goes on, 'My Lord Archdruid Bathurst ordered me to meet him at dinner. . . .' On this wonderful autumn day everyone was a Druid.[385]

Mrs Peirson must be explained. She was the married sister of the Rev. Mr Foote, with whom Stukeley came into contact over coins of Carausius, and under the name of Miriam constantly appears in the journals and letters of this period. There is a panegyric in his Journal about her, a 'bosom friend, one exactly of one's own disposition . . . a female of a most inlarg'd understanding' who 'enters readily into the secret of religious antiquity',[386] and one recalls the poem of a century later, with its telling lines –

> On firmer ties his joys depend
> Who has a polished female friend.[387]

There is no doubt that Stukeley, now between sixty-five and seventy years of age and his second wife still alive (she died aged seventy in 1757), was indulging in a tender romantic friendship with the middle-aged and intellectual Miriam. There is an odd letter in which he quotes with approval a dictum of Apollonius that it becomes a wise man and a philosopher to deceive the world, and urges prudence so that their relationship should be 'out of sight and the understanding of the Vulgar'.[388] It would not do for gossip to centre on the Rector of St George's.

In 1755 Stukeley was to make a visit to Oxford for the first time since his interview with Hearne, and under rather interesting circumstances. One of his parishioners, living in East Street near Red Lion Square, was a scholar named St Amand, who died in 1754 and bequeathed his library and manuscript notes to the Bodleian Library, and Lincoln College, Oxford, with Stukeley as one of his executors. On St Amand's death he therefore set about having the library catalogued, and for this work found a literary hack who was none other than Alexander Cruden, the author of the famous Biblical Concordance, who the year before had recovered from the third of his periods of insanity and was still, to say the least of it, an eccentric character, styling himself 'The Corrector' of the morals of the people of England.[389]

In May 1755 Stukeley set out personally for Oxford with the St Amand collection in twenty-seven packing-cases, and on the 23rd of that month dined with the Vice-Chancellor, George Huddesford, after handing over the collection and obtaining the signatures of Huddesford and of Isham, Rector of Lincoln, to a form of receipt on the fly-leaf of one of the two copies of the catalogue that Cruden had produced.[390] He returned to London, and in July sent a further box of St Amand's coins and papers to the Bodleian with a covering letter to Mr Owen, Bodley's Librarian.[391] Later in the month he writes to an unnamed correspondent in Oxford, who must be either Owen or Huddesford, thanking him for a letter which had been delivered by Cruden – 'I am glad the books are safe, but you are not to give any person any premium concerning them. The terms of the will require that everything should come free to the University. We design to give Mr Cruden his two guineas.'[392] From this it appears that Cruden had tried to obtain money from somebody in Oxford on account of his compilation of the catalogue; he is known to have come to Oxford on 9 June 1755 and to have stayed there nearly a month in a vain attempt to correct the morals of the University, and to have dined more than once with the Vice-Chancellor and with Mr Owen at Jesus.[393] It is an interesting and unexpected glimpse of one of the outstanding eccentrics of the time.

The last ten years of Stukeley's life were to be relatively uneventful. His wife died in 1757, his daughters were married, and he lived at the Rectory of St George's, Queen's Square, looked after by a housekeeper. There were still the meetings of the Antiquaries to attend, where he might discourse on British coins or prove the Druids no idolaters, but people laughed, and there had been that difficulty

144

when he was amoved from the Society for non-payment of subscriptions, in 1740, though he was readmitted in November 1754 without payment of a fine.[394] He compiled a History of the Society of Antiquaries in 1752 (Soc. Ant. MS. xi; another version dated 1760 in Bodl. MS. Eng. Misc. e. 396), but it tells one nothing not already contained in Hearne's edition of the *Curious Discourses* and in the other sources referred to above. But on one occasion at least the Society seems to have supported Stukeley against his critics. Mr Willis of Andover, who as we have seen made certain very pertinent criticisms of Stukeley's woefully inaccurate plan of Roman Silchester, had gone so far as to prepare an abstract of his points of disagreement, and to have this read at a meeting of the Antiquaries by the Hon. James West in the 1750s, but 'it was not so well regarded by those Gentlemen, as I had been too free in exposing the errors of so worthy a Member'. It is rather unfortunate that Mr Willis's strictures all seem to have been well founded.[395]

At the Royal Society again there was trouble – his papers were turned down, and were not printed in the *Transactions*, although they showed so conclusively that sponges were not living creatures or that the Deluge took place in the autumn.[396] However, there was a new attraction in the recently opened British Museum Library, where there were still but few readers – two or three literary hacks and a nervous, shy man who would spend four or five hours a day there, and to whom Stukeley gossiped, little knowing he was talking to the poet Thomas Gray, who was in his poems to give a wide currency to the romantic ideas about Druids and bards that Stukeley had unwittingly started with his megalithic investigations in the 1720s. Gray was scornful of Stukeley and his 'nonsense', and was irritated by the garrulous old man interrupting his reading in the Museum with 'coffee-house news', but his debt to the Druids was enormous, if unacknowledged, and the influence of *Stonehenge* and *Abury* can be traced in his work.[397]

The royal patronage, so delightfully begun that October day at Kew, was continued within the next few weeks following his first visit. There were further audiences with the Princess and with Prince Frederick: she was presented with a copy of the *Carausius* book and *Oriuna* bound in gold and purple. At one audience she asked Stukeley why he did not go abroad and study antiquities there: 'I answered that I loved my own country and that there was curiosity and antiquity enough at home to entertain any genius.' He then drew the Princess's attention to the fact that the Roman Wall was at that moment being pillaged for stone to build the new military roads in Scotland, and followed this up with a very directly worded letter urging legislation to stop the destruction. 'Is it not to be regretted', the letter runs, 'in an age of Building and Architecture, that this British boast and glory should be destroyed.' And as for seeing the monuments of the Roman Empire, 'must we send our Nobility and young folks innumerable, to spend immense sums of money yearly in foreign countrys for that purpose, and have our own unvisited, but what is worse, doomed to be destroyed, and *that* under a public sanction?'[398] The appeal has a modern ring, and though it was foredoomed to be ineffective, we can recall with gratitude this determined effort by Stukeley to interest authority in ancient monuments.

In November 1757 Stukeley had occasion to bring this matter of the destruction of Hadrian's Wall to the Society of Antiquaries in a lively report[399] which details the depredations from Newcastle to Carlisle 'all under sanction of the Government, which we may well accuse of supine indolence, as to this affair'. And, in addition to this, he has another instance of a threatened ancient monument to bring to the attention of the Society.

It appears that at Stukeley's instance oak posts had been set up near the base of Waltham Cross, to preserve it from injury by traffic passing too close. First one and then another of these had been broken, and on his last visit he had found that the ground had been dug away so as to endanger the actual stability of the Cross. He 'found, on enquiry, that the authors of this unworthy violation of so noble a monument, were the Commissioners of the turnpikes, or their senseless agents', and so he wrote to the owner, Lord Monson. He had taken instant action, Stukeley had met his steward on the site, and a sound brick wall had been built to protect it. But he goes on

I shall make this general reflexion, that with grief I discern us dropping into Gothic barbarism. The revival of learning came among us, with Reformation of Religion. We are now become tired of Religion, in its honest and open dress, true religion, and with it goes backward true learning. One species of it we have here before us, the neglect and defacing antient monuments.

Much of the archaeological work done during his last years is worthless, though of interest for the curious development of his religious theories (as in the essay on 'The Brill', a rectangular earthwork enclosure which he conceived to be a Roman camp at St Pancras),[400] yet there is one piece of work worth mentioning for its own sake. The evidence for this survives rather mysteriously in a set of engravings which were never published and for which I can trace no notes or original drawings: of the engravings, the only set seems to be that in the Chelmsford Public Library. It consists of five unique proofs from Stukeley's drawings made in 1759, engraved by Benazech, of earthworks at Colchester which in the main are now known to belong to the fortification of the Belgic capital at that place. We know from a brief note in Stukeley's Journal that on 13 August 1759 he 'survey'd the wonderful works of Cunobeline' at Colchester and Lexden, and he is known to have been a friend of Morant, the Colchester historian, who in 1748 had published an earlier survey of the earthworks made in 1722. His drawings, which survive in these five engravings, have considerable value as a representation of the remains as he saw them, for here no religious partisanship could intrude to alter the archaeological facts.[401]

At home, in the intervals of parochial duties, there was always writing to be done. So many ideas came into his head – 'I invented a new method of military tents without the embaras of rope staked into the ground. 'Tis after the fashion of the Mosaic tabernacle' he notes in his Journal one day, and on another, 'I found out the true nature of Solomon's Temple',[402] and, again, 'I observe derry down, the burden in Robin Hood songs, is a remain of the Druids'. Aaron's Pectoral, the Origin of Letters, Ovid's Banishment, and Zoophytes – quire after quire of small quarto paper was filled with his distinctive, clear writing,[403] now becoming large as his eyesight weakened, though he did not wear spectacles until 1763, and on his first appearance in them in church preached, with his charming touch of humour, on the text 'Now we see through a glass, darkly.'[404]

His sermons must have been remarkable, even in an age of churchmanship in which the most varied philosophical dissertations were expected from the pulpit. Some were topical – 'On the Fast for the War', 1762; 'On the Peace', 1763; 'On the Eclipse of the Sun' in the same year.[405] On this last occasion he postponed his morning service until after the celestial event, and wrote to the papers advocating this action in all churches on the line of the eclipse. But others were more mysterious – 'Melchisedec' for example – or the remarkable group of three Vegetable Sermons.

The Vegetable Sermon was an institution peculiarly characteristic of the eighteenth-century Church. It had been founded in 1729 by Mr Fairchild of Hoxton, who bequeathed a sum of money to pay for a sermon in St Leonard's, Shoreditch, on the Tuesday in Whitsun week on 'The Wonderful Works of God in the Creation; or the Certainty of the Resurrection of the Dead, proved by certain changes in the animal

The Druid.

Oh quis me gelidis in vallibus Haemi
Sistat —   Virgil.

From grinding care, & thrift secure,
arriv'd at years of life mature,
unenvy'd for a Fortune great;
above contempt, for low estate;
let the remainder of my days,
in private life, serenely pass.
     unnotic'd, I wd. chuse to dwell,
yet in a house, & not a Cell;
not in a rustic, lone retreat.
be the *Metropolis* my seat.
let me with men & manners live,
where Sciences, & learning thrive;
where best Society we find,
toward improvement of the mind.

12 *Opening page of an unpublished poem,* The Druid, *by
Stukeley, dated 19 October 1758 and signed 'Chyndonax'. It has a
retrospective quality, for the Virgilian quotation from Georgics II
488 is the opening of the lines he used on the title-page of his
draft Stonehenge and Avebury of thirty-five years earlier (plate 19)
and he recalls his old nickname Chyndonax of the Roman
Knights. Later in the poem (not shown) 'Mount Haemus' is
Hampstead, and Phoebe is invited to visit him in the last couplet.*

and vegetable parts of the Creation.'[406] The first sermon under these curious terms of reference was preached in 1746, and Stukeley preached at St Leonard's in 1760, 1761, and 1763, publishing the sermons in *Paleographia Sacra, or Discourses on Sacred Subjects* (1763), which included five other sermons among which 'Balaam Druid: A Theological Question' stands out as an even odder subject than the rest.

The volume was dedicated to the Princess Augusta under the rather unexpected appellation of Veleda,[407] Archdruidess of Kew, and the dedication is signed by Chyndonax of Mount Haemus, Druid. The preface takes up the theme of the Vegetable Discourses: 'Christianity is a republication of the patriarchal religion. For which reason I have not scrupled to introduce Druids before a Christian audience. They were of the patriarchal religion of ABRAHAM, . . . and have a right to assist at a Vegetable Sermon.' Then follows a paragraph on Sunday observance, and this truly remarkable preface ends up with an appeal to all readers who have British coins in their possession to lend them to Dr Stukeley, divine and Druid, for drawing and engraving.

The first sermon begins well enough with Solomon's Temple, but soon the Druids come in, with allusions to their temples at Avebury, Stonehenge, and Shap. The Shoreditch congregation is then given a direct reference to *Abury*, Chapter xv, and the concluding doxology runs 'as once of old in groves, so here in their representative fabrics, we adore the three sacred persons of the deity, Father, Son and Holy Ghost, to whom be ascribed all honour and glory now and for ever, Amen'. Surely never was a sermon ended more strangely. In the subsequent discourses, the Druids, mistletoe, and Balaam 'who was really a Druid' are all present – whether or not they had a right, they certainly assisted at the Vegetable Sermons.

In 1760 the literary world was taken by storm by an unpretentious small octavo volume of seventy pages entitled *Fragments of Ancient Poetry* and purporting to be the remains of epics by the ancient Gaelic poet Ossian, handed down by oral tradition and gathered and translated by one James Macpherson. One need not discuss here the intriguing question of the Ossian inventions of Macpherson, so adroitly presented in 'measured prose' with just the right touch of romanticism to assure enthusiastic reception in the 1760s.[408] *Fingal* appeared in 1761, *Temora* in 1763: Gray was 'extasié' though sometimes suspicious of their authenticity. But Ossian had taken hold of England and was soon to extend his influence to the Continent, where later Napoleon was to travel ever accompanied by his patchouli and snuff-scented copy of Macpherson's rhapsodies, and Bernadotte, christening his son Oscar, gave to the throne of Sweden a king with a name taken from the first-fruits of Gaelic romanticism.

The romantic in Stukeley naturally delighted in *Fingal* and *Temora* – the books had been sent him by the Bishop of St Davids – and though 'some suspicious critics pretend to doubt of it' he had no such qualms. The descriptions of heroes, of battles, of barbaric funerals on the moors, recalled to his mind the barrows he had excavated when a young man with Lord Pembroke at Stonehenge, and he wrote a pamphlet on Cathmor's Shield, addressed to Macpherson and containing a drawing of the shield as he visualized it – even less convincing than Macpherson's poems themselves.[409]

He was now seventy-six years of age, but by no means lacking in spirit. Miriam seems to have been replaced by Phoebe –

> That Phoebe's my friend, my delight and my pride,
> I always have boasted, and seek not to hide.
> I dwell on her praises, wherever I goe;
> They say I'm in love, but I answer No. No.

or Mrs Eliza, Druidess of Caen Wood, addressed in verses less arch than those to Phoebe, with a rather pleasing opening –

> Grant me, ye Fates, a calm retreat
> Where I may pass my days
> Far from the low, mean follys of the Great
> Free from the Vulgar's envious hate
> And Careless of their praise.[410]

He had bought a cottage at Kentish Town, then a pleasant country district, in 1759, and spent much of his time laying out the garden there. He could still take a vivid interest in everything that he saw – in April 1759 he notes in his diary: 'At Kentish town to my new house by the castle. Heard the cuckoo, saw a fine painted land newt in a bank just by its hole.'[411] The warm spring day is held in the phrase as bright and gleaming as the lizard, and one thinks instinctively of Gilbert White.

He moved about as vigorously as ever: early in 1765 he walked from Bloomsbury to Grosvenor Square to call on his old friend Warburton to inquire about his chances of a prebendal stall at Canterbury likely to become vacant. 'One never dies the sooner, you know, for asking preferment', he observed cheerfully, to Warburton's amusement.[412] At the end of February he had been at the Kentish Town cottage, but had come in for a vestry meeting, and after this returned to the Rectory.

According to his usual custom, he lay down on his couch, where his housekeeper came and read to him; but some occasion calling her away, on her return, he with a cheerful look said 'Sally, an accident has happened since you have been absent'. 'Pray what is that, sir?' 'No less than a stroke of the palsy.' She replied 'I hope not so, sir' and began to weep – 'Nay, do not trouble yourself' said he, 'but get some help to carry me upstairs, for I never shall come down again but on men's shoulders.'[413]

He was carried to his bed, where he lay in a coma for three days, and on the 3rd of March 1765, a Sunday, he died.[414]

VII
The Man and his Work

AFTER HIS DEATH, Bishop Warburton was to write a character sketch of Stukeley which deftly and sympathetically portrays the man as he appeared to his friends.

> You say true [he writes to Hurd] I have a tenderness in my temper which will make me miss poor Stukeley; for, not to say that he was one of my oldest acquaintance, there was in him such a mixture of simplicity, drollery, absurdity, ingenuity, superstition and antiquarianism, that he afforded me that kind of well-seasoned repast, which the French call an *Ambigu*, I suppose from a compound of things never meant to meet together. I have often heard him laughed at by fools, who had neither his sense, his knowledge, or his honesty; though it must be confessed, that in him they were all strangely travestied.[415]

Warburton's estimate is confirmed by the intimations of Stukeley's character we can recover from his letters and his published work: there is an immensely likeable quality about him, with all his foibles, and it is not surprising that when he was laid up in bed on one occasion in Queen's Square, over 120 friends and parishioners visited him or sent him messages of condolence.[416]

To his contemporaries, he must have appeared as a learned man, despite the fanciful ideas of his later life, and the mass of seemingly erudite theory with which he loaded his published works undoubtedly passed for the authentic expression of a scholar. His really valuable work in archaeology, as we are now able to perceive it in the perspective of two centuries, is, of course, his objective fieldwork at Avebury and Stonehenge and other sites during the years around 1718–24. But this was unappreciated by other mid-eighteenth-century antiquaries, who were in no position to distinguish this from the fanciful etymologies and the Biblical analogies with which he smothered the basic fieldwork in his published books. It must be admitted that he was not a good scholar: he was uncritical of his literary sources and his reading was discursive rather than profound. His value to archaeology in his own day and now lies in his capacity to observe and record facts in the open air. In historical studies of the same period he may perhaps best be compared with Hearne, whose meticulous editions of medieval texts still win the approval of modern scholars, but whose efforts as an historian were uncritical and often valueless. Stukeley's surveys, drawings, and notes of Avebury are sources which we can use with the same confidence as a chronicle edited by Hearne, but, apart from the fortunate survival of many of these in manuscript form, we have to dig out the remaining facts from the mass of absurdity which loads the pages of *Abury* and, to a lesser degree, *Stonehenge*.

The recognition of two periods in Stukeley's intellectual life, the first, to 1725, reliable and objective, and the second, from his ordination to his death, speculative and fantastic, almost enables us to assess the value of any archaeological records of his that survive on the criterion of date. It is exceedingly fortunate that Avebury engaged his attention in 1718 and not in 1728.

But let us recognize the very great importance of the work he did in the 1720s. Quite apart from its value at Avebury as a record of structures now destroyed – and Stukeley was acutely conscious of this aspect of his work – it is, with the exception of Aubrey's remarkable pioneer efforts of sixty years before, the first evidence for a branch of field archaeology which in Britain has taken on a peculiar importance. It is pure fieldwork and survey carried out in the open air, with a minimum of excavation. This is a technique in which today British archaeology is outstanding: with this fieldwork goes a high standard of draughtsmanship and the visual presentation of evidence which is in direct descent from Stukeley. It is not for nothing that this study is one of the open air, and it seems to me intimately bound up with the English approach to the countryside which was developed unconsciously side-by-side with the Romantic movement in literature and the arts, and which touches also on fieldwork in other studies such as natural history.

Stukeley's delight in the English countryside is an endearing feature. It is not the thrill of the wild, the sublime, the mountainous and horrid that we encounter in his writing, but an almost sensuous pleasure in the mild English landscape of the Wiltshire Downs. His field-notes include such passages as this:

To take in all the beautys of Abury we must widen our imagination and think with the antients and behold the most stately strife between art and nature. Major rerum mihi nascitur ordo. The avenues are well contrived for though they run in a valley yet never along the lowest ground but with a little declivity from them to the bottom that the rain may never lodge . . . on each hand a high hill, Windmill Hill and the corner of Hackpen called Whitehill. That easternmost is highest to keep off the keen winds which are indeed sharp at this place, the air commonly very fine.[417]

Or again, of Windmill Hill itself:

'Tis a pretty round apex, the turf as soft as velvet. There is the sign of a very old camp cast up on one half of it but unfinished. The air here extremely fragrant.[418]

and of the pleasure of walking on the downs:

The strolling for relaxed minds upon these downs is the most agreeable exercise and amusement in the world especially when you are every minute struck with some piece of wonder in antiquity. The neat turn of the huge barrows wraps you up into a contemplation of the flux of life and passage from one state to another and you meditate with yourself of the fate and fortune of the famous personages who thus took care of their ashes that have rested so many ages.[419]

And, finally, this delightful appreciation of fieldwork in the Avebury district:

I have an infinite number of times remarked the fine breathings or streams sweeter than can be imagined saluting the nostrils most agreeably and recreating the spirits like taking snuff, though fatigued in walking, for it has been common with me to walk 10 mile before dinner, as much before night, and all the while upon Nature's tapistry more easy than a plane floor, being yielding to the weight of the impressed foot and rebounding again with an elasticity which saves half the labour of walking, and I have never found any sultry heats, but breezes very inconvenient for drawing as blowing the paper about and that in the calmest weather I ever found here.[420]

In Stukeley we find one of the first Englishmen to enjoy and to describe in pleasant prose the unexciting landscape, and we can see in him the lineal ancestor of Richard Jeffries and Hudson.

With regard to the unfortunate episodes of his later days – the Richard of Cirencester forgery, the Oriuna fatuity, the wild guesses about Carausius and the British kings – we can at least say that he was no worse than his contemporaries. Nothing comes out more strongly from a study of Stukeley's life and work than the changed intellectual temper in England after about 1730. This has been commented on in the realm of historical studies as well as in palaeontology and geomorphology, and with Stukeley we can find a parallel decline in antiquarian pursuits.[421] He is all too significantly a child of his age, and his own intellectual history but lives out the melancholy story of that of British learning at large.

One cannot help feeling that had he been born fifty years earlier, he might have carried on the high tradition of his early studies into later life. His Avebury and Stonehenge work was done in the last years of the great historical tradition surviving from the Restoration, and by 1724 there were few, if any, with whom he could share his interest in exact record and detailed draughtsmanship. There were no young men to train, as he had trained old Lord Winchelsea, in taking bearings, making plans, and sketching prospects – the interest was lacking and his own work unappreciated. It must have been this that acted as one of the contributory causes of his retirement from London to Grantham: a lone enthusiast, no one could understand his concern for the preservation of Avebury or share with him a delight in its details of planning and construction. As I have suggested elsewhere, 'perhaps we should see William Stukeley's greatness as a field archaeologist not in his being an innovator, but in his being provincial, old-fashioned and out-of-date, continuing the high tradition of Restoration antiquarianism unaware of the changed intellectual mood of the metropolis.'[422]

He moved with the times all too readily, and the easy opportunity of recognition afforded by religious controversy was too seductive to be resisted. The Deists were without difficulty made into a redoubtable foe against whom one might fight with every honour to learning and the Established Church, and his sense of the historical associations of the Church of England may have been among the causes that led him to take orders and to turn in controversy against those who wished to undermine a venerable English institution.

A puzzling character even to his friends such as Warburton, at the remove of two centuries Stukeley still remains an enigmatic, tragicomic figure. We can today appreciate far better than his contemporaries the valuable work he did as a young man – work that they poked fun at or ignored – but perhaps less well than they can we understand the high esteem in which he was held on account of his published writing. It is an uncomplimentary tribute to an age of decadence in learning that they did not start laughing at the Antiquaries before they did. In an age of more vigorous and accurate scholarship criticism might have prevented Stukeley from perpetrating many of his follies, rather than encouraging him as a whimsical dilettante.

But one cannot ignore the fact that the indirect influence of his work was enormous, and with the most unexpected results upon English imaginative literature of the late eighteenth and early nineteenth centuries. The indebtedness of Gray, Collins, Mason, and other poets to Stukeley's ideas on Druids has long been recognized, but the debt owed by William Blake to the Stonehenge and Avebury volumes is only beginning to be appreciated. M. Denis Saurat seems to have been the first to notice the connection between Stukeley and the Prophetic Books, especially *Jerusalem*, and others have taken the matter further.[423]

In the interval between Stukeley's death and Blake's poetical compositions, the Druidic theories had, of course, been adopted and developed by other writers. When the Welsh bard, Edward Williams, published his *Poems* in 1794, for instance, he could write naturally of 'The Patriarchal Religion of Ancient Britain, called Druidism', while another Welshman, Edward Davies, in his *Celtic Researches* (1804), takes it as a matter of course that the Druids had inherited a religious tradition from Adam and Noah. But these ideas really owe their origin to Stukeley, and when we find Blake, in his description of his picture 'The Ancient Britons', making the categorical statement 'Adam was a Druid, and Noah also', it is to *Stonehenge* and *Abury* that we must turn in seeking his inspiration for so striking an observation.

To anyone familiar with Stukeley's work there comes, in reading *Jerusalem*, a moment of relief as at glimpsing a familiar landscape, after trudging through a wood thick with obscure mythological undergrowth, when he reaches the end of Chapter I. Here he finds the sudden invocation:

To the Jews
Jerusalem the Emanation of the Giant Albion! Can it be? Is it a Truth that the Learned have explored? Was Britain the Primitive Seat of Patriarchal Religion? If it is true, my title-page is also True, that Jerusalem was & is the Emanation of the Giant Albion. . . .
All things Begin and End in Albion's Ancient Druid Rocky Shore.
Your Ancestors derived their origin from Abraham, Heber, Shem and Noah, who were Druids, as the Druid Temples (which are the Patriarchal Pillars & Oak Groves) over the whole Earth witness to this day.
You have a tradition, that Man anciently contain'd in his mighty limbs all things in Heaven & Earth: this you received from the Druids. . . .

This is the authentic utterance of the 'Archdruid': perhaps he would have thought it a little too enthusiastic for a Vegetable Sermon, but he would have approved of the sentiments, phrased as they are nearly as quotations from his own works.

And so throughout the great, formless rhapsody in which Blake's visionary mind has turned the ideas of the speculative mythologists of the seventeenth and eighteenth centuries into a wild vision of a personal apocalypse, Stukeley's Druids constantly appear and reappear in one form or another. 'The Serpent Temples thro' the Earth, from the wide Plain of Salisbury' are illustrated by a remarkable allegorical plate of which the background is formed of a 'Dracontium' based, as Ruthven Todd has seen, on Stukeley's reconstruction of the Avebury plan, but in which, instead of individual standing stones, Stonehenge trilithons are introduced. The 'Druid Patriarchal rocky Temples' stand side by side with the 'Dragon Temples,' and the Druidic wicker image used for holocausts, so well attested by classical writers and so inconvenient to supporters of the sublime Druidic Patriarchs, is turned into 'The Wicker Man of Scandinavia' and so removed into a safely barbarous sphere.

After Chapter II of *Jerusalem* comes an attack on the Deists, which again may owe something to Stukeley, and from then on the references to Stonehenge and the Druids are frequent. A specific Stukeley contact must certainly exist in the line 'They look forth from Stone-henge: from the Cove round London Stone', for 'Cove' is the peculiar word invented by Stukeley as a name for the settings of three stones such as those within the northern of the two extant inner circles at Avebury, and is otherwise meaningless.

In *Milton* again, Blake brings in his Druids, and in one line must be referring to the dimensions of Stonehenge as worked out by Stukeley with his Druid Cubit. The victims are being prepared for the sacrifice in South Molton Street and Stratford Place (with that disconcerting use Blake makes of banal London street-names side-by-side with his wildest extravagances),

. . . and their inmost palaces
Resounded with preparation of animals wild & tame,
(Mark well my words: Corporeal Friends are Spiritual Enemies)
Mocking Druidical Mathematical Proportion of Length, Bredth, Highth;
Displaying Naked Beauty. . . .

Of all destinations for archaeological fieldwork surely this is most odd – odder even than Stukeley's own use in later life of the careful and detailed observations of his younger days when he and Lord

Winchelsea tired themselves out with the delightful task of accurately measuring Stonehenge for the first time. Without Stukeley's enthusiastic championing of the patriarchal origins of the British Druids, Blake's passionate belief in a mystical Holy Land on British soil might never have taken root in his fantastic mind. As an old man, Stukeley was certain he had found Julius Caesar's camp near St Pancras, but it was left to William Blake to discover the New Jerusalem 'Near mournful ever-weeping Paddington'.

Another curious by-way of British eccentricity that survives today owes its origin to Stukeley and his ideas about Druids. In 1781 a society under the name of 'The Ancient Order of Druids' was founded by a man called Hurle – probably Henry Hurle, a London carpenter and builder who died in 1795. Originally a speculative and 'secret' society, after a secession in 1833 it was transformed into the Benefit Society which still continues to exist under the original name. But the picturesque aspects of Stukeley's white-robed priests are still retained by others, and each returning Midsummer Eve sees ceremonies carried out at Stonehenge which, while they certainly bear no relation to the performances of the Celtic Iron Age priesthood, probably come near to realizing the dreams of Stukeley.[424]

But Blake was only one – the greatest – of those later influenced by Stukeley's theories. On the basis of his first ideas, derived from Aubrey and Toland, that the Druids built stone circles, he had erected a fantastic fabric of theory around which even more queer romantic pavilions and turrets were piled up in the course of the second half of the century. The Druids became the philosopher-priests who championed ancient liberty against the brutal Romans; they knew the secrets of the universe and the mysteries of the heavens. They were waiting ready in the wings to make appropriate entries into the Romantic drama at any point, sometimes as more or less authentic Druids, sometimes as Bards, Scalds, or Fates. By the opening years of the nineteenth century Stonehenge, the Edda, the poems of Taliesin, the lost tribes of Israel, and the Bards of the Isle of Britain were all competing for prominence. It was a Druidic dream-world which has left an oddly tangible relic today in the Welsh Eisteddfod with the Gorsedd Circle, invented and introduced into its ceremonies by Iolo Morganwg in response to romantic Welsh patriotism a century or so ago, but in the end to be derived from Stukeley, patiently measuring the circles at Avebury so that posterity might know what Tom Robinson had destroyed.

Appendices
Sources
Notes and References
Further Reading
List of Illustrations
Index

Appendix I

Reconstructed Journals of the Tours
1721–5

The following Journals have been reconstructed from the dated drawings either in manuscript or engraved as plates in the *Itinerarium Curiosum*, I and II (abbreviated to IC(1) and IC(2), followed by the plate number, in the references below), and serve to give a chronological framework to the text as published in this work.

1721

14 AUGUST Drew Reading Abbey Gate (IC (1), 23, 26; Bodl. Top. gen. d. 13, f. 5).

15 AUGUST Drew Marlborough Mound (Bodl. Top. gen. d. 13, f. 7).

16–18 AUGUST At Avebury and Stonehenge (see separate journals).

20 AUGUST Drew gardens at Wilton House (Bodl. Top. gen. d. 13, f. 10).

23 AUGUST Copied Roman inscription at Cirencester (Bodl. Top. gen. d. 13, f. 14).

24 AUGUST At Gloucester, drew Black Friars (IC (1), 22); White Friars (IC (1), 32); cloisters (Bodl. Top, gen. d. 13, f. 15).

30 AUGUST At Worcester, drew gateway (IC (1), 23; Bodl. Top. gen. d. 13, f. 18).

2 SEPTEMBER At Malvern, drew gatehouse (Bodl. Top. gen. d. 13, f. 19).

7 SEPTEMBER At Hereford, drew view of city (Bodl. Top. gen. d. 13, f. 22).

9 SEPTEMBER Made plan of Kenchester (IC (1), 85).

14 SEPTEMBER Drew Leominster Priory (Bodl. Top. gen. d. 13, f. 29).

16 SEPTEMBER Drew view of Ludlow (Bodl. Top. gen. d. 13, f. 30).

21 SEPTEMBER Drew monuments in Tenbury Church (Bodl. Top. gen. d. 13, f. 20ᵛ).

23 SEPTEMBER Drew Blackston Cave (IC (1), 13); Hermitage (Bodl. Top. gen. d. 13, f. 33).

30 SEPTEMBER Drew Littlechester, Derby (IC (1), 86; Bodl. Top. gen. d. 13, f. 39).

1 OCTOBER Drew view of Derby (Bodl. Top. gen. d. 13, f. 39ᵛ).

3 OCTOBER Drew Nottingham Castle (Bodl. Top. gen. d. 13, f. 40).

7 OCTOBER Drew monuments in Tuxford Church (Bodl. Top. gen. d. 13, f. 46ᵛ).

10 OCTOBER Drew view of Newark (Bodl. Top. gen. d. 13, f. 47).

12 OCTOBER Made drawings at Grantham (Bodl. Top. gen. d. 13, ff. 48–51); at Great and Little Stukeley (Bodl. Top. gen. d. 13, f. 58).

13 OCTOBER Drew Colsterworth Church (Bodl. Top. gen. d. 13, f. 51ᵛ).

1722

23 JULY–AUGUST At Avebury and Stonehenge (see separate journals).

1 AUGUST Drew Sarum Cross, Broughton, and Wallop River (Bodl. Top. eccles. d. 6, f. 87); drew view and made plan of Old Sarum (Bodl. Gough Maps 229, 56; IC (1), 65).

4 AUGUST Made plan of Silchester (IC (1), 61).

5 AUGUST Drew Silchester (IC (1), 45).

20–1 AUGUST Drew Hobson's Conduit (Cambridge) (Bodl. Top. gen. d. 14, ff. 5, 5ᵛ); made plan of Chesterford (IC. (1), 59); drew Roman Camp at Littlebury (Walden) (IC (1), 45).

23 AUGUST Drew Ivy Cross, Sutton St James (Bodl. Top. eccles. d. 6, f. 80).

26 AUGUST Drew Holbeach Church (Bodl. Top. eccles. d. 6, f. 32ᵛ).

28 AUGUST Drew Spalding Town Hall (Bodl. Top. gen. d. 14, f. 6).

29 AUGUST Drew Boston Stump (IC (1), 19).

1 SEPTEMBER Drew 'Banovallum' (IC (1), 89).

3 SEPTEMBER Drew Newport Gate, Lincoln (IC (1), 54).

4 SEPTEMBER Made plan of Lincoln (IC (1), 88); plan of Roman Lincoln (Bodl. Gough Gen. top. 15, 59).

6 SEPTEMBER Drew view of Newark (Bodl. Top. gen. d. l4, f. 6ᵛ).

7 SEPTEMBER Drew 'Ad Pontem' (IC (1), 90); drew 'Crocolana' (near Newark) (IC (2), 21).

8 SEPTEMBER Drew Burrow Hill, Leics. (IC (2), 22); Nether Broughton (IC (1), 91), Leicester Roman Wall (IC (2), 23); Bowbridge at Leicester (Bodl. Top. gen. d. 14, f. 7); made plan of Leicester (IC (1), 92); drew Long barrow at Cassington, Notts. (Bodl. Top. gen. b. 53, f. 14ᵛ).

9 SEPTEMBER Drew Raw Dykes (IC (2), 27); drew 'Bennonis' (Bodl. Top. gen. d. 14, f. 73) and made plan (IC (1), 93); drew Bowbridge (IC (1), 94); view of Bowbridge (Bodl. Gough Gen. top. 15, f. 32).

10 SEPTEMBER Drew Raw Dykes, Leicester (IC (2), 25, 26)

11 SEPTEMBER Drew Dunstable Church (Bodl. Top. eccles. d. 16, f. 32).

14 SEPTEMBER Drew Leominster Priory (IC (1), 22).

20 SEPTEMBER Drew Claremont (Bodl. Top. gen. d. 14, f. 7ᵛ).

22 SEPTEMBER Drew earthworks at Pinner (Soc. Ant. Lond. Roman Prints iii).

SEPTEMBER Drew Little Burgh (IC (1), 87).

4 OCTOBER Drew Rochester Castle (IC (1), 6).

5 OCTOBER Drew Faversham Abbey (IC (1), 27); made plan of Canterbury (IC (1), 96).

6 OCTOBER Drew St. Augustine's, St. Gregory's, and Ethelbert's Chapel, Canterbury (IC (1), 25); St Augustine's (IC (1), 24); Worth Gate, Canterbury (Soc. Ant. Lond. Roman Prints iii; IC (1), 54); Roman Gate at Canterbury (Bodl. Top. gen. b. 53, f. 44).

7 OCTOBER Drew two views of Dover (Bodl. Top. eccles. d. 6, f. 31ᵛ); drew Richborough (Soc. Ant. Lond. Roman Prints iii; IC (2), 35; IC (1), 97); Deal (Soc. Ant. Lond. Roman Prints iii).

8 OCTOBER Drew Pharos at Dover (IC (1), 46, 48); Snaregate Street (Soc. Ant. Lond. Roman Prints iii).

9 OCTOBER Drew Lymne (IC (1), 99).

10 OCTOBER Drew Roman barrow on Barham Down (IC (1), 55); Chilham and Julaber's Grave (IC (2), 54); square earth-work on Barham Downs (IC (2), 53).

15 OCTOBER Drew Kit's Coty (IC (2), 31, 32, 33; Bodl. Top. gen. b. 53, f. 19ᵛ).

7 NOVEMBER Made plan of Roman London (IC (1), 57).

1723

28 JUNE Drew Speen (IC (1), 60); made plan of Speen (IC (2), 10).

29 JUNE Drew Lord Hertford's House at Marlborough (Gough Maps 33, f. 9ᵛ; IC (1), 3); Marlborough (IC (1), 63); made plan of Marlborough (IC (2), 11).

30 JUNE–2 SEPTEMBER At Avebury and Stonehenge (see separate Journals).

2 JULY Drew Great Bedwyn (IC (1), 64).

6 JULY Drew Martinsell (IC (1), 44); made plan of Marlborough Mound (IC (1), 62).

11 JULY Drew Oldbury (IC (1), 42).

17 JULY Drew Devizes (IC (1), 69); Lansdown Monument, Bath (Bodl.

Top. gen. d. 14, f. 8).

18 JULY Drew Heddington (IC (1), 68).

21 JULY Drew Bath (IC (1), 71).

23 JULY Drew Stanton Drew (IC (2), 77, 78, 79).

JULY Made plan of Bath (IC (1), 70).

JULY Drew Stanton Drew (Bodl. Top. gen. b. 53, ff. 3–4).

1 AUGUST Drew view of Old Sarum (IC (1), 66).

3 AUGUST Drew Clarendon (Bodl. Gough Maps 33, f. 28; IC (1), 9).

15 AUGUST Drew Cadbury Castle (Camelot) (IC (1), 43).

16 AUGUST Drew Tor and Kitchen at Glastonbury (Bodl. Top. eccles. d. 6, f. 37).

17 AUGUST Drew view of Glastonbury (Bodl. Top. gen. b. 53, ff. 69–70; Bodl. Top. gen. d. 14, f. 9); Glastonbury Abbey (IC (1), 33, 36); Abbot's Kitchen (IC (1), 34); made plan of Ilchester (IC (1), 72).

19 AUGUST Made plan of Exeter (view, pl. 74) (IC (1), 74); drew view in Somerset (Montagu Hill) (IC (1), 44).

20 AUGUST Drew Seaton (IC (1), 75).

21 AUGUST Drew Lyme Regis (IC (1), 76).

22 AUGUST Drew Winterborne nine stones (IC (2), 92); Dorchester: made plan (IC (1), 77) (view, pl. 78); made plan of Maumbury (IC (1), 50).

25 AUGUST Drew Figsbury (IC (1), 41).

26 AUGUST Drew Salisbury from Harnham Hill (Bodl. Top. gen. d. 14, f. 9^v); Sarum from Harnham Hill (IC (1), 67).

5 SEPTEMBER Drew large view of Wilton House (Gough Maps 33, f. 19^v).

9 SEPTEMBER Drew Winchester Cross (Bodl. Top. gen. d. 14, f. 10^v).

11 SEPTEMBER Drew Southampton (IC (1), 79); drew view of Portsmouth (Bodl. Top. gen. d. 14, f. 11).

12 SEPTEMBER Drew Porchester (IC (1), 80).

13 SEPTEMBER Drew Portsmouth (IC (1), 82).

14 SEPTEMBER Made plan of Chichester (view, pl. 82) (IC (1), 81).

15 SEPTEMBER Drew Chichester Cross

(Bodl. Top. gen. d. 14, f. 10^v); Trundle (IC (1), 43).

16 SEPTEMBER Drew Farnham (IC (2), 44); view and plan of Staines (IC, (1), 84).

1724

8 MAY Drew Roman amphitheatre at Silchester (IC (2), 43).

9 MAY Drew Barrows on Brimpton Common (Bodl. Gough Maps 231, 33).

11 MAY Drew Total eclipse of Sun on Haradon Hill (IC (1), 172).

11 MAY JUNE At Stonehenge and Avebury (see separate Journals).

7 JUNE Drew view of Ogbury (Bodl. Gough Maps 229, 173).

9 JUNE Drew Druids' House at Deadman's Den (Bodl. Gough Maps 229, 57^v); hill-fort at Bere Regis (IC (2), 45).

14 JUNE Drew Romsey Church (Bodl. Top. eccles. d. 6, f. 9); drew Ringwood (IC (2), 46).

21 JUNE Corrected proof of Maumbury and made notes (Bodl. Top. Wilts. c. 4, f. 123).

10 JULY Drew six barrows at Stevenage (IC (2), 85); Ravensbury, near Hexton (IC (2), 63).

11 JULY Drew view of Castor (IC (2), 13); spring at Uffington, Lincs. (Bodl. Top. gen. d. 14, f. 11^v).

13 JULY Drew view of Stamford (Bodl. Top. gen. d. 14, f. 12); Brigcasterton (IC (2), 14).

14 JULY Drew Crowland Bridge (Bodl. Top. gen. d. 14, f. 12^v); Crowland Abbey (IC (2), 4).

20 JULY Drew view of Ancaster (IC (2), 15).

24 JULY Drew Wintringham (IC (2), 16); Ferriby Sluice (Bodl. Top. gen. d. 14, f. 13); 'Aukborough' (IC (2), 17).

25 JULY Drew 'Alate' temple at Barrow, Lincs. (Bodl. Top. gen. b. 53, f. 10).

26 JULY Drew Gaunt's Palace at Lincoln (Bodl. Top. gen. d. 14, f. 13^v); Caister, and the spring at Caister, Lincs. (IC

(2), 19, 20); Thornton College Gate (IC (2), 18).

8 SEPTEMBER Drew 'Antiquity Hall' at Oxford (Bodl. Top. gen. d. 14, f. 14).

9 SEPTEMBER Drew Blenheim (Bodl. Top. gen. d. 14, f. 14ᵛ).

13 SEPTEMBER Drew view of Banbury (IC (2), 8).

14 SEPTEMBER Drew view of Thame (IC (2) 7); Berkhampstead (IC (2), 29).

16 SEPTEMBER Drew Ludlow Castle (IC (1), 5).

6 OCTOBER Made notes on Noviomagus (Bodl. Gough Maps 229, 38).

7 OCTOBER Drew Rochester Roman wall (IC (2), 30); Roman amphitheatre at Richborough (IC (2), 36); Dover (IC (2), 39).

11 OCTOBER Drew Julaber's Grave (IC (2), 56).

13 OCTOBER Drew Wilton (Bodl. Top. gen. d. 14, f. 15).

17 OCTOBER Drew Malling Abbey (IC (2), 97); Eltham (Bodl. Top. gen. d. 14, f. 15ᵛ).

1725

24 MAY Drew Julaber's Grave (IC (2), 57).

27 MAY Drew Richborough from Amphitheatre (Soc. Ant. Lond. Roman Prints iii).

28 MAY Drew view of Downs near Eastwell, dated 1726, but in error for 1725 (Soc. Ant. London. Roman Prints iii.).

29 MAY Drew views of Dover (Soc. Ant. Lond. Roman Prints iii).

31 MAY Drew Watling Street from Barham Downs (Soc. Ant. Lond. Roman Prints iii).

5 JUNE Drew views of Downs near Aylesford and Wye (Soc. Ant. Lond. Roman Prints iii).

4 JULY Drew Tothill Castle, Dunstable (Bodl. Top. d. 14, f. 16ᵛ).

6 JULY Drew 'Benavona' (IC (2), 28).

7 JULY Drew view of Warwick (IC (2), 9); Chapel and Hermitage at Guy's Cliffe (Bodl. Top. gen. d. 6, f. 18).

17 JULY Drew Stafford Castle (Bodl. Top. gen. d. 14, f. 17).

20 JULY Drew Tutbury Castle (Bodl. Top. gen. d. 14, f. 17ᵛ).

26 JULY Drew Chatsworth cascade and Pool's Hole (Bodl. Top. gen. d. 14, ff. 18, 18ᵛ).

27 JULY Drew view of Buxton (Bodl. Top. gen. d. 14, f. 19).

2 AUGUST Drew Roman gate at Chester (IC (2), 65; Bodl. Top. gen. b. 53, f. 44).

3 AUGUST Drew Roman carving on rock at Chester (IC (2), 67).

4 AUGUST Drew Roman altar in Chester (IC (2), 66).

14 AUGUST Drew Kendal church and castle (Bodl. Top. gen. d. 14, f. 20).

15 AUGUST Drew Mayborough and Arthur's Round Table (Bodl. Top. gen. b. 53, ff. 15ᵛ, 16).

16 AUGUST Drew Long Meg stone circle (Bodl. Top. gen. b. 53, f. 13ᵛ).

1 SEPTEMBER Drew Chester-on-the-Wall (IC (2), 75).

4 SEPTEMBER Drew Roman Wall at Newcastle (IC (2), 77).

12 SEPTEMBER Drew Prior's Kitchen at Durham (Bodl. Top. gen. b. 53, f. 58).

13 SEPTEMBER Drew Scruton House (Bodl. Top. gen. d. 14, f. 20ᵛ).

14 SEPTEMBER Drew Devil's Arrows at Boroughbridge (IC (2), 90); Market Place at Ripon (Bodl. Top. eccles. d. 6, f. 50).

20 SEPTEMBER Drew Robin Hood's Well (Bod. Top. gen. d. 14, f. 21).

Appendix II

Reconstructed Journals of Fieldwork at Avebury and Stonehenge

From Stukeley's dated drawings and notes, and incidental references in his published works, it is possible to reconstruct a fairly detailed Journal of the sequence of his work at Avebury, and to a less extent at Stonehenge, which gives an interesting insight into the progress of his work, and the changing theories that passed through his mind at the time. The more detailed Avebury evidence is given first.

The Avebury Journal

1718

I have already pointed out that the references to a first visit to Avebury in 1718 (*Abury*, 24; SS iii, 273) must be a confusion with the year 1719 – both references were made twenty years or more after the event. On 10 December 1718 he finished copying out Gale's transcript of Aubrey's *Monumenta* MS. into his Commonplace Book (Devizes MS.) with the Avebury plan.

1719

19 MAY 'Rude general sketch' made of Avebury (Devizes MS, f. 41). This seems to have been Stukeley's first visit, made with the Gales.

1720

'In the year 1720, I saw several stones just taken up there', i.e. in the Kennet Avenue (*Abury*, 30).

1721

16 AUGUST Measured circumference of Great Ditch with Roger Gale (*Abury*, 20).

Drew 'Cove' of North Inner Circle (*Abury*, Tab. XV); North and South entrances (Bodl. Top. gen. d. 13, ff 7ᵛ, 8); 'Cell of Celtic Temple' (Hearne's *Collections*, x, 187).

AUGUST Drew plan of Avebury with 'Solar' and 'Lunar' temples (Bodl. Gough Maps, 231, f. 22).

4 SEPTEMBER Made fair drawings of Avebury while staying at Worcester (SS iii. 280).

1722

23 JULY Stukeley, Vandergucht, and Pine set out for Avebury (SS iii. 273).

26 JULY Drew general view of Avebury (Bodl. Gough Maps, 231, f. 325); another view from south (Bodl. MS Eng. misc. b. 65). Sketch of Tom Robinson, 'Stone-Killer' (Bodl. Gough Maps 231, f. 241).

AUGUST In this month he made drawings of the South Entrance (*Abury*, Tab. XII); North Inner Circle (ibid., Tab. XIII); 'Temple of the Moon' (Inner Circle) (Bodl. Gough Maps 231, f. 39); View from North (ibid., f. 218); South Entrance (ibid., f. 308); South Entrance (Hearne's *Collections*, x, 187).

In 1722 (no month stated) he first recognized the (probable) Beckhamptton Avenue (*Abury*, 34), and recorded of the Great Circle that of 100 original stones 'there was left in the year 1722, when I began to write, above 40' (ibid., 22).

1723

30 JUNE Drew Devil's Den (Bodl. Gough Maps 231, f. 206; *Abury*, Tab. XXXIV).

1 JULY Another drawing of same (Bodl. Gough Maps 231, ff. 203–4; *Abury*, Tab. XXXIII).

6 JULY Earl of Winchelsea and Lord and Lady Hertford visited Stukeley at Avebury (SS iii. 246, 273); Stukeley drew Old Chapel Long Barrow (Bodl. Gough Maps 231, ff. 4ᵛ, 10, 224).

8 JULY Drew 'The Sanctuary' as 'Temple of Ertha' (Bodl. Gough Maps 231, f. 227; Bodl. MS Eng. misc. d. 444, f. 62); 'I came hither 8 July 1723' (Bodl. MS Eng. misc. c. 323, 1).

10 JULY Drew 'Cove', 'South Obelisk', Millbarrow, 'Lunar Cove', 'Solar Temple' (Bodl. Gough Maps 231, ff. 16, 41, 45, 237; *Abury*, Tab. XIV, XVI, XXX).

11 JULY Drew Silbury Hill (Bodl. Gough Maps 231, f. 264; *Abury*, Tab. XXVII).

12 JULY Drew north-west side of Great Circle (Bodl. MS Eng. misc. b. 65, f. 19); Lord Winchelsea writes to Stukeley 'at the Catherine Wheel, at Abury', mentioning the Temple of Earth (SS iii. 244; Nichols, *Illus.* ii).

14 JULY Drew Beckhampton Avenue 'from top of an haycock' (Bodl. Gough Maps 231, 233).

15 JULY Drew Roman Road cutting disc barrow; Roundway Hill (*Abury*, Tab. IX, X); 'Solar Temple' (Bodl. Gough Maps 231, f. 48); 'A view of the South Temple' (*Abury* Tab. XVII).

17 JULY Drew West Kennet Long Barrow (Bodl. Gough Maps 231, ff. 14, 242).

18 JULY Drew Roman Road and disc barrow (Bodl. Gough Maps 231, f. 36).

19 JULY Drew Silbury Hill (Bodl. Gough Maps 231, f. 252); general view of Avebury (Bodl. MS Top. gen. b. 53, f. 31); view of Avebury from south (ibid., f. 57); altered title on Beckhampton Avenue view from 'Spot of the Temple' to 'Spot of the Termination of the Bekampton Avenue' (Bodl. MS Eng. misc. d. 444, f. 61; *Abury*, Tab. XXV).

22 JULY Stukeley writes from Bath to Roger Gale of his fortnight's work at Avebury, where he had 'taken a world of drawings' and worked out the Beckhampton Avenue (SS iii. 245–7).

In 1723 (no date) the 'Geometry of Silbury' drawing was made (*Abury*, Tab. XXVIII).

1724

12 MAY Drew Avebury from Wansdyke (Bodl. Gough Maps 231, f. 2ᵛ).

13 MAY Drew Silbury (Bodl. Gough Maps 231, 251; *Abury*, Tab. XXVI) and saw stones carted from 'The Sanctuary' (Bodl. Gough Maps 231, f. 8ᵛ).

14 MAY Drew entrance of West Kennet Avenue to Avebury (Bodl. Gough Maps 231, f. 292); took bearings from Waden Hill (ibid., 33ᵛ).

15 MAY Drew West Kennet Avenue from Hackpen Hill (*Abury*, Tab. XXII); Beckhampton Cove (Bodl. Gough Maps 231, f. 33); view of Sanctuary entitled 'The place of lustration and cophoria at Kennet' (ibid., f. 31).

16 MAY Drew West Kennet Long Barrow (Bodl. Gough Maps 231, f. 243).

18 MAY Altered proof engraving of The Sanctuary (*Abury*, Tab. XXI) from 'Temple of Ertha' to 'Temple of Overton Hill', but without the subtitle 'The Hakpen or head of the Snake in ruins' with which is it published (Bodl. MS Eng. misc. d. 444, f. 62).

29 MAY Drew 'Old Chappel upon Temple Down' (Bodl. Gough Maps 231, f. 222).

The Stonehenge Journal

The information on the Stonehenge work is much less detailed than that on Avebury: there are no dated drawings of 1720.

1719

18–19 MAY 'I was at Stonehenge . . . with Mr. Rog. and Sam. Gale. The first time I saw it'; drew plan (Bodl. Gough Maps 33, f. 2ᵛ).

1721

18 AUGUST With Roger Gale at Stonehenge, drew views (Bodl. Top. gen. d. 13, ff. 9, 9ᵛ; Bodl. Gough Maps 229, f. 147).

AUGUST Drew ground-plan with Avenue (Bodl. Gough Maps 229, f. 16); another plan dated 1721 only (ibid., f. 105).

1722

AUGUST Drew various views (Bodl. Gough Maps 229, ff. 78, 92, 94, 104, 118; *Stonehenge*, Tab. XVII, XIX, XX).

1723

4 JULY Drew rough plan (Bodl. Gough Maps 229, f. 41); view from top of trilithon with Lord Winchelsea (ibid., f. 149).

5 JULY Drew view (*Stonehenge*, Tab. XXXII).

29 JULY Drew view (*Stonehenge*, Tab. XXXIII).

6 AUGUST Drew view of Cursus (Bodl. Gough Maps 229, f. 128); view of Stonehenge (ibid., f. 50); various views (*Stonehenge*, Tab. XXIII, XXIX).

7 AUGUST Digging barrows (Bodl. Gough Maps 229, f. 45); drew view (*Stonehenge*, Tab. XXVI).

9 AUGUST Drew view at 7 am (Bodl. Gough Maps 229, f. 150).

18 AUGUST Drew view of 'cell' (Bodl. Gough Maps 229, f. 146).

28 AUGUST Drew east end of Cursus (Bodl. Gough Maps 229, f. 127).

2 SEPTEMBER Drew barrows near Stonehenge (Bodl. Gough Maps 229, ff. 40, 129; *Stonehenge*, Tab. XXXI).

1724

11 MAY Drew view looking towards Ratfyn (Bodl. Gough Maps 229, f. 169).

2 JUNE Drew circular view from Stonehenge (Bodl. Gough Maps 229, f. 15); view from Avenue (ibid., f. 36).

3 JUNE Drew view along Avenue (Bodl. Gough Maps 229, f. 172); Vespasian's Camp (ibid., f. 42).

4 JUNE Drew rough plan (Bodl. Gough Maps 229, f. 18).

6 JUNE Drew view of Stonehenge and Avenue (Bodl. Gough Maps 229, f. 24); view into Sanctum Sanctorum (ibid., f. 142).

8 JUNE Drew views of Avenue and Ratfyn (Bodl. Gough Maps 229, f. 171; *Stonehenge*, Tab. XXV).

Sources

The material available for a biographical study of Stukeley is enormous, and the task is one of selection rather than that of an unrewarding search for meagre scraps. In 1766, the year after his death, his library was sold in London, and this included a number of manuscript items, some of which seem to have come into the hands of such topographers as John Britton and Richard Gough.[425] The collections of the latter were acquired by the Bodleian Library, Oxford, in the nineteenth century, and those included a number of very important Stukeley manuscripts. But the bulk of the Stukeley papers passed into the hands of a member of the family, and in 1877 belonged to the Rev. Harris Fleming St John of Dinmore Court, near Leominster, the descendant of William Stukeley through the female line. In that year the Surtees Society decided that a selection of this material, and other manuscripts relating to the Gale family, into which Stukeley had married, should be edited by the Rev. W. C. Lukis. This was accordingly done, and three volumes of the Society's publications were devoted to these papers and appeared between the years 1882 and 1887.[426]

Before this, a large amount of correspondence with Stukeley had been published by John Nichols in his *Literary Anecdotes* and his *Illustrations of Literary History* (1812–15 and 1817–58), and in the *Bibliotheca Topographica Britannica* (1750–1800), together with various anecdotes and other material relating to Stukeley and his friends.

The Stukeley papers at Dinmore Court remained intact until the 1920s. A preliminary examination of them, with particular reference to the Avebury material, was made by O. G. S. Crawford,[427] but in 1924 and 1931 the entire collection was put up for sale at Sotheby's and dispersed.[428] Some were acquired for the Bodleian,[429] others by Alexander Keiller, but the majority were sold to booksellers. Some of these were eventually recovered by Keiller, whose collection of Stukeley MSS was presented to the Bodleian in 1955, a year before his death.[430] Captain Cragg of Threekingham Hall also collected together a number of manuscript items which are now divided between the British Library, Corpus Christi College, Cambridge, and the Bodleian Library. There are various other smaller collections in public and private libraries, notably the Society of Antiquaries of London and the Gentlemen's Society of Spalding.

For this study I have used as a basis the published material in the Surtees Society's volumes and in Nichols's publications, but where possible have worked at first hand on the manuscripts. The first fruits of this study appeared in 1935,[431] and the only other recent work on Stukeley and his archaeology is a treatment of the Richard of Cirencester forgery by Mr. H. J. Randall in 1933.[432] I have in this study deliberately concentrated on Stukeley's work as an antiquarian and as the founder of British field archaeology, and within these limitations have been mainly concerned with his work on prehistoric Britain. His contributions to the study of Roman Britain, some of which were noted by Haverfield in his 1907 Ford Lectures, could be discussed in further detail by those more qualified than I to do so. With regard to his very wide range of non-archaeological interests, here again I have not attempted to deal with, for instance, his astronomical interests, reflected by a special group of letters in the Surtees Society's volumes.[433]

In addition to this material directly connected with William Stukeley, and that contained in his published works, my debt to other sources is reflected in the footnotes which document the text. I have utilized unpublished manuscripts in the Bodleian in connection with the relations between John Aubrey, John Toland, and Stukeley, and those in the Clerk of Penicuik papers in the Scottish Record Office for his friendship with Sir John Clerk. Stukeley's published works from *An Account of a Roman Temple...* in 1720 to his *Letter to Mr. Macpherson* in 1763, are given in the second (1776) edition of the *Itinerarium Curiosum* and most of these are referred to with comment in the preceding study. Additional unpublished papers, mainly read or intended for reading to the Royal Society or the Society of Antiquaries, are in the libraries of these bodies and in the Bodleian. The small scientific value of his writings after about 1740 makes detailed comment unnecessary except in so far as they throw incidental light on his wide range of interests and on the development of his antiquarian theories in later life.

Notes and References

1 *Anecdotes of British Topography*, ii (1780), 373.

2 O. G. S. Crawford, in Crawford and Keiller, *Wessex from the Air* (1928), 211.

3 *A Letter to Dr. Mead concerning some Antiquities in Berkshire* (Oxford 1738), 7.

4 Cf. Strickland Gibson in *Oxoniensia*, i (1936), 173.

5 Thomas Hearne, *Collections* (Oxford Hist. Soc.), viii, 111.

6 Joan Evans, *A History of the Society of Antiquaries* (1956).

7 Alexander Gordon, *Itinerarium Septentrionale* (1726), preface.

8 David C. Douglas, *English Scholars* (1939), *passim*.

9 Sir Henry Savile, *The Ende of Nero and Beginning of Galba, Fower Bookes of the Histories of Cornelius Tacitus. The Life of Agricola.* (Oxford 1591.)

10 Clement Edmonds, *Observations Vpon Caesar's Commentaries* (1604).

11 *Henry V*, III, ii.

12 Cf. S. Piggott, *Ruins in a Landscape* (1976).

13 The Visitation is in the College of Heralds, MS C 39. For the monuments, cf. Bersu in *Trans. Cumb. & West. Arch. Soc.* N.S. xi (1940), 169–206. Dugdale's MS was known to John Aubrey, who made notes from it in his *Monumenta* MS, and his copy of Dugdale's plan of King Arthur's Round Table is reproduced by Bersu, pl. 1 E.

14 *The Roman Occupation of Britain* (1924), 75. For Horsley, see also G. Macdonald and R. C. Bosanquet in *Arch. Aeliana*, 4th S. x (1933), 1–81.

15 For Gibson, see Norman Sykes, *Edmund Gibson* (1926); S. Piggott, *Proc.* Brit. Acad. XXXVII (1951), 199; *Ruins in a Landscape* (1976), 33.

16 For Rollright, G. Lambrick, *The Rollright Stones* (1983).

17 For Anstis and his notes on Cornish antiquities, see below.

18 A. Powell, *John Aubrey and his Friends* (1948); for the Avebury and Stonehenge work, see *Wilts. Arch. Mag.* iv (1858), 309–63; vii (1861), 224–6.

19 *Dict. Nat. Biog.* xi, 1096; the remark is quoted by N. Owen, *British Remains* (1777), 131–84.

20 For Toland, see below.

21 For Paschal, see, for example, a letter to John Aubrey printed in *Miscellanies on Several Curious Subjects* (1714), 15–19. William Musgrave published *Antiquitates Britanno-Belgicae* (1719); for John Strachey, cf. *Dict. Nat. Biog.* 1st Supp. iii, 334; Moyle's letters were published in his posthumous *Works* (1726).

22 *Mona Antiqua Restaurata* (1723).

23 *Antonini Iter Britanniarum* (1709).

24 *An Account of the Isles of Orkney* (1693).

25 *A Description of the Western Islands of Scotland* (1703).

26 *Itinerarium Septentrionale* (1726); the Clerk Papers are largely unpublished, but cf. I. G. Brown, *Antiquity* LI (1977), 201; *The Hobby-Horsical Antiquary* (Nat. Library of Scotland 1980).

27 Somner, *Roman Ports and Forts in Kent* (1693); John Batteley, *Antiquitates Rutupinae* (1711).

28 Cf. *Diary of Ralph Thoresby* (1677–1724), ed. Hunter 1830.

29 A copy of these proposals is in Bodl. Wood 658, f. 780; Michael Hunter, *John*

Aubrey and the Realm of Learning (1975).

30 *Phil. Trans.* I (1666), 186.

31 Bodl. MS Aubrey 4, ff. 243–4. Mr Powell drew attention to this questionnaire in *John Aubrey and his Friends* (1948), 152, but wrongly attributed it to a scheme for revising William Camden's *Britannia.* The first volume of Ogilby's book of this name was published in 1675, though no further volumes appeared. Camden's work had to wait for its revision until Gibson undertook the task in 1693–4.

32 This sheet of queries is in Bodl. MS Ashmole 1820ª, f. 226. Machell continued his antiquarian interests after he had become Rector of Kirkby Thore in Westmorland, and his MS collections for the history of Cumberland and Westmorland are now in the Dean and Chapter Library at Carlisle. He died in 1698. (See Eric Birley in *Trans. Cumb. & West. Arch. Soc.* NS XLVI (1947), 129, 155; J. M. Ewbank, *Antiquary on Horseback* (1963).

33 Bodl. MS Rawlinson B.323.

34 A. Powell, *John Aubrey* (1948), 166.

35 Bodl. MS Ashm. 1820ª, f. 228. Lhuyd sent this outline of his projected work in an undated letter to Martin Lister, and it was subsequently printed as a broadsheet.

36 Ibid., ff. 76 et seqq. Many of these sheets of printed queries have the replies from the Welsh clergy and others written in the frequently quite inadequate spaces provided. The details of antiquities are usually very vague, if given at all.

37 For an admirable study, D. E. Allen, *The Naturalist in Britain* (1976).

38 'All over England the appreciation of scenery, the experiencing of romantic emotions, and the perception of the sublime in nature, increased in direct ratio to the number of turnpike acts' (C. Hussey, *The Picturesque*, 101). To this one might add, the investigation of ancient monuments in the field.

39 R. Gale, *Tour through several Parts of England 1705*, printed in a revised form of 1730 by Nichols, *Bibl. Top. Brit.*, vol iii.

40 *Itinerarium Septentrionale* (1726), preface.

41 *Hist. Druids* (1814 edn), 134.

42 Quotations from *Lincolnshire: a Poem* (Anon 1720). This is in fact a pirated version, with a change of place-names etc., of William Diaper's poem *Brent*, evidently from an MS copy, as *Brent* was not published (in Curll's *Miscellanea*) until 1727. (Information from Miss Dorothy Broughton.)

43 A remarkably full account of Stukeley's childhood is contained in his *Commentarys* (1720), published in SS i. 1–48 (see note 426 below), and quotations in the ensuing section are from this unless otherwise documented.

44 Bodl. Mus. e. 33.

45 W. Stukeley to A. Pimlow, 17 Apr. 1705 (SS i. 142–4 – see note 426 below).

46 Bodl. MS Eng. misc. e. 135, f. 8. This is from an entry in his diary of 1754 when he was making a sentimental pilgrimage to Cambridge and recalling his undergraduate days.

47 Cf. *Englishmen at Rest and Play*, ed. R. Lennard (1931), for a discussion of river-bathing in the late seventeenth century.

48 For Vigani, see H. S. Peele in *Camb. Ant. Soc. Comms.* xxxiv (1934), 34–9.

49 L. T. More, *Isaac Newton* (1934), 252.

50 John Stukeley to William Stukeley, 14 Dec. 1705 (SS i. 144).

51 John Stukeley to William Stukeley, 14 Jan. 1705/6 (SS i. 145).

52 For 'keeping Acts' and the attendant ceremonies on degree conferring, see C. Wordsworth, *Scholae Academicae* (1877), *passim.*

53 Bodl. MS Top. gen. e. 61.

54 For Richard Mead cf. *Dict. Nat. Biog.* s.v.

55 Bodl. MS Eng. misc. e. 121, ff. 26, 28.

56 For Maurice Johnson, see *Dict. Nat. Biog.* s.v., and Nichols, *Illus. and Lit. Anec. passim.* For the Gentlemen's Society of Spalding, *Lit. Anec.* vi. 1 ff.;

H. J. J. Winter, 'Scientific Associations of the Spalding Gents. Soc. . . . 1710–1750', in *Archives Internat. d'Hist des Sciences* no. 10 (1950), 77; D. M. Owen (ed.) *The Minute Books of the Spalding Gentlemen's Society 1712–1755* (Lincoln Record Soc. 1981).

57 Spalding Gentlemen's Society, Minute Book, vol. i.

58 Johnson to Stukeley, 6 Apr. 1714 (Bodl. MS Eng. misc. c. 113, f. 225).

59 The *Iter Boreale* of 1725 was published posthumously in the second edition (1776) of the *Itinerarium*.

60 Bodl. MS Top. gen. e. 61, f. 85 rev. ff. All quotations dealing with this tour are from this source unless otherwise documented.

61 The attribution of both buildings is complex but Henry Bell (1647–1711) seems to have been mainly responsible, together with Edward Edwards in 1677–88 (H. M. Colvin, *Biog. Dict. British Architects 1600–1840* (2nd edn 1978), 105, 214).

62 *It. Cur.* I, 44–5

63 *Oxoniensia* II (1937), 74.

64 A. Burl, *Stone Circles of the British Isles* (1976), 292; G. Lambrick, *The Rollright Stones* (1983).

65 *It. Cur.* I, 51–61 (*Iter Cimbricum*).

66 Quoted by R. A. Aubin, *Topographical Poetry in XVIIIth Century England* (1936), 202. This splendid confusion reminds one of Payne Knight on the origin of Gothic architecture, 'manifestly a corruption of the sacred architecture of the Greeks and Romans, which is formed out of a combination of Egyptian, Persian and Hindoo' (*Enquiry into the Principles of Taste* (ed. 1805), 162).

67 For the sale catalogue of Stukeley's library, 1766, see *Sale Catalogues of Eminent Persons: 10, Antiquaries*, ed. S. Piggott (1974), 419–62.

68 *It. Cur.* 1–34.

69 For the Car Dyke in Cambridgeshire, see J. G. D. Clark, *Antiq. Journ.* xxix (1949), 145; in Lincolnshire, Phillips in *Antiquity*, v (1931), 106; *Arch. Journ.* xci (1934), 118.

70 Stukeley to Maurice Johnson, 19 May 1714 (Gents. Soc. Spalding MSS).

71 Stukeley to Maurice Johnson, 6 June 1716 (ibid.).

72 For the Camden engravings of Stonehenge, see E. H. Stone, *Stonehenge* (1924), 147–8.

73 Stukeley to Maurice Johnson, 29 Nov. 1719 (Gents. Soc. Spalding MSS). He had visited Stonehenge for the first time on 18 May 1719 with Roger and Samuel Gale (Gough Maps 33, f. 2ᵛ).

74 See below, p. 152.

75 Cf. W. T. Whitley, *Artists and their Friends in England, 1700–1799* (1928), i. 28.

76 For the Gales, *Dict. Nat. Biog.* s.v. Thomas, Roger, and Samuel Gale; Nichols, *Illus. and Lit. Anec., passim*; 'Reliquae Galeanae' in *Bibl. Top Brit.* iii.

77 David C. Douglas, *English Scholars*, 221.

78 Stukeley, as a fellow Lincolnshire man, became on very friendly terms with Newton, and in 1752 wrote *Memoirs of Sir Isaac Newton's Life*, the original manuscript of which is now in the possession of the Royal Society (App. xxxvi), and was published under the original title, edited by A. Hastings White, in 1936. In the library of The Spalding Gentleman's Society, in a volume of manuscript collections made by John Nichols, is Stukeley's original letter written to Mead from Grantham on 16 June 1727, giving reminiscences and a pedigree of Newton. It is to Stukeley that we owe the first authentic record of the story of Newton's discovery of gravitation by observing a falling apple.

79 Joan Evans, *A History of the Society of Antiquaries* (1956).

80 Ibid., vi. 1 et seqq. (Maurice Johnson to Ducarel, 4 Feb. 1754); SS i. 181; Ellis, *Letters of Eminent Literary Men* (Camden Soc. 1843), 100–2. Douglas, op. cit., 131–3.

81 Society of Antiquaries MS 265 is a minute-book and record of exhibits made by Stukeley in 1719, and contains

various drawings of antiquities. There is also a list of eighty-three of the earlier members with their autograph signatures, including Stukeley as secretary, Roger Gale, Thomas Rawlinson, George Vertue, Maurice Johnson, William Warburton, Humphrey Wanley, Isaac Whood, Alexander Gordon, Lords Winchelsea and Hertford, and White Kennet. This list must date from c.1725–30. The first of the formal minute-books (vol. i) is in Stukeley's hand up to 1725.

82 Kirkall to Stukeley, 17 Nov. 1725 (Bodl. MS Eng. misc. c. 114, f. 2).

83 For the decline of English historical studies after about 1730, cf. Douglas, op. cit., chap. xiii.

84 Douglas, op. cit., 70.

85 John Aubrey to Anthony Wood, 3 Dec. 1692 (Bodl. MS Tanner 456, f. 41). In Thomas Gale's copy of the 1610 edition of Camden's *Britannia* (Bodl. Gough. gen. top. 51) there are various manuscript notes derived from Aubrey's information, for example: 'At Wayland Smyth near ye white horse in Berkshire and at Luckington in Wiltsh. are to be seen certain vaulted houses. J. Aubury', on fly-leaf at end of volume. (The reference is to the chambered tombs of Wayland's Smithy, Berks., and Giant's Cave, Luckington; T. C. Darvill, *Megalithic Chambered Tombs of the Cotswold–Severn Region* (1982)).

86 Michael Hunter, op. cit.; a very unsatisfactory edition of the *Monumenta Britannica* has been published, edd. J. Fowles and R. Legg, I (1980); II (1982)

87 Aubrey to Wood, 7 Mar. 1679/80 (Bodl. MS Tanner 456, f. 23).

88 Aubrey to Wood, 19 May 1692 (Bodl. MS Tanner 456, f. 40).

89 Bodl. Wood 658, f. 780.

90 Thomas Warton, *Life . . . of Ralph Bathurst D.D.* (1761), 150–1. I am indebted to Dr E. A. O. Whiteman for drawing my attention to this reference.

91 I am indebted to the Librarian of Trinity College, Cambridge, for searching among the Gale MSS which were bequeathed by Gale to Trinity in 1744.

92 This manuscript is now in the Library of the Wilts. Archaeological and Natural History Society at Devizes and is cited in ensuing pages as 'Devizes MS' or 'Devizes Common-place Book'.

93 Devizes MS f. 37.

94 e.g. ff. 29 and 31.

95 SS iii. 273, quoting from Journal.

96 *Abury*, p. 24.

97 I. Smith, *Windmill Hill and Avebury* (1965); A. Burl, *Prehistoric Avebury* (1979).

98 Bodl. MS Top. gen. e. 61, f. 49^v.

99 Devizes MS, f. 41.

100 For the evolution of the Bath Road, see *Wessex from the Air* (1928), 235 and fig. 57. By 1772 the road had been moved to run a mile south of the Avebury circles, and the Catherine Wheel Inn, where Stukeley had stayed, was shut up for want of custom. (John Whittaker to Dr Ducarel, 13 June 1772: Nichols, *Illus.* IV, 855).

101 Camden's *Britannia*, first English trans. 1610.

102 *Abury*, 15.

103 Bodl. MS Eng. misc. c. 323, f. 173.

104 Thomas Hearne, *Collections* (Oxford Hist. Soc.), VII, 37.

105 R. Gale to Arthur Charlett, 13 Oct. 1719 (Bodl. MS Rawlinson A. 275, f. 110).

106 W. S. to Roger Gale, 12 July 1719 (*Reliq. Galeanae*, ii, pt 1, 112).

107 B. M. Fagan, *Antiq.* XXXIII (1959), 279.

108 M. I. Guenebault, *Le Réveil de l'Antique Tombeau de Chyndonax, prince des Vacies, Druides, Celtiques, Dijonnois* (Dijon 1623).

109 T. D. Kendrick, *The Druids* (1927), 20.

110 The Society was instituted on 23 July 1722 (Bodl. MS Eng. misc. e. 121) and survived until 1725. Its minutes were printed in part in *Lincs. Notes and Queries*, Apr. 1909, 177. (Bodl. MS Eng. misc. c. 401.)

111 Nichols, *Lit. Anec.* vi 228; Douglas, op. cit., 133.

112 The list of members in 1722 is as

follows: Lord Pembroke (Carvilius), Lord Winchelsea (Cingetorix), Lord Hertford (Segonax), Roger Gale (Venutius), William Stukeley (Chyndonax), James Hill (Caradocus), Samuel Gale (Cunobelinus), William Hulet (Brennus), Vandergucht (Indutiomarus), J. Pine (Adminius), Thomas Bawtree (Scribonius), J. Warburton (Asclepiodotus), Alexander Gordon (Galgacus), Nicholas Haym (Varro), Sir John Clerk (Agricola), and Maurice Johnson (Prasutagus) (Bodl. MS Eng. misc. c. 401).

113 Dr. Joan Evans suggested to me that the fact that women were admitted to certain Italian 'Academies' of the time may be relevant in this regard.

114 Sir John Clerk to Roger Gale, 12 May 1736 (Clerk Papers). The last phrase evidently pleased Sir John: it is in fact the final line of his long unpublished poem *The Country Seat*, which was written in 1727 and was now being revised after the appropriately Horatian nine years (S. Piggott, 'Sir John Clerk and "The Country Seat"', in H. M. Colvin and J. Harris (edd.) *The Country Seat* (1970), 110). For the changes in the significance of the word 'Gothic' between the 16th and 18th centuries, cf. E. S. de Beer in *Journ. Warburg & Courtauld Insts.* XI (1948), 142; A. O. Lovejoy, 'The first Gothic revival....', *Essays in the History of Ideas* (1948), no. VIII.

115 S. Gale to Stukeley, 3 Aug. 1728 (Bodl. MS Eng. misc. c. 113, f. 137). This was written after Stukeley's marriage in 1727 and, as we have seen, Cartismandua is Mrs Stukeley.

116 Algernon Seymour, Lord Hertford (1684–1739/40), *Complete Peerage*, iv. 227. Segonax is the Kentish princeling *Segovax* of Caesar (*Bell. Gall.* v. 22).

117 Lord Winchelsea to Stukeley, 14 Oct. 1723 (Nichols, *Illus.*, ii. 769 et seqq.). Cyngetorix is again from Caesar's *Cingetorix*, a Belgic prince (*Bell. Gall.* v. 22).

118 Heneage Finch, fifth Earl of Winchelsea (c.1656–1726). His wife Anne was well known for her poems (*Com-*

plete Peerage, viii. 179).

119 Lord Winchelsea to Stukeley, 1 Jan. 1723/4 (Nichols, loc. cit.)

120 From the same to the same, 27 Dec. 1722 (Nichols, loc. cit.).

121 Bodl. MS Eng. misc. d. 459.

122 Lord Winchelsea to Stukeley, 26 Oct. 1723 (Nichols, loc. cit.). Julaber's Grave is a Neolithic long barrow near Chilham (*Antiq. Journ.*, xvii (1937), 122; xix (1939), 260).

123 *Poems* (London, ed. 1800), I, 138.

124 A copy of the printed Ode with this manuscript footnote is pasted into the MS History of the Society of Antiquaries written by Stukeley in 1760 (Bodl. MS Eng. misc. e. 396). Ramsay had probably received his archaeological details from Sir John Clerk, who visited Stonehenge in 1727 and had evidently discussed it with Stukeley (*Journey to London 1727* (Clerk Papers); *Memoirs*, ed. Scottish Hist. Soc. 1892, 128).

125 H. M. Colvin, op. cit., 29.

126 W. Stukeley, *An Account of a Roman Temple and other Antiquities near Grahams-Dike in Scotland* (1720). In the Haverfield Library of the Ashmolean Museum in Oxford is a set of proofs of this pamphlet, with copious annotations by Stukeley. For Jelfe, H. M. Colvin, op. cit. 456.

127 K. A. Steer, *Arch. Journ.* CXV (1960), 99; I. G. Brown, *Antiq.* XLVIII (1974), 283.

128 Steer, loc. cit. 109.

129 The house at Penicuik (gutted by fire in 1899) and the stables were all built to Sir James's designs, the drawings for which still survive (H. M. Colvin, op. cit., 220).

130 W. Stukeley, *Essay towards the Anatomy of the Elephant* (1723).

131 Hearne, *Collections*, ix. 99.

132 Avebury drawings dated 16 Aug. 1723 in Bodl. MS Top. gen. d. 13, ff. 7^v, 8; Stonehenge, ibid., f. 9.

133 *It. Cur.* 63.

134 Ibid., 67. Hardly a confession for a Roman Knight to make!

135 Ibid., 72.

136 Diary, 23 July 1722 (SS iii. 273).

137 *Dict. Nat. Biog.* s.v.

138 Ibid.; Whitley, *Artists and their Friends . . . passim.*

139 Bodl. MS Eng. misc. e. 136, f. 34.

140 Bodl. Gough Maps 231, f. 244.

141 Ibid., f. 225.ᵛ

142 Maurice Johnson to Peter le Neve, 5 July 1746. Nichols, *Bibl. Top. Brit.* iii.

143 Reproduced in *Antiq.* x (1936), pl. VI opp. 424.

144 Hearne, *Collections,* x. 187 (entry of 13 Oct. 1729).

145 The Stonehenge engravings are on the whole less successful than those of Avebury: several engravers, many anonymous, worked on Stukeley's plates.

146 The itinerary of this tour can be reconstructed from the dated plates in the *Itinerarium* and drawings in Bodl. MSS Top. gen. b. 53, Top. eccles. d. 6, and Gen. top. d. 14.

147 *It. Cur.* 77.

148 Ibid. 87–8.

149 Ibid. 83.

150 Ibid. 99.

151 Ibid. 115.

152 Reconstructed from the published text and dated plates in the *Itinerarium* with a few drawings in Bodl. MS Top. eccles. d. 6 and Top. gen. d. 14.

153 Lord Winchelsea to Stukeley, 12 July 1723 (Nicholas, *Illus.* ii. 769 ff.; SS iii. 244).

154 For Strachey, see below, p. 82. An account of the Stanton Drew circles was written in 1723 as 'The Weddings', but not published until the posthumous 1776 edition of the *Itinerarium.*

155 A. Burl, *Stone Circles of the British Isles* (1976), 105.

156 This note was written *c.*1740 by Stukeley inside the cover of the attempted catalogue (Bodl. MS Top. Wilts. e. 6).

157 *It. Cur.* 163.

158 Ibid. 189.

159 In *Abury* (1743), *passim.*

160 For Poundbury, see B. Cunliffe, *Iron Age Communities in Britain* (1974), 232.

161 *It. Cur.* 141.

162 Ibid. 188.

163 *It. Cur.* 189, *Stonehenge, passim.* These views were adopted by Edwin Guest in the 1850s (*Arch. Journ.* viii (1851), 143) more or less without acknowledgment of their source.

164 D. Bonney, 'Early boundaries in Wessex', in P. J. Fowler (ed.) *Archaeology and the Landscape* (1972), 168.

165 Bodl. MS Eng. misc b. 65.

166 *Arch. Journ.* xcix (1943), 22. In one instance in south Wales it was possible to prove geologically that all the materials of a Bronze Age cairn on a false crest were derived from the side from which it was sited.

167 *It. Cur.* 130.

168 M. Guido & I. F. Smith, *Wilts. Arch. Mag.* LXXVI (1982), 21.

169 *It. Cur.* 130.

170 Ibid. 181.

171 For Ogbury and its fields, see *Wessex from the Air,* 150; for prehistoric fields in general, P. J. Fowler in S. Piggott (ed.), *Agrarian History of England & Wales* I.i. (1981), 63.

172 For Stukeley's Masonic career, see Gould in *Ars Quatuor Coronatorum,* vi; A. M. Broadley, *The Visit of W. Bro. Dr. W. Stukeley to Dorchester* (privately printed, Weymouth 1913). Broadley reprints Stukeley's account of the amphitheatre from a copy in the British Library: it was reproduced in facsimile by the Quatuor Coronati Lodge in 1925.

173 R. Bradley, *Archaeologia* CV (1976), 1.

174 *It. Cur.* 193.

175 *Antiquity,* VII (1933), 290.

176 Diary, 20 Dec. 1723 (SS ii. 72).

177 Douglas, *English Scholars,* 338.

178 He remained so until 1726, when he left London (Nichols, *Lit. Anec.* v. 333). Alexander Gordon succeeded him.

179 Soc. Antiqs. Minute Book I, 3 Jan. 1721/2; 1 Apr. 1722; 30 May 1722. Nichols, *Lit. Anec.* vi. 157; D. F. Allen, *Numis. Chron.* 7th s. x (1970), 117.

180 *Abstract of my Life* (SS i. 51).

181 *Diary of Ralph Thoresby 1677–1724* (ed. Hunter 1830), ii. 323, 359, 380.

182 The tour is reconstructed from these and dated drawings in Bodl. MSS Top. eccles. d. 6; Top. gen. d. 14; Top. gen. b. 53.

183 Hearne, *Collections*, viii. 4.

184 Ibid. 265.

185 Published in *It. Cur.* Tab. 61, opp. p. 177.

186 *Memoirs* (Scottish Hist. Soc. 1892), 122.

187 Richard Willis to Stukeley, 18 September 1750 (Bodl. MS Eng. misc. c. 114, f. 323).

188 Richard Willis to Stukeley, 11 July 1760 (ibid., f. 325).

189 Stukeley planned a *Centuria II*, of which an incomplete draft dated 1760 exists (Soc. Ant. MS 494 (2)), but this was neither completed nor published. The *Centuria II* published posthumously in 1776 contains many additional plates.

190 Hearne, *Collections*, VIII, 383.

191 Ibid. 350, 357; IX, 15.

192 Ibid., 23.

193 Published as 'Iter Boreale' in the 1776 edition of the *Itinerarium*. The original MS of the journal is in Bodl. MS Eng. misc. e. 384.

194 *It. Cur.* II, 41.

195 *It. Cur.* 48. Potted char had been recognized as an attraction of the Lake District since the time of Celia Fiennes's visit in the late seventeenth century, but the appreciation of the romantic elements in the landscape seems not to date before the late 30s of the eighteenth (cf. C. Hussey, *The Picturesque*, 97).

196 For the stone circles of Long Meg and Keswick, see A. Burl, *Stone Circles of the British Isles* (1976), 55. Avenues at Shap may have existed, but the site is much destroyed and scattered over a wide area. Stukeley wrote up a separate account of Shap in *c.*1750–60, embodying his 'serpentine' theories (Bodl. MS Eng. misc. e. 389). Cf. Crawford in *Antiq.* VIII (1934), 328 for the accuracy of the Long Meg drawings.

197 *It. Cur.* II. 76–7.

198 He wrote on a sketch of the hills near Wye in Kent, 'The last of my expeditions', with the date 28 May 1726, but this must be an error for 1725 when he was in this part of Kent between 24 May and 5 June (Soc. Ant. Lond. Roman Prints, iii).

199 In his retrospective journal of this period of his life he refers to the 'irresistible impulse' that prompted him to leave London, and makes an odd reference to the decision being made as he gazed one night at the Milky Way (SS i. 77).

200 This horse was so named from his being 'a Roman squire, under the appellative and title of Squire Dick' and so a junior member of the Society of Roman Knights (Stukeley to S. Gale, 6 Feb. 1726/7; SS i. 190).

201 Stukeley to S. Gale, 6 Feb. 1726/7 (SS i. 188).

202 *Journey to London in 1727* (Clerk Papers).

203 Sir John Clerk to R. Gale, 11 June 1726 (*recte* 1727) (*Bibl. Top Brit.* iii, *Reliq. Galeanae*, p. 241).

204 Bodleian MS Top. Wilts. c. 4, f. 2.

205 *Vertue Notebooks*, Walpole Soc. xx (1932), 31.

206 R. Gale to Stukeley, 6 Feb. 1727/8 (SS i. 200–2). A self-portrait of Stukeley and his wife Frances is in Bodl. MS Eng. misc. d. 452 and is reproduced in *Antiquity* IX (1935), pl. i, opp. p. 22.

207 Stukeley to S. Gale, 14 Oct. 1728 (SS i. 208).

208 Stukeley to Sir Hans Sloane, 24 Sept 1729: (Nichols, *Illus.* ii. 769 et seqq.).

209 Stukeley to ?, 4 Feb. 1728 (Nichols, *Bibl. Top. Brit.* iii, twenty-fifth letter in the Stukeley group – the pagination of the book precludes a page citation).

210 e.g. R. Gale to Stukeley, 7 Dec. 1726 (SS i. 186); Warburton to Stukeley, 10 Feb. 1732/3 (Nichols, *Illus.* II. 1 et seqq.).

211 Stukeley to S. Gale, 6 Feb. 1727 (SS i. 190). Sir John Clerk implies that he was working on a book incorporating the Avebury and Stonehenge material in 1733 (see p. 111).

212 Hearne, *Collections*, x. 339. Entry of 3 Oct. 1730.

213 S. Piggott, in *I Celti e loro cultura* ... (Accad. Naz. dei Lincei, Quaderno 237 (1978), 37.)

214 S. Piggott, *The Druids* (1975); A. L. Owen, *The Famous Druids* (1962).

215 S. Piggott, *Sale Catalogues of Eminent Persons*, 10 (1974), 419. The sale was held at Essex House for five successive evenings, and the catalogue lists 1,121 items, mainly printed books, but about fifty manuscripts, including many of Stukeley's notes and drawings of antiquities. Some of these were presumably acquired by Gough in due course and from him have come to the Bodleian.

216 For a complete bibliography of Stonehenge and Avebury to 1901, see W. J. Harrison in *Wilts. Arch. Mag.* xxxii (1901), 1–169.

217 Paschal to John Aubrey, 2 Dec. 1689 (*Miscellanies on Several Curious Subjects*, 1714, 18–19).

218 In the Devizes MS Stukeley has copied a plan of Stanton Drew 'As represented by Dr. Musgrave from Mr. Strachey': this plan is published in Musgrave's book, vol. i, pl. xiv (opp. 209).

219 *Dict. Nat. Biog.* i. 515–16; British Library Stowe MSS 1023, 1024. Anstis is, unfortunately, mainly remembered by Lord Chesterfield's exasperated outburst – 'You foolish man, you don't even know your own foolish business!'

220 Lhuyd's MSS apparently comprised at least 40 folios, 10 quartos, and over 100 smaller books of notes and drawings. They were offered at his death to Jesus College, Oxford, and the University, but were refused owing to a quarrel among the personalities concerned. The Irish manuscripts are now in Trinity College, Dublin, and certain Welsh manuscripts passed into Lord Macclesfield's library in the eighteenth century. The remainder were sold at Sotheby's in 1807 and were largely destroyed after purchase by a fire at the binder's at which they were lodged (*Dict. Nat. Biog.* s.v.; *Gents. Mag.* 1807, i. 419).

221 *Allgemeine Deutsche Biographie*, xv (1882), 702; P. H. Stemmermann, *Die Anfänge der Deutschen Vorgeschichtsforschung ... 16 u. 17. Jahrhunderts* (1934), 109 et seqq. Stukeley has in the Devizes MS drawings copied from 'my friend Mr. Keysler's book'.

222 *Dict. Nat. Biog.* xix. 918 and the Life prefixed to Huddleston's edition of the *History of the Druids* (1814) are the main published sources for Toland's life. There are, however, considerable unpublished MS sources for his earlier life and his stay in Oxford in 1694 in Bodl. MSS Tanner 25; Ballard 27; Rawlinson 923, 377, 401. Quotations from some of these with detailed references are given below. See also Ellis, *Letters of Eminent Literary Men* (Camden Soc. 1843), 226–30.

223 The story is often quoted – for example, Abbey and Overton, *English Church in the XVIII Century*, i. 183, with reference to Hunt, *Religious Thought in England*, ii. 244.

224 Stukeley to R. Gale, 25 June 1730 (SS iii. 267).

225 *Dict. Nat. Biog.* xix. 918.

226 These letters are mainly in Tanner MS 25 and have, of course, been drawn upon, with the other Bodleian MS sources for Gibson's life, by Professor Norman Sykes in his *Edmund Gibson* (1926), especially chap. i.

227 Gibson to Tanner 12 Apr. 1694 (MS Tanner 25, f. 134).

228 Gibson to Charlett 9 Apr. 1694 (MS Ballard 5, f. 27).

229 Gibson to Tanner 20 Apr. 1694; ibid. 26 Apr. 1694 (MS Tanner 25, ff. 138, 140).

230 Gibson to Tanner 22 May 1694 (MS Tanner 25, f. 154).

231 Toland, *Hist. Druids.* (1814 edn), 159; John Britton *Memoir of John Aubrey* (1845), 6–7.

232 This is in the British Library (c. 45, c.1), and there is also a complete transcript of the original notes in the Bodleian (Gough Scotland 185), made by Joseph Ames (1689–1759), an antiquary and 'deist by conversation', into a copy

of the second (1716) edition of Martin's work. Gough acquired this book from Ames's library, but the original, in the British Library, was in the sale of Dr Mead's library in 1755. (See Nichols, *Lit. Anec.* v. 263.) The marginalia are initialled 'J.T.' or 'L.M.' and there is a prefatory note by Toland dated Putney, September 1720, with a postscript of 21 Oct. 1721.

233 M. Martin, *A Description of the Western Islands of Scotland* (1703), 365.

234 *History of the Druids* (1814), 138.

235 Entry in Diary 12 May 1729 (SS ii, 302).

236 Gough Maps 231, f. 22.

237 Stukeley to Ambrose Pimlow, 18 Aug 1729 (SS i, 223)

238 Bodl. MS Eng. misc. c. 323.

239 SS i. 227.

240 Devizes MS f. 6.

241 Available in Zwicker, *Fontes Religionis Celticae* (Berlin 1934).

242 *Nero Caesar or Monarchie depraved. An Historical Work* (1624), 181. This work was published anonymously. Gibson in his edition of Camden gave a summary of these and other views that had been held on Stonehenge during the seventeenth century (*Britannia*, 1695 edn, p. 108).

243 *Natural History of Staffordshire* (1686).

244 Bodl. MS Eng. misc. c. 323; Cardiff Public Library MS 4.253.

245 Bodl. Gough Maps 231, f. 127.

246 T. Twining, *Avebury in Wiltshire, the Remains of a Roman Work* . . . (1723). The book was dedicated to Lord Winchelsea and demonstrated that Avebury was a Roman temple to Terminus. The great circle had been added by Agricola in commemoration of his having sailed round the Orkneys.

247 Samuel Bowden, *Antiquities and Curiosities in Wiltshire and Somerset,* 1733, quoted by R. A. Aubin, *Topographical Poetry in XVIII century England* (New York 1936), 198. For Hearne's view, cf. his *Collections*, x, 187.

248 *Nat. Hist.* xxxv. 14 (49). Genera

eorum fiunt tria – Lydion, quo nos utimur . . . longum sesquipedem, latum pedem. . . .

249 William Stukeley, *Account of a Roman Temple* . . . (1720), 18.

250 *Stonehenge*, 6.

251 Stukeley to Roger Gale, 26 July 1723 (SS iii, 249–50). He was also helped in his Stonehenge surveys by his friend Henry Flitcroft, the builder and architect. (Bodl. Gough Maps 229, f. 139.)

252 *Stonehenge*, 15. He also experimented with a 'Celtic Foot' as a unit – cf. *It. Cur.* II, pls. 81, 83.

253 F. E. Manuel, *Isaac Newton Historian* (1963), 161, 294.

254 D. C. Heggie, *Megalithic Science* (1981); A. Burl, *Prehistoric Avebury* (1979), 150; C. Chippindale, *Stonehenge Complete* (1983), 137.

255 R. J. C. Atkinson, *Stonehenge* (1979); Royal Comm. Hist. Mons. (England), *Stonehenge and its Environs* (1979); C. Chippindale, *Stonehenge Complete* (1983).

256 *Stonehenge* (1740), 35.

257 First published by O. G. S. Crawford in *The Observer* July 22, 1923, later in *Antiq. Journ.* IV (1924). See also *Air Survey and Archaeology* (1924), 13 and *Wessex from the Air* (1928), 222.

258 Royal Comm. Hist. Mons. (England), *A Matter of Time* (1960), 24, with list and map to which many additions could now be made.

259 Both quotations from *Stonehenge*, 44.

260 Gough Maps 229, f. 45.

261 We may compare the instructions in a Council of Nantes in the late ninth century – *lapides quoque, quos in ruinosis locis et silvestribus, daemonum ludificationibus decepti venerantur, ubi et vota vovent et deferunt, funditus effodiantur, atque in tali loco projiciantur, ubi nunquam a cultoribus suis inveniri possint.* (Council of uncertain date, but assigned by Mansi to *c.*896: *Sacr. Concil. Coll.* xviii (1902), 172; quoted by Thurnam in *Arch.* XLII. 242.)

262 Gough Maps 231, f. 5; reproduced in

Antiquity, X (1936), pl. vi between p. 424–5.

263 Bodl. Gough Maps 231, f. 25ᵛ.

264 The original drawing for this is in Bodl. MS Eng. misc. b. 65.

265 Gough Maps 231, f. 22.

266 The Solar and Lunar temple theory was developed in some detail in Stukeley's account of the stone circles at Stanton Drew in Somerset, written in March 1723/4 and published posthumously in the second edition of the *Itin. Cur.* (1776), 169–77. The original is in Bodl. MS Eng. misc. c. 321.

267 *Wilts. Arch. Mag.* XLV (1931), 300. The site was identified from Stukeley's drawings used on the ground. For recent interpretation, I. F. Smith, *Windmill Hill and Avebury* (1965), 244.

268 Bodl. MS Eng. misc. d. 452, no. 62. I discussed this sequence of ideas at Avebury at greater length in *Antiq.* IX (1935), 22.

269 H. R. Ellis Davidson, *Gods and Myths of Northern Europe* (1964), 94, 106.

270 *Danicorum Monumentorum Libri Sex*, 12.

271 Bodl. Gough Maps 231, f. 9ᵛ and f. 54ᵛ.

272 Lord Winchelsea to Stukeley, 12 July 1723 (SS iii, 244)

273 Stukeley to Roger Gale, 22 July 1723 (SS iii, 246).

274 I. F. Smith, *Windmill Hill and Avebury*, 217; A. Burl, *Prehistoric Avebury*, 191.

275 Bodl. MS Eng. misc. b. 65.

276 Bodl. MS Eng. misc. d 452.

277 Bodl. Gough Maps 131, f. 9ᵛ and f. 54ᵛ.

278 Devizes MS, f. 46.

279 Stukeley to Abp. Wake, 3 June 1729 (SS i. 216).

280 Abp. Wake to Stukeley, 10 June 1729 (SS i. 217).

281 For this, cf. especially Professor Norman Sykes's comments in *Church and State in the XVIII century in England, passim*.

282 Stukeley to Abp. Wake, 25 June 1729 (SS i. 221).

283 Abp. Wake to Stukeley, 3 July 1729 (SS i. 221).

284 Stukeley to Abp. Wake, 6 July 1729 (Rawlinson MS A 275, f. 110). This letter is in a volume of Wake correspondence which seems to have strayed from the remainder of the Wake papers in the Library of Christ Church, Oxford. By the courtesy of the Wake Trustees, through the then Librarian, Mr J. N. L. Myres, I examined these, but could trace no additional papers relating to Stukeley's ordination. The originals of the letters published in the Surtees Society's volume are now in the Bodleian, MS Eng. misc. c. 114.

285 R. Gale to Stukeley, 14 June 1729 (SS i. 219).

286 Hearne, *Collections*, x. 165.

287 Referred to in Abp. Wake to Stukeley, 26 Sept. 1729 (SS i. 225).

288 Stukeley to Sir Hans Sloane, 24 Sept. 1729 (Nichols, *Illus*, ii, 769 et seqq.).

289 Bodleian MS Eng. misc. e. 121.

290 Stukeley to Mrs Stukeley, 16 Oct. 1729 (SS i. 225).

291 B. Willey, *The Eighteenth Century Background* (1940); A. O. Lovejoy, 'The Parallel of Deism and Classicism' in *Essays in the History of Ideas* (1948), no. VI; S. Piggott, *The Druids* (1975), 151.

292 For this summary, cf. J. M. S. Tompkins in *Review Eng. Studies* XXII (1946), 1; E. B. Hungerford, *Shores of Darkness* (1941), 67.

293 Conveniently available to Stukeley in *Opera Omnia*, 3 vols, 1712. His two main works were *Geographia Sacra* (1646–7) and *Hierozoicon* (1663), the first dealing with the dispersion of mankind after the Flood and the second with the primeval language used by Adam to name the beasts.

294 Under the title of *De Antiquitatibus Insulae Monae* it was seen by Richard Richardson, a correspondent of Hearne's. (S. Briggs, *Antiq. Journ.* LVIII (1978), 250). For Rowlands, C. L. Hulbert-Powell, *Trans. Anglesey Ant. Soc.* 1953, 21.

295 This view was solemnly reiterated in 1865 by the Rev. Samuel Lysons in his book, *Our British Ancestors*, in which the Neolithic chambered tombs of the Costwolds are called in as witnesses.

296 *Delphi Phoenicizantes* (1655)

297 J. M. S. Tompkins, *Review of English Studies* XXII (1946), 1; S. Piggott, *The Druids* (1975).

298 *Hist. Druids* (1814 edn.), 59.

299 In addition to J. M. S. Tompkin's and E. B. Hungerford's works already referred to, see Ruthven Todd, *Tracks in the Snow* (1946), 47 et seqq.

300 Stukeley to R. Gale, 25 June 1730 (SS iii. 266). Gale found this information 'new and surprising' and felt that 'it promises at the same time both the utile and the dulce'. (R. Gale to Stukeley, 30 June 1730 (SS i. 237).)

301 Mr Howard Colvin points out to me that Stukeley's imaginary reconstructions of Solomon's Temple in Bodl. Gough Maps 41°, ff. 74–5, make it look curiously like an eighteenth-century church!

302 Cf. *Dict. Nat. Biog.* s.v. Richard Mead.

303 *Stonehenge* (1740), preface.

304 Ibid.

305 David C. Douglas, *English Scholars* (1939), 356, 361.

306 See p. 86 and p. 111.

307 *Abury* (1743), 64.

308 *Antiquity*, IX (1935), 31, with reproductions of the relevant drawings.

309 Commonplace Book, SS i, 77, 107.

310 SS i, 105.

311 F. E. Manuel, *Isaac Newton Historian* (1963); *A Portrait of Isaac Newton* (1968).

312 *Stonehenge* (1740), 66. Edmund Halley, Astronomer Royal, helped Stukeley here.

313 Stukeley to S. Gale, 24 Dec. 1739 (SS i. 226). The original slip of paper with these titles written out is in the library of the Spalding Gentlemen's Society.

314 William Stukeley, *An Account of a Large Silver Plate . . .* (London 1736). In the Bodleian copy (Douce S. 501) is a

letter to Stukeley from an unknown correspondent dated 2 Dec. 1729 on the inscription on the plate. For a modern account of the find, C. Johns, *Antiq. Journ.* LXI (1981), 53.

315 Letters between Stukeley and Warburton from 1722 to 1764 are printed by Nichols, *Illus*, II, 1 et seqq.

316 Corpus Christi Coll. Cambridge MSS 618, 619.

317 'A Toure into England in the year 1733' (Clerk Papers).

318 Sir John Clerk to Roger Gale, 11 June 1733 (*Memoirs*, ed. Scottish Hist. Soc. (1892), 142 n.).

319 Cf. A. L. Owen, *The Famous Druids* (1962), 129.

320 Bodleian MS Eng. misc. e. 122. For the Brasenose knocker, cf. C. E. Mallett *Hist. Univ. Oxford*, i (1924), 157.

321 Stukeley to Maurice Johnson, 15 Feb. 1728–9 (Spalding Gentlemen's Soc. MSS).

322 The blank books destined for the minutes of the Brazen Nose Society and afterwards used by Stukeley for his own Journal are Bodleian MSS Eng. misc. e. 122–40.

323 Stukeley to S. Gale, 2 Feb. 1737/8 (SS i. 299).

324 R. Gale to Stukeley, 5 May 1738 (SS i. 300).

325 For Mrs Stukeley's marriage portion, see newscutting in Bodl. MS Eng. misc. c.314, dated 13 Jan 1739 – 'a Lady of great Beauty, and a fortune of 10,000 l.' The marriage took place in Gray's Inn Chapel. For gossip, J. Whitaker, *Hist. of Richmondshire* (1823), II, 71. I am indebted to Mr Cyril Preston for this reference.

326 Bodl. Gough Maps 230, f. 411.

327 *Flowers of Parnassus* (1736), 82, quoted by R. A. Aubin, 'Grottoes, Geology and the Gothic Revival', in *Studies in Philology* XXI (1934) 408; J. D. Hunt, *The Figure in the Landscape* (1976); P. Willis, 'Charles Bridgeman: the Royal Gardens', in P. Willis (ed.), *Furor Hortensis* (1974), 41; B. Allen, *Country Life* 3 Nov. 1983, 1248. For con-

temporary Gothic, A. O. Lovejoy, *Essays in the History of Ideas* (1948), no. VIII; S. Piggott, *Ruins in a Landscape* (1976).

328 Bodl. MS Eng. misc. e. 122.

329 C. R. Weld, *A History of the Royal Society* (1848), i, 424 et seqq.

330 Stukeley's Commonplace Book (SS i. 98–100). 'Mrs. Bracegirdle' was, in fact, Mrs Lucretia Bradshaw, 'a handsome woman, probably only of second-rate abilities', as the *Dict. Nat. Biog.* article on Folkes crushingly remarks.

331 Sir John Hill, *A Review of the Works of the Royal Society of London* (1751).

332 Stukeley was amoved from the Society of Antiquaries for non-payment of subscriptions in 1740/1 and did not attend meetings again until his re-admission in 1754.

333 Bodl. MS Eng. misc. e. 124, f. 85; J. D. Wortham, *British Egyptology 1549–1906* (1971), 38.

334 Dict. Nat. Biog. s.v.

335 K. Thomas, *Man and the Natural World* (1983), 190, 209; Mrs Arthur Colville, *Duchess Sarah* (1904), 285.

336 *Memoirs of the Duchess of Marlborough*, ed. W. King (1930), 304.

337 *Private Correspondence of Sarah Duchess of Marlborough*, ii (1838), 196.

338 Walpole to Mann, 24 July 1749 (*Letters*, ed. Toynbee, ii, 400).

339 SS i. 114.

340 Bodl. MS Eng. misc. e. 126, f. 30.

341 Ibid., f. 68. This beginning of landscape gardening at Boughton at Stukeley's instance is interesting: Shenstone's Leasowes was laid out in 1745 and Capability Brown was laying out roads in

'. . . that peculiar curve
Alike averse to crooked and to straight
Where sweet Simplicity resides. . . .'

soon after (cf. C. Hussey, *The Picturesque*, 141).

342 William Goodhall to Stukeley, 15 Oct 1742 (SS ii, 196).

343 V. C. H. *Hertfordshire* III, 254, with photographs of the sculpture; S. P.

Beamon & L. G. Donel, *Proc. Cambs. Ant. Soc.* LXVIII (1978), 47.

344 *Place-Names of Hertfordshire* (Eng. Place-Name Soc., vol. xv, 1938), 161. The early forms are against an identification with Roisia wife of Eudo Dapifer. The base of the cross which the early forms of the place-name imply still exists.

345 G. Burton to Stukeley, 30 Apr. 1747 (Bodl. MS Eng. misc. c. 113, ff. 41 et seqq).

346 Bodl. MS Eng. misc. e. 123, f. 78.

347 William Woty, *Church-Langton* (c.1770), quoted by Aubin, *Top. Poetry in XVIIIth Cent. England* (1936), 182: the reference here is, incidentally, not to a medieval building, but to the designs for a grandiose Gothic revival church.

348 For these aspects of the early Gothic revival, cf. Kenneth Clark, *The Gothic Revival, passim*; A. O. Lovejoy, loc. cit. In the discussion of Stukeley's Gothic designs I owe much to conversations with Mr. Howard Colvin and the late Sir John Betjeman.

349 Clark, op. cit. It is interesting to note that Sanderson Miller provided Borlase with notes on Rollright (William Borlase, *Antiquities . . . of Cornwall* (1769), 202).

350 Thomas Eayre to Stukeley, 30 Nov. 1744 (SS i. 368); P. I. King, *Northants Past & Present*, 2, no. 5, (1952), 11.

351 Bodl. MS Top. gen. d. 14, f. 50.

352 Bodl. Gough Maps 230, f. 409.

353 Stukeley to S. Gale, 12 June 1747 (SS i. 390).

354 Bodl. MS Eng. misc. e. 126.

355 Bodl. MS Eng. misc. e. 128, f. 4.

356 Bodl. MS Eng. misc. e. 126, f. 64.

357 K. Thomas, *Man and the Natural World* (1983), 110. Bodl. MS Eng. misc. e. 126, ff. 73–75 contains the whole story of Stukeley's move from Stamford.

358 For earlier accounts of the forgery, H. J. Randall, *Antiq.* VII (1933), 49–60; J. E. B. Mayor, introduction to Richard of Cirencester *Speculum Historiale* (Rolls Series) 1869, vol. ii; A. L. F. Rivet & C. Smith, *Place-names of Roman Britain* (1979), 182. The main sources are Bodl. MS Eng. letters b. 2 (letters from Bertram

to Stukeley 1746–63); MS Top. gen. g. 1 ('transcript' of 'original'); Gough Maps IA, f. 5ᵛ (map). For the vicissitudes of the MSS, cf. *Antiq.* VII (1933), 222. Stukeley's narrative is in his *Account of Richard of Cirencester* (1757).

359 I am indebted to Mr John Griffiths of Jesus College Oxford for establishing this fact.

360 SS iii, 204.

361 For the sources, A. L. F. Rivet & C. Smith, *The Place-names of Roman Britain* (1979), Part I; 'Richard of Cirencester' is discussed 182–4.

362 *In litt.* 19 July 1947.

363 The MS is now in the Royal Library of Denmark (Ny kgl. Saml. 4894 4°) and has been described and illustrated by G. Henningsen, *Skalk* no. 4 (1976), 18; *Geog. Mag.* (June 1978), 594.

364 *Royal Charter and Statutes of the Society of Antiquaries of London* (1946), 5–11.

365 Cf. letter from Charles Godwyn to John Hutchins, 23 Dec. 1763: 'He [Stukeley] sometimes tries the patience of the Antiquarian Society with a dissertation, which never fails of exciting laughter' (Nichols, *Lit. Anec.* viii. 240).

366 *The Downfall of Westminster-Bridge: or My Lord in the Suds. A New Ballad* (n.d.).

367 For the Westminster Bridge controversy, see John Summerson, *Georgian London* (1945), 95–8.

368 John James, *A Short Review of the several Pamphlets and Schemes . . . in relation to Building a Bridge at Westminster* (1736).

369 Anon (but B. L. Catalogue suggests Labelye), *The Present State of Westminster Bridge . . .* (1743).

370 Batty Langley, *A Survey of Westminster Bridge, as 'tis now Sinking into Ruin* (1748).

371 Bodl. MS Eng. misc. e. 127, f. 66ᵛ.

372 *The Medallic History of Carausius*, Book I, 1757, Book II, 1759, and various drafts, &c., in e.g. Bodl. MSS Eng. misc. e. 377; e. 380; d. 442.

373 *Histoire de Carausius, Empereur de la Grande-Bretagne* (Paris 1740).

374 Documented by entry in Journal, Aug. 1750 (Bodl. Eng. misc. e. 128; original sketch of coin on f. 59ᵛ).

375 G. C. Boon, *Numis. Circular* LXXXII (1974), 428.

376 H. Mattingley, *Antiq.*, XIX (1945), 122.

377 D. F. Allen, *Numis. Chron.* 7th S. X (1970), 117.

378 Corpus Christi Coll. Cambridge MSS 613, 614. Cf. Allen loc. cit.

379 *Twenty-three Plates of the Coins of the Ancient British Kings* (n.d.)

380 John Evans, *The Coins of the Ancient Britons* (1864), chap. i.

381 Derek Allen in *Archaeologia*, XC (1944), 20, n. 3.

382 Journal, 3 Oct. 1758 (SS ii. 8). I drew attention to this identification in *Antiquity*, viii (1934), 230. (For the Uffington White Horse, ibid., v (1931), 37–46; M. Marples, *White Horses and other Hill Figures* (1949).)

383 Walpole to Mann, 19 May 1750 (*Letters*, ed. Toynbee, i. 447).

383 Journal, 1753/4 (SS iii. 210–12).

385 Journal, 5 Oct. 1754 (Bodl. MS. Eng. misc. e. 135, f. 14).

386 Bodl. MS. Eng. misc. e. 121, f. 102.

387 The Rev. Cornelius Whur, *Village Musings on Moral and Religious Subjects* (1837).

388 Stukeley to 'Miriam' (Mrs Peirson) 2 Oct. 1754 (SS i. 86–9).

389 One of the two copies of the catalogue of the St Amand bequest in Bodl. Library Records is headed 'The Catalogue taken in September 1754 by Alexander Cruden, M.A.' For Cruden's life, see Edith Olivier, *The Eccentric Life of Alexander Cruden* (1934).

390 Journal (Bodl. MS Eng. misc. e. 135, partly printed in SS iii. 166, 274) and catalogues in Bodl. Library Records.

391 Note in St Amand Catalogue by Stukeley.

392 Bodl. MS Rawlinson Letters 108, f. 223.

393 Edith Olivier, op. cit., p. 175. *Alexander the Corrector's Earnest Ad-*

dress to the Inhabitants of Great Britain (1756), 22.

394 Society of Antiquaries Minutes, 22 Jan. 1740/1; 2 Nov. 1754; 14 Nov. 1754. Despite his amoval, Stukeley is recorded as attending a meeting on 19 Nov. 1741, but he may have come as a guest.

395 Richard Willis to Stukeley, 11 July 1760 (Bodl. MS Eng. misc. c. 114, f. 325).

396 Cf. Weld. *Hist. Roy. Soc.* i. 326.

397 Gray to Rev. James Brown, 8 Aug. 1759 (*Letters*, ed. Tovey (1904), ii. 95). For Gray and the Druids, cf. E. D. Snyder, 'Thomas Gray's interest in Celtic', *Modern Philology*, xx (1914), 559–79; ibid., *The Celtic Revival in English Literature* (Cambridge, Mass. 1923), esp. chap. iii.

398 Bodl. MS Eng. misc. e. 135, ff. 19 et. seqq.

399 Society of Antiquaries MSS.

400 There was in fact no Roman camp at St Pancras, and the earthworks are now destroyed (F. Celoria & B. W. Spencer, *Trans. London & Middlesex Arch. Soc.* XXII, i, (1968), 23).

401 Attention was first drawn to these engravings by Mr E. J. Rudsdale; for Colchester and the earlier surveys of the earthworks (including these), see C. F. C. Hawkes and M. R. Hull, *Camulodunum* (Soc. Ant. Research Committee Reports, 1947), 8. The four letters from Stukeley to Morant in the British Library (Add. MSS 37222, ff. 123, 125, 134, 172) throw no light on these drawings.

402 Journal 1748/9 (Bodl. MS Eng. misc. e. 128)

403 Cf. many essays now in Bodl. MSS Eng. misc. d. 453–7; Royal Society MSS II/13; III/88; IV/69.

404 Journal 30 Oct. 1763 (Bodl. MS Eng. misc. e. 139).

405 Bodl. MS Eng. misc. e. 379.

406 For the Vegetable Sermons, see Weld, *Hist. Royal Soc.* I, passim. Cf. K. Thomas, *Man and the Natural World* (1983): the sentiments implicit in their foundation suggest comparison with Harvey's *Meditations in a Garden* (1746).

407 This is a name taken from Tacitus (*Germ.* VIII). She was a Germanic tribal leader.

408 J. S. Smart, *James Macpherson, an episode in literature* (1905).

409 *A Letter from Dr Stukeley to Mr Macpherson on his publication of Fingal and Temora* (1763).

410 Poems entitled 'Druid Song' and dated Oct. 1758 (Bodl. MS Eng. misc. d. 450) and 'The Druid', dated 16 Apr. 1759 (Bodl. MS Eng. misc. e. 138, f. 48).

411 Ibid., f. 49.

412 Warburton to Hurd, 4 Mar. 1765 (Nichols *Illus.*, II, 59)

413 Memoir by Peter Collinson in *Gents. Mag.* 1765, 211.

414 For his will, F. W. Steer, *Antiq.* XXV (1951), 213.

415 Warburton to Hurd, 4 Mar. 1765 (Nichols *Illus.* II, 59).

416 Bodl. MS Eng. misc. e. 137, f. 80.

417 Notes on back of the 'Great Prospect' of Avebury, Bodl. MS Eng. misc. b. 65.

418 Bodl. Gough Maps 231, f. 33.

419 Bodl. MS Eng. misc. b. 65.

420 Bodl. Gough Maps 231, f. 9.

421 S. Piggott, *Ruins in a Landscape* (1976), 117.

422 S. Piggott in J. D. Evans et al. (edd.) *Antiquity and Man: Essays in honour of Glyn Daniel* (1981), 24.

423 Denis Saurat, *Blake and Modern Thought* (1929), especially Part ii, 'Celts and Druids'; R. Todd, *Tracks in the Snow* (1946) 48; S. Piggott, *The Druids* (1975).

424 S. Piggott, *The Druids* (1975).

425 For the vicissitudes of the Stukeley MSS in the early nineteenth century, cf. *Antiquity*, VII (1933), 222.

426 *The Family Memoirs of the Rev. William Stukeley, M.D.*, ed. by W. C. Lukis, Surtees Society, vols lxxiii (1882); lxxvi (1883), and lxxx (1887). These volumes are cited in footnotes as SS i, ii, and iii.

427 Cf. his remarks in *Wessex from the Air*, 211.

428 The material is listed in Sotheby's Sale Catalogues of 15 July 1924 and 1 April 1931.

429 *Bodleian Quarterly Record*, IV (1924), 149.

430 *Bodleian Library Record* V (1956), 256.

431 *Antiquity* IX (1935), 22.

432 *Ibid.* VII (1933), 49.

433 Cf. J. R. Milburn, *Annals of Science* XXXI (1974), 511.

Further Reading

Documentation is given in the notes for all the detailed subject-matter of the book, but the following selection of sources may be useful as a guide to further reading. For a general survey of the history of ideas within which Stukeley's life and work play their part, see Basil Willey, *The Seventeenth Century Background* (London 1934) and *The Eighteenth Century Background* (London 1940); A. O. Lovejoy, *Essays in the History of Ideas* (Johns Hopkins 1948); with for antiquarianism, S. Piggott, *Ruins in a Landscape* (Edinburgh 1976). The historians of the period are the subject of D. Douglas, *English Scholars* (London 1939), and seventeenth-century science and antiquarianism are discussed by M. Hunter, *John Aubrey and the Realm of Learning* (London 1975) and *Science and Society in Restoration England* (Cambridge 1981). J. M. Levine, *Dr Woodward's Shield: History, Science and Satire in Augustan England* (University of California 1977), and M. 'Espinasse, 'The Decline and Fall of Restoration Science', in Charles Webster (ed.) *The Intellectual Revolution of the Seventeenth Century* (London 1974), 347–68, cover the main aspects of the decline of learning and antiquarianism in the eighteenth century, while D. E. Allen, *The Naturalist in Britain: a social history* (London 1976) covers natural history from the seventeenth to the nineteenth centuries. The Druids of antiquity and later imagination are displayed in S. Piggott, *The Druids* (rev. edn, London & New York 1975) and A. L. Owen, *The Famous Druids* (Oxford 1962) and at Stonehenge by C. Chippindale, *Stonehenge Complete* (London & New York 1983). The current views on the purely archaeological background of Stukeley's work is given here and in R. J. C. Atkinson, *Stonehenge* (Harmondsworth 1979); A. Burl, *Prehistoric Avebury* (New Haven & London 1979) and *The Stone Circles of the British Isles* (New Haven & London 1976), and over the wider field of British archaeology, J. V. S. Megaw & D. D. A. Simpson, *Introduction to British Prehistory* (Leicester 1979).

List of Illustrations

All illustrations followed by the abbreviation Bodl. and a manuscript number have been reproduced by kind permission of the Bodleian Library, Oxford.

TEXT FIGURES

PLATES

Index

Bold numerals refer to text figures; *italic* numerals indicate plates

Index

Walpole, Horace 15, 118, 119, 142
Waltham Cross, Essex 72, 146
Wanley, Humphrey 41, 43, 71
Wansdyke, Wilts 68
Warburton, William 84, 111, 125, 150, 152, 24
Webb, J. 81
Weekley, Northants 123
West Kennet, Wilts 47–9, 95
Westminster Bridge 139
Whood, Isaac 76
Widmore, R. 132
Williams, Edward 156
Willis, Browne 19, 122
Wilton House, Wilts 66

Winchelsea, Fifth Earl of 54, 56–7, 60, 64, 71, 90, 95
Wise, Francis 13, 33
Wood, Anthony 44
Worm, Ole 81, 87, 95

Y

York Minster 122

Z

Zodiac Club 53